PRIVATE WARRIORS

PRIVATE WARRIORS

KEN SILVERSTEIN

RESEARCH BY
DANIEL BURTON-ROSE

VERSO

New York • London

First published by Verso 2000
© Ken Silverstein 2000

V

VERSO

UK: 6 Meard Street, London W1V 3HR
USA: 180 Varick Street, New York, NY 10014-4606

Verso is the imprint of New Left Books

Design by POLLEN
Printed by R.R. Donnelley

ISBN 1 85984 756 0

British Library Cataloguing-in-Publication Data
A catalogue record for this book is available
from the British Library

Library of Congress Cataloging-in-Publication Data
A catalog record for this book is available
from the Library of Congress

Contents

Acknowledgments

FIRST AND FOREMOST, I wish to thank the Florence and John Schumann Foundation for the generous support that allowed me to research and write this book. I would also like to thank the Joseph Handleman Foundation for the timely last-minute grant that allowed me to complete it.

Private Warriors would have been impossible to write without the prodigious and superb efforts of Daniel Burton-Rose. He played a vital role in researching and reporting the book, as well as in helping write the final chapter. Ian Urbina provided invaluable help after Daniel's departure.

Thanks also to Colin Robinson of Verso for his support and enthusiasm; Daniel Nelson, who suggested the idea for such a book almost three years ago (fortunately, he was too busy to write it himself); Dieter Meier, for generously sharing the remarkable research he has conducted over the past five years through the Freedom of Information Act; and Jason Vest, for his suggestions and help as the book progressed.

Prologue

IN LATE-1998, the *Washington Post* ran a lengthy front-page article ominously titled "Idled Arms Experts in Russia Pose Threat." The story told of one of the "least understood but most significant consequences of the end of the Cold War," namely the collapse of the former Soviet Union's military apparatus. As a result of that collapse, thousands of Russian arms experts have been "thrown onto the street" and are now selling their services to the highest bidder. Those include rogue states that the Russians are assisting to develop weapons systems and to build nuclear capabilities. Thanks to these displaced Russian free-lancers, the world is a less stable, more dangerous, place.

It was an alarming story, to be sure. At the same time, neither the *Post* nor the rest of the American media has noted a parallel and equally significant phenomenon closer to home. In America, as in Russia, the Cold War witnessed the construction of an enormous and richly funded military-industrial complex. A Brookings Institute study puts Pentagon spending between 1940 and 1998 at $19 trillion, a figure that dwarfs the second highest government expenditure for the period, $7.9 trillion for social security payments. And as in Russia, a similar if not identical process of military retrenchment and downsizing has taken place in the United States during the past decade. Like those dispossessed Russian arms experts, vast numbers of America's Cold War veterans—Pentagon bureaucrats, national security establishment staffers, intelligence operatives and soldiers—have been cast adrift by the fall of communism. So, too, have the arms dealers, including many foreigners, who grew rich by supplying arms for CIA-sponsored Cold War covert-operations.

Of course, the United States won the Cold War, and its military machine remains far more vibrant than does its Russian counterpart. Hence, plenty of old hard-liners remain entrenched at the Pentagon and other national security posts. Many more have moved on to military-related jobs in the private sector. Former Defense Department officials serve as consultants to the arms industry, helping lobby for needless Cold War-era weapons systems and promoting greater arms sales to foreign regimes. Retired generals form private corporations that train the armies of foreign nations and encourage US entanglements abroad. Arms dealers linked to US intelligence agencies still trot the globe hawking their wares, sometimes in support of government operations, sometimes acting strictly as private businessmen. Intellectuals who gained their names by hyping the Soviet threat still counsel our political leaders. The advice they offered during the Cold War was of dubious value, and it has decidedly less merit today.

These Private Warriors have a financial and career interest in war and conflict, as well as the power and connections to promote continued hard-line policies. Their collective influence is one reason that the United States seems incapable of making the transition to the post-Cold War world. In the words of Dan Nelson, a professor at the George C. Marshall European Center for Security Studies in Garmisch, Germany, and a former visiting scholar at the Departments of State and Defense, "We created a Cold War military infrastructure and infrastructures die hard. What we've seen is an assiduous effort on the part of the men who staffed that infrastructure to maintain their income, their influence and their ideas. In doing so, they advocate the same laws and policies that underpinned the Cold War."

One simple barometer of the Cold War's continued hold on policymakers is the Pentagon's budget, which in 2000—a decade after the fall of the Berlin Wall and with no credible "enemy" in sight—sits at $268 billion. That's four times more than Russia spends and about eight times more than China. As this book goes to press, the Pentagon is simultaneously planning three new tactical aircraft programs—the Joint Strike Fighter, the F/A-18E/F fighter-bomber, and the F-22—at a cost of about $400 billion. Then there's the B-2 bomber, which was originally designed to penetrate the air defenses of the Soviet Union, a nation that no longer exists. At $2.5 billion a copy, it costs more than its weight in gold and will eat up another $50 billion or so in total program costs. As new weapons systems roll off production lines, the Pentagon can't even use, let alone store, its entire current arsenal. The Defense Department "has been dumping old tanks like an Army/Navy surplus store conducting frantic going-out-of-business sales," William Greider recounts in *Fortress America: The American Military and the Consequences of Peace*. During the past few years, the United States gave away hundreds of tanks to foreign allies and sold hundreds more at ten cents on the dollar. In 1999, the Pentagon dumped dozens of old M-60 and M-48 tanks off the Alabama coast to form artificial reefs. Meanwhile, the world's largest air force—other than the Pentagon's—sits moth-balled at the Davis Mountain Air Force Base in Arizona. Known as the "Boneyard," the Davis Mountain site is a broom closet for old planes so that new aircraft can be delivered and deployed.

Even some conservative analysts agree that it's time to rein in the Pentagon. Doug Bandow, a senior fellow at the conservative Cato Institute and a former special assistant to Ronald Reagan, wrote in 1999, "The world remains dangerous, [but] it isn't particularly dangerous to the United States . . . The US and her allies account for eighty percent of the world's military expenditures. By itself, the US accounts for about one-third of all military outlays worldwide . . . America faces no serious conventional threat. Russia's armed forces are but a pale shadow of what they were under the Soviet regime. China has potential, and the advantage of sheer manpower, but it will take years to create a truly world-class military. Pariah regimes such as Iraq and North Korea are poor, isolated and imploding. Those nations aren't capable of making war on America."

Yet in early 1999, the Clinton administration announced that during the next six years, it would grant the Pentagon an additional $112 billion over and above the generous blandishments Congress had already authorized for the period—the biggest proposed increase in military spending since the Reagan years. In justifying the hike, Clinton pointed to the need to retain personnel and to a "readiness crisis" that is said to be hampering American forces. But only a small amount of the taxpayers' money will go to addressing those issues (for example, by raising salaries and improving medical care for troops). Nor will it confront real threats to national security, such as the spread of weapons of mass destruction. Instead, the Pentagon will use the biggest chunk to jack up its procurement budget for new weapons by more than half—from $49 billion to $75 billion—between 1999 and 2005. Since Congress has mandated that new government spending must be offset by cuts in other areas, the Pentagon's slush will come at the expense of social programs, which have already been shredded during the past two decades.

Of course, the Private Warriors' continued influence isn't the only factor that accounts for the still vigorous health of the military-industrial complex. Between 1997 and 1998, four major defense firms—Boeing, Lockheed Martin, Northrop Grumman, and Raytheon—donated roughly $4 million to elected leaders and political parties, spreading the money among Republicans and Democrats alike (that doesn't include individual contributions from the companies' executives). Defense firms are also generous when it comes to hiring Washington lobbyists. As of 1998, the four firms mentioned above had more than 250 influence peddlers on their combined payrolls. Their collective spending to lobby the federal government that year topped $22 million.

That kind of money buys a lot of influence in Congress, which is always willing to lend the military-industrial complex a helping hand. During the Reagan and Bush years, when the Pentagon's budget climbed into the stratosphere, lawmakers approved ninety-five percent of all funding requested by the presidents. More recently, Congress has been larding the arms makers with huge subsidies to help cushion the blow from a post-Cold War fall-off in government orders. *Corporate Welfare for Weapons Makers: The Hidden Costs of Spending on Defense and Foreign Aid*, a report from the Cato Institute, found that in 1999, industry received about $35 billion in government-funded military research and development assistance. That same year, Congress provided defense manufacturers with more than $7 billion to subsidize arms exports and billions more to underwrite industry mergers and low-cost, government-funded factories and equipment.

Many in Congress view the Pentagon's budget as a jobs and pork program for their home states. In 1998, Senate Majority Leader Trent Lott added $1.5 billion to a defense appropriations bill to pay for an assault ship that the Pentagon didn't even ask for, to be built in shipyards at Pascalgoula, Mississippi. Some of the Congressionally directed pork doesn't even pay for military items or projects. One of Lott's colleagues, Senator Daniel Inouye, managed to win millions of dollars to fund a Pentagon drive to keep the brown tree snake out of his native Hawaii.

At the same time, the activities and continued sway of the men discussed in this book are an important, overlooked factor in understanding why the United States can't seem to put the Cold War to rest. *Private Warriors* will examine how a small number of Cold War hawks continue to influence policy in a profound and disastrous manner. It will also show how the arms brokers and covert networks employed by the Pentagon and the CIA during the Cold War have not only survived but flourished in the post-Communist era.

The six chapters of this book are self-contained units that mainly focus on one man or institution. The first looks at how some key Cold Warriors remain entrenched at government agencies and how those agencies themselves continue to formulate policy as if the Cold War had never ended. Andrew Marshall, a fixture of the military-industrial complex for nearly half a century, is a central figure here. One of the original nuclear intellectuals, Marshall worked in the 1950s with Herman Kahn at the RAND Corporation. (Marshall and a few colleagues were instrumental in concocting the "missile gap" used so successfully by John Kennedy during the 1960 election.) Since the mid-1970s, he has headed the Defense Department's Office of Net Assessment, which is supposed to objectively rate threats to American national security. During the Cold War, Marshall systematically overstated Russian power and painted fearsome scenarios about US vulnerability to the Communist menace. Now he promotes the Revolution in Military Affairs, a doctrine that holds that today's arsenal needs to be augmented with billions of dollars in state-of-the-art hardware suitable to the twenty-first-century battlefield. The chapter will also look at America's continued domination of the international weapons trade and how the government helps companies like Lockheed and Boeing arm the world.

Chapter Two considers the role of private arms dealers who grew rich during the Cold War and who prosper to the present day in the weapons trade. Here the focus will be Ernst Werner Glatt, a right-wing German who, for many years, was one of the Pentagon's preferred gun-runners. He helped funnel arms to American-backed guerilla forces and client regimes during the Cold War, and was also the leading supplier for the Foreign Materiel Acquisition Program, a "black" operation that secretly procured Soviet Bloc weapons for the Pentagon. Glatt has been slowed by age and health troubles, but he remains active in the arms trade and as a helper to the United States. Though Glatt's politics are very different from my own, he is a fascinating subject, and I confess to having developed a certain respect for his diverse talents.

Chapter Three concerns a Nazi war hero named Gerhard Mertins, another German arms dealer used by the United States. Headquartered in Bonn, his company, Merex, opened a US office in 1966. Mertins's business contacts at that time included former SS commando Otto "Scarface" Skorzeny, and Klaus Barbie, the ex-Gestapo chief known as the "Butcher of Lyons." During the 1980s, Mertins supplied the contras in Nicaragua (including a deal engineered by Oliver North), and like Glatt, helped obtain Soviet Bloc material for the Pentagon. Mertins died in 1993, but his previously unreported story illustrates the continuing synergistic relationship that the government maintains with private arms dealers. Furthermore, a number of Mertins's former business collaborators remain active in the arms trade, demonstrating the ongoing importance of the old Cold War weapons networks.

Chapter Four examines the rapidly emerging Mercenary, Incorporated field. The term refers to the private corporations that offer military training and assistance to America's foreign allies, as well as working directly in support of the Pentagon's sensitive overseas operations. Though private, these companies have strong links to the government—they are licensed by the State Department and are staffed by former military officers—effectively serving as an extension of foreign policy. The most prominent is Military Professional Resources Inc. of Alexandria, Virginia, where a score of retired generals are listed as directors or corporate officers. MPRI has trained the armies of Croatia and Bosnia, and is seeking to expand in Eastern Europe and Africa. As one critic says, "The only difference between what these firms do and what mercenaries do is that the companies have gained the imprimatur of government for their actions."

Chapter Five reports on the hordes of Cold War veterans who now work as consultants and lobbyists for the arms industry. Defense contractors find it especially useful to hire military officials upon their retirement because they know the ropes of the domestic procurement process and have contacts abroad—often with dictatorial governments that the US supported during the Cold War—which can lead to foreign sales. The post-government career of General Alexander Haig, a veteran of the Nixon and Reagan administrations, is the centerpiece of this chapter. Today, Haig runs Worldwide Associates, a consulting firm in downtown Washington. He has helped companies like Sikorsky Aircraft, maker of the Black Hawk helicopter, and defense giant Boeing sell their goods abroad. He also seeks to win political support for corrupt foreign leaders—

like those in China and Turkmenistan—who he directly represents or who head nations where his corporate clients have significant business interests.

Chapter Six discusses the Cold War strategists who now work in think tanks and consulting firms, where they crank out the intellectual scaffolding needed to gird continuing Cold War policies. Frank Gaffney, a former Defense Department staffer and nuclear arms zealot under Ronald Reagan, now heads the Washington-based Center for Security Policy. That think tank—funded heavily by defense contractors—promotes "Star Wars"-style missile defense, as well as the B-2 bomber and other weapons boondoggles. Gaffney's political allies these days include Richard Perle, an assistant secretary of defense during the Reagan years, and Keith Payne, a so-called Nuclear Use Theorist. Payne once suggested that the US should initiate a first strike against the Soviet Union in order to ensure victory in an atomic war—with "victory" defined as leveling Russia while limiting American dead in a nuclear counterstrike to twenty million. "Frank is the conservatives' rapid deployment force for national security," Robert Andrews, a Washington lobbyist for Rockwell International, told the *National Journal*.

All of this helps explain why US national security policy in the post-Cold War era looks very much like it did twenty years ago, when Europe was divided and much of the Third World was a battleground between East and West. Back then, the Pentagon and its supporters could at least pinpoint a significant threat to national security (even if they exaggerated it dramatically). Today, with Pyongyang and Havana standing in for Moscow, that's no longer the case. Moving beyond the Cold War, then, requires recognizing the influence of

Private Warriors. Only by doing so can we construct a defense policy based on real issues and threats, rather than one shaped, in part,
by the profit motives and egos of a small group of hard-liners.

Two final notes. First, I sought to have sources for this book
speak on the record, but a number would talk to me only on background. (This was especially so in researching the two chapters on
private arms brokers.) As Bob Woodward writes in *Veil*, his book
about the CIA, "The simple reality is that people will not discuss
intelligence and security matters without this protection." I sometimes left out material—even if I strongly believed it to be true—if
I could not find additional sources to confirm it or solid documentary evidence. Second, much of the material presented here comes
from my original research, but I have relied in some cases on previously published accounts. As a journalist rather than an academ-
ic, I am not fond of footnotes. Hence, where possible, I have cited
sources in the text itself.

ONE

ARMS AND THE STATE

The Clinton administration "accepts the premise that conventional arms sales by American suppliers are a legitimate and important business."

—Frank Wisner, Undersecretary of Defense for Policy

RUTH HARKIN, a senior vice president for the defense manufacturer United Technologies and the wife of Senator Tom Harkin, kicks off the blue pumps that accessorize her matching business suit and climbs into the cockpit of a F-16 fighter plane. Wearing a look somewhere between grim determination and mild embarrassment, she heads the plane down the runway and takes off to do battle with two enemy jets. With a flick of her hand, she fires a pair of sidewinder missiles from the F-16's wing. As the enemy planes erupt in flames, Harkin coolly returns to base.

Harkin's display of Top Gun prowess came in the spring of 1999, as NATO planes were bombing Yugoslavia. Harkin's bombing run, though, was not in the skies above Belgrade, but aboard a flight simulator built by F-16 manufacturer Lockheed Martin, which was on display at the Latin American Defentech 99, an arms show held for four days in Rio de Janeiro. About 200 firms from around the world came to Rio in hopes of drumming up business with Brazil, the region's biggest arms importer, as well as other Latin nations.

Defentech is one of several dozen annual stops on the international arms circuit, with exhibition sites on every continent outside of Antarctica. Though largely a mixture of hype and machismo—at the mammoth International Defense Exhibition in Abu Dhabi, there's a live-fire range where attendees can sip umbrella drinks while observing surgical strikes on dummy targets—arms shows provide industry sales personnel with the opportunity to make the hard sell to potential clients. "A friend of mine sells medical supplies and goes out door to door," Sherry Butcher of a US defense company called Merex explained to me. "There are a lot of military people coming through here so this gives us a chance to interface with the end-users."

Thousands of people milled through the invitation-only Defentech, including members of eighteen official delegations stuffed with high-ranking defense officials from as far away as Saudi Arabia and Mozambique. At booths spread across a vast 30,000-square foot exhibit hall, would-be buyers perused displays trumpeting the virtues of a vast array of weapons: British tanks, Finnish armored vehicles, South African attack helicopters, German air defense electronics, Dutch howitzers, American planes, Swedish torpedoes, and Spanish warheads.

The equipment on display is top-of-the line, and just about anything is available short of nuclear, chemical and biological weapons. Sales reps from Seattle-based Boeing were talking up the company's Super Hornet fighter, a plane that's still in production and that won't be fully deployed in the US military for the better part of another decade. The craft is so new that the company hasn't even received permission from the government to sell it abroad. But Boeing is wasting no time in drumming up interest since, as one salesman told me, authorization of foreign sales down the road is a "slam dunk."

(Boeing's promotional material for the plane raved about its super-capacities, but salesmen were no doubt tight-lipped about an array of problems surrounding it. In 1996, pilots flying pre-production models reported that when maneuvering in combat simulation, they found the craft flipping suddenly on its side, a problem known as "wing drop." Senator Russ Feingold of Wisconsin has charged that the plane is only marginally better than an earlier version, which costs $50 million—$20 million less than the Super Hornet. In response to complaints from Feingold, the Navy appointed a three-member "independent" investigating panel. In addition to two retired generals, the panel included Carl Smith, a defense industry consultant. Smith's clients included Boeing—one of his jobs was to promote the Super Hornet on Capitol Hill—with which he cut ties only after being named to the Pentagon review. Predictably, the panel came back with a report highly favorable to the fighter. A June 1999 report from the General Accounting Office (GAO), Congress's watchdog agency, was far more critical. It identified eighty-four deficiencies with the plane and suggested that the Pentagon slow the program until Boeing corrected them.)

As Defentech got underway, industry representatives were heartened when Brazilian Air Force Minister Walter Werner Brauer confirmed that his country was planning to spend several billion dollars to buy a new fleet of fighter planes. Meanwhile, the Brazilian Army and Navy are drawing up expensive modernization plans of their own. "That's why you see these companies here marketing like hell," said a defense staffer from the US consulate. "There's a lot of money at stake."

Overall, though, the relatively depressed state of the post-Cold War global arms market produced a decidedly melancholy atmosphere. "When the Berlin Wall came down there just wasn't an enemy any longer," Jan Olierook, a manager for the Dutch firm RDM, said disconsolately. I inquired if the war in Yugoslavia had a beneficial effect on the market, a hope I had heard expressed by several other Defentech attendees. "No, I'm afraid not," Olierook replied with a shake of the head, before quickly adding, "Actually, I probably shouldn't say that."

WAR AND MILITARY tension is good for weapons makers and, as Olierook's comment indicates, the collapse of the Soviet Union has put arms merchants in a tough position. That's especially true in the US, where during the Cold War, the Pentagon needed only to point to the rampaging Russian Bear to get Congress to pass yet another expensive defense program. The Defense Department still has plenty of friends on Capitol Hill, but it's become hard to justify Cold War levels of military spending when the enemy you've been touting for the past half-century has suddenly disappeared from the map.

In the early 1990s, industry trade magazines were nervously reporting that the Pentagon's budget could fall as low as $150 billion by 1996, about half of its average during the Cold War. Government funding for domestic weapons procurement had already fallen dramatically. Between 1987 and 1994, the Pentagon's budget for new weapons fell by fifty-six percent. In 1986, at the height of Reagan's arms build-up, the military bought 387 warplanes. By 1998, that figure had plunged to thirty-three.

For arms makers, the whole affair was alarmingly similar to what occurred in the aftermath of World War II. That conflict had brought unprecedented profitability for the aircraft companies, whose sales climbed from $250 million in 1939 to $16.7 billion in 1944. When the shooting stopped, so did the companies' sales. From its Number One domestic economic ranking in 1943, the industry dropped to Forty-Four by 1947. "The situation in the aircraft industry today ... is pretty grim," Robert E. Gross, then-president of Lockheed, wrote in a letter to a friend that year. "The companies have no idea where any real business is coming from. The commercial market has proved to be far less than one would have thought, and everybody of any standing is fiercely competing to get what orders are offering. We have cut some 6,000 people out of the place in the last few weeks and are about to take at least as big a cut again." By the following year, Gross was even more despondent. In another letter, this one to former Secretary of State Edward Stettinius, he wrote: "While the problems of the war were great and the pressure upon airplane manufacturers to produce was incessant, I feel that the hazards experienced then were never comparable to the ones we have had to face up to since. We had one underlying element of comfort and reassurance in the war—we knew we would get paid for whatever we built. Today we are almost entirely on our own, the business is extremely speculative and with a narrowed market, the competition is very keen."

As the crisis dragged on, *Business Week* proclaimed that only the equivalent of a federal bailout could save the arms makers from financial ruin. "[T]he aircraft builders, even with tax carrybacks, are near disaster," the magazine reported. "Right now the government is their only possible savior—with orders, subsidies, or loans."

Help was not long in coming. As described by Frank Kofsky in his marvelous book *Harry S. Truman and the War Scare of 1948*, the arms industry—with help from friends at the Pentagon and other government agencies—solved its post-World War II slump by drumming up a huge and vastly exaggerated Red Scare. Never mind that the Soviet Union was still recovering from devastating wartime losses, the scare's proponents argued, Stalin was poised to roll across Western Europe at a moment's notice. The campaign worked to perfection. In mid-1948, Truman increased the Pentagon's budget by thirty percent. "No president since—not even Ronald Reagan at his most influential—has ever even come close to expanding military expenditures so spectacularly in time of peace," writes Kofsky.

(Little of the money extracted by the war lobby during the build-up to the Korean crisis was used to benefit soldiers serving in Korea.

Instead the defense establishment spent heavily on weapons such as the B-47, the first nuclear bomber—of little use in Korea where fighter planes were most needed—and on vast numbers of tanks which, like the B-47, were sent off to the quiet European front. Meanwhile, ground forces in Korea were miserably equipped. Half of all US casualties—this category includes the wounded—in Korea were caused by frostbite, because troops weren't supplied with decent boots. American troops would raid Chinese trenches to strip dead peasants from the poorest nation on earth of their footwear. Soldiers desperately needed a good anti-tank weapon, but had to make do with vintage World War II arms.)

With no credible threat to national security, tackling the post-Cold War crisis has been decidedly trickier. General Colin Powell alluded to the problem when he told Congress in 1991, "I'm running out of demons. I'm down to Kim il Sung and Castro." Hence, the Pentagon and the arms makers have devoted considerable time and resources to lining up a new "threat" that can be used to bludgeon Congress and public opinion into supporting continued levels of Cold War spending.

For a time, the arms lobby conceded that the world situation had improved but argued that the United States must remain vigilant against a possible resurrection of Russian power. That position became increasingly untenable during the last decade as the Red Army entered a state of virtual collapse. By the summer of 1998, it was in such abysmal straits that Russian officers were ordering troops to gather mushrooms, berries and other foodstuffs growing in the wild. The following year, the State Department's annual report to

Congress on international military expenditures stated that Russian army readiness was in a state of "rapid decay" and that the average Russian soldier is "only marginally combat capable." It said that Red Army troop strength had dropped from 3.7 million in 1989 to 1.7 million in 1998, and was expected to fall to about 1 million by 2000.

The threat inflaters also pointed to "rogue nations" such as North Korea, Iraq and Iran. This strategy never galvanized the public much, especially after American-led forces routed Saddam Hussein's troops during the Gulf War. Meanwhile, Iran, the most potent "rogue," spends only about one percent what the US does for defense while North Korea appeared to be facing mass starvation as the millenium dawned.

Next up was China, which Pentagon planners sometimes refer to as The Khan (as in Genghis). "The gradual growth of Chinese power-projection capabilities will unsettle regional security and demand US attention, even if no hostile Chinese intentions are evident," says a mid-1998 report published by the National Defense University's Institute for National Strategic Studies. "A US-China showdown over Taiwan could materialize by 2018, and it is imperative that the United States have the offensive and defensive forces that would actually be used in such a crisis." China has a horrendous human rights record and represses its own citizens, but as a military threat it, too, comes up short. China's troop strength has been cut in half to two million since the 1970s, and most of its soldiers field weapons that are a quarter-century old. Beijing's Air Force doesn't have a single long-range bomber and, according to a *Time* magazine story from June 1999, its entire nuclear arsenal "packs about as much explosive power as what the US stuffs into one Trident submarine. China's ballistic missile sub (singular, not plural) hasn't been to sea for a year and would be sunk in minutes in a battle with a US attack sub."

With threat options running out, the Pentagon is becoming increasingly desperate. More recently, military planners have started talking up a new danger, something they refer to as GET, Generic Emerging Threat—a menace as yet undefined but against which the US had better arm itself. Pentagon officials also allude to dangers posed by "asymmetric niche competitors." This could be an ethnic tribe, a drug lord, or an organized crime or terrorist group. "They can't come up with any big threat so now they're trying to find an itty-bitty threat," says Chuck Spinney, a thirty-year Pentagon veteran. "The point is the same: to make sure that there's no threat to the defense budget."

ANDREW MARSHALL is an aging but still sprightly Cold Warrior whose work in the Pentagon is vital to lubricating the flow of funds to the defense contractors. He heads up the Pentagon's Office of Net Assessment, an outfit charged with projecting threats to national security decades into the future and making sure the United States is prepared to deal with them. It's a small shop by Pentagon standards—the ONA has a staff of about a dozen—but an influential one. A slew of Marshall's former staffers have moved on to senior posts in industry, academia and defense think tanks.

Marshall is the primary theorist behind the so-called Revolution in Military Affairs (RMA), a doctrine which holds that high-tech weaponry—combined with strategic and organizational innovations—is transforming warfare in the same way as occurred with the advent of the musket in the 1600s or the use of atomic weapons in 1945. Hence, today's "platforms"—tanks, aircraft carriers, and manned bombers—are hopelessly outdated and must be replaced with a whole new set of immensely expensive, 21st-century "brilliant" weapons.

Marshall appears infrequently in the press, but when he does he is treated with the sort of reverence normally reserved for incoming presidents and beauty queens. A 1998 article in *Defense News* called his Office of Net Assessment (ONA) an agency that "funds innovative studies on futuristic threats, often ones that the rest of the Pentagon is fearful of tackling." A *Wall Street Journal* profile a few years earlier described Marshall as someone "struggling to save the US armed forces from becoming paralyzed by their own successes in the Cold War and Desert Storm."

More sycophantic still was an April 1999 *Washingtonian* article by Jay Winik (author of *On the Brink*, a cartoon-book history of the Cold War that argues that four caped crusaders who served in the Reagan administration, Elliot Abrams, Jeanne Kirkpatrick, Richard Perle, and Max Kampelman brought down the Soviet Union). Sprawling over eleven pages, Winik's story described Marshall as "The most influential man you've never heard of," "a legend among the national security elite," "a key figure, even the central figure, in reshaping America's military for the next century," as well as "one of the towering figures in the whole story of American security and defense thinking in the last era." Not only is Marshall the foremost military genius of his time, argues Winik, but also a man so graced with powers of foresight that he was one of the first people on the planet to understand the risk posed by AIDS. "This is going to be much bigger than anyone realizes," Winik has Marshall telling his staff at the ONA in the early 1980s. "Let's do something about this." Soon Marshall's office was on the phone with the Center for Disease Control, urging the agency to devote more resources to the emerging scourge.

A closer look reveals Marshall—who declined a request for a formal interview—to be one of the most effective pork-seeking missiles ever deployed by the military brass. "Andy's a one-man RAND," an ex-Pentagon staffer and long-time Marshall watcher says. "He's one of those defense intellectuals who's always there to come up with the stuff that backs the needs of industry." That, say others, is precisely what the RMA is all about—specifically, the Pentagon's desire to keep the money spigot open in the post-Cold War period. "The RMA has nothing to do with warfare and everything to do with budgets," says Pierre Sprey, a former weapons designer who quit consulting for the Pentagon during the Reagan years in disgust over pork-barreling. "It's just an excuse to funnel money to the defense contractors by funding a whole new generation of high-tech weapons."

Marshall grew up in Detroit and received a graduate degree in economics from the University of Chicago. He took a job at the RAND Corporation in 1949 and worked with nuclear intellectuals such as Herman Kahn and Albert Wohlstetter. While there, Marshall and several colleagues played an important if hidden role in the 1960 presidential election when they served as advisors to John Kennedy and concocted the fraudulent "missile gap" which JFK used to pillory Richard Nixon.

In 1972, Henry Kissinger hired Marshall to work at the National Security Council. Two years later, he was appointed head of the Pentagon's newly created ONA, which was charged with rating the threat to national security posed by the Soviet Union. In his book *The Wizards of Armageddon*, Fred Kaplan writes that Marshall turned the ONA "into an intermediate contracting house that wrangled money from other divisions of the Pentagon and handed it out to consultants for studies of strategic ideas that interested Andy Marshall."

Marshall saw his mission at the ONA as drumming up timely worst-case scenarios to help out the boss. One of his earliest studies found that the CIA was seriously underestimating Soviet defense spending and power. Schlesinger promptly used the report to press Congress for more money.

Another ONA specialty was rigging the conventional balance of forces with simple bean counts of weaponry that stressed Moscow's numerical strength while ignoring the clear technological superiority of American equipment. Hence, Marshall's crew would tote-up every Russian tank ever made—possibly including those perched on World War II memorials in Siberian villages—to show that the West lay naked and exposed to a Soviet blitzkrieg across Western Europe.

(For the threat-inflation crowd, the Russian T-72 tank was a dire threat to anything in the US arsenal. In fact, the Israelis pulverized the T-72 during fighting with Syrian forces in 1982. The T-72 had a number of operational problems that greatly diminished its battlefield utility. Foremost among them was an automatic loader that was supposed to greatly increase its rate of fire. Unfortunately, a mechanical arm on the device had a tendency to load the gunner's arm or leg, as opposed to ammunition, into the breech, which slammed shut automatically. In his book *The Threat: Inside the Soviet Military Machine*, Andrew Cockburn cites a US Army officer who suggested that the automatic loader was "how the Red Army Chorus gets its soprano section." Following a number of unplanned amputations, the Russians decided that manual loading had some advantages after all. As a result, the T-72's real rate of fire was less than one-third that of NATO's best tanks.)

Marshall also remained involved in the world of nuclear strategy. One of his inspirations at the ONA was to promote new technology that would make the Navy's sea-launched missiles as accurate as the Air Force's ICBMs. His efforts led directly to the Trident II nuclear-armed missiles fielded by America's submarine fleet. During the Reagan years, Marshall helped author a secret document that called for the US to develop the capability of fighting and winning a nuclear war with Russia. America should "be able to force the Soviet Union to seek earliest termination of hostilities on terms favorable to the United States," said the study. Marshall has also been an enthusiastic supporter of Star Wars and related schemes. In 1998, he was one of the experts called before the Rumsfeld Commission, which concluded that the United States could face a ballistic missile threat from countries such as Iraq or North Korea within a very short period of time. The clear if unstated conclusion was that America should speed up development of a multi-billion dollar ballistic missile shield to ward off the impending menace.

Marshall's admirers portray him as a man always one step ahead of the competition. "Well ahead of most Sovietologists, Mr. Marshall noticed weaknesses of Soviet society," reads the *Wall Street Journal* profile. "In 1977, he focused on the environmental and demographic crises that were undermining the Soviet system." Associates have no recollection of Marshall ever having expressed such views. "Until the very end he was a major promoter of the line that 'The Russians are coming and they're ten feet tall,'" says the ex-Pentagon man. Eternally vigilant, Marshall in late-1989—after the fall of the Berlin Wall and shortly before Mikhail Gorbachev's ouster in the Soviet Union—was insisting that high levels of defense spending were as urgently needed as ever. "It's going to take us several years of careful watching and monitoring to see how much change takes place," he said. "I don't think I've ever seen so much uncertainty about the future as there is today."

Since the collapse of Communism, Marshall has spent much energy hunting for a suitable "threat" to replace the Russians. He first turned his attention to North Korea, with a 1991 ONA report concluding that, in the event of war, Pyongyang's troops would be rolling into Seoul within two to three days and US forces would be unable to do much to stop them.

After it became apparent that North Korea was on the verge of collapse, Marshall turned his attention to China. An ONA study from the mid-1990s stated that Beijing's military was modernizing so rapidly that the Peoples Liberation Army would soon be able to defeat the US in a regional conflict in Asia. Marshall's nightmare vision was laid out in the *Journal*'s story, which opened with a classified Pentagon war game that pitted America versus a resurgent China in 2020. To the horror of US officials, Chinese forces pitilessly peppered American forces with high-tech weaponry while satellite-guided anti-ship missiles showered the US fleet. By sundown, the once proud American armada had sunk beneath the waves of the South China Sea and the Middle Kingdom ruled once more.

A second ONA report on China, prepared for the agency by RAND, estimated that Beijing is spending about $140 billion a year on defense. That figure is about two-and-a-half times that of other high-end estimates and seven to eight times greater than low-end ones. In 1997, yet another ONA-sponsored study concluded ominously that China viewed the US as a declining superpower and was scheming to exploit this weakness. One possibility: a Communist takeover of Taiwan. "Chinese military officers and analysts are writing very unfriendly things about the United States," Michael Pillsbury, the analyst who conducted the study, breathlessly told the Senate Intelligence Committee in reporting on his findings. (Pillsbury made his conclusions after translating hundreds of Chinese military books and journal articles that had been provided to him by authorities in Beijing. "Far from hiding these writings, Chinese authorities openly gave them to the Pentagon and promised to provide more," a baffled *Associated Press* reporter wrote of Pillsbury's testimony.)

Marshall's pivotal position in the defense network became clear in 1997, when incoming Defense Secretary William Cohen—apparently unaware of Marshall's years of intellectual toil on behalf of the military-industrial complex—proposed downgrading the ONA's status. Immediately, a group of Congressional hawks and defense executives led by Jim Roche, a former Marshall aide now at

Northrop Grumman, mounted a fierce counterattack to preserve their man's influence. Marshall's friends in the press also weighed in, with letters and articles appearing in outlets such as the *Washington Times, Aviation Week*, the *Weekly Standard* and the *Wall Street Journal.* "Americans don't go to sleep at night worrying about how we'll win the next war," Paul Gigot wrote in the latter. "Andy Marshall does, which is why Americans ought to worry that he's being banished to outer Siberia by a witless and bureaucratic Pentagon." Cohen swiftly backed off and Marshall remained fixed at his threat-inflation post.

In recent years, Marshall's primary task has been promoting the RMA and the high-tech arsenal that girds it. "Over the next twenty to fifty years a military revolution will transform the way wars are fought," Marshall told Congress in 1995. "Rather than closing with an opponent, the major operational mode will be destroying him at a distance."

One sub-component of the RMA is something Marshall calls "Rapid Dominance." In 1998, he funded a project on the concept, with a review panel comprised of retired and active duty hawks from the defense establishment. At a conference that year sponsored by the National Defense University, one member of Marshall's study group, Harlan Ullman, defined the aim of Rapid Dominance: "to control the will and perception of adversaries, from privates to princelings, by applying a regime of shock and awe." Other panelists talked excitedly of creating "Bedlam Brigades" composed, as *Defense News* put it, "of highly mobile and lethal units that could be rapidly deployed and whose sole aim is to inject disarray and upheaval into an enemy's command arrangement and forces." Of course, all of this will require "a new generation of vehicles and soldier equipment," as John Foster, the former head of the Defense Science Board and another panelist, put it. One future weapon envisioned by the panel is called "very long-range global artillery," which would fire 1,000-pound warheads "with pinpoint accuracy," producing "unexplained explosions or light shows that could take place over an enemy's principle cities causing confusion and bewilderment among civilian populations."

During the past few years, the RMA has become one of the hottest buzzwords at the Pentagon. Back in 1997, the Clinton administration's National Defense Panel recommended spending between $5 billion and $10 billion annually to implement the doctrine. In his report to the president and Congress the following year, Secretary of Defense William Cohen said that the Pentagon's "willingness to embrace the Revolution in Military Affairs—to harness technology to ultimately bring about fundamental conceptual and organizational change—is critical" to meeting future national security challenges. The whole concept is now so sacrosanct that military commanders find that invoking the RMA is the surest way to get funding for a desired project. "Some people at the Pentagon take it very seriously as a means of planning for the future and others use it loosely to serve their bureaucratic purposes," says Professor Tom Mahnken, a former staffer at the Office of Net Assessment and an RMA expert at the Naval War College in Newport, Rhode Island. "It's become fashionable to justify your pet rock by calling it part of the RMA."

The vision of space-based surveillance systems ordering up precision strikes from "brilliant" weapons stationed far from the field of combat is dear to military planners because it suggests that future wars can be fought largely without the need for ground troops. Hence, the Pentagon can reduce overseas deployments and casualties without limiting America's ability to intervene abroad. It's a vision that also finds favor with industry officials, who understand that the Buck Rogers-type hardware favored by Marshall opens the door for especially heavy profiteering. A Pentagon official, who spoke about the RMA on condition of anonymity, concedes that weapons associated with the doctrine are pricey, but argues that it's money well spent. "Precision weapons are always going to be more costly on an individual basis than dumb bombs . . . but they are significantly more effective," he said. The RMA has also been embraced by many in Congress, including former House Speaker Newt Gingrich. "Virtually every soldier in combat in 2010 will have somewhere on their body a personal telephone linked by satellite to a world telephone network," he said in a speech before he abruptly resigned in 1999. "That telephone will probably be a . . . personal communication system that will also have a computer capability, faxing capability, so during lulls they can arrange a date."

Unfortunately, high-tech weapons systems seldom work as promised and can often be defeated with simple and far cheaper countermeasures. An early example came during the Vietnam War, when the Air Force dropped remote sensors by parachute into trees along the Ho Chi Minh Trail. The devices were supposed to monitor Viet Cong traffic, but couldn't differentiate between human porters carrying weapons and herds of wild deer. A recording made by one of the sensors captured the sound of a

North Vietnamese man walking up to the tree in which it was caught, taking it down, unzipping his pants and urinating on it. A more recent setback for the high-tech crowd came during the war in Yugoslavia, when Serb forces used a 1963 model Russian missile to shoot down the Air Force's vaunted F-117 "stealth" fighter, a plane supposedly all but invisible to enemy radar, that carries a price tag of $45 million.

One of Marshall's ideas is that the best way to halt an Iraqi ground attack is with a submarine launching from 100 miles away "brilliant" missiles that zero in on the sound of Russian-built tank engines. Acoustic homing has been contemplated—and rejected as being too easy to fool—since World War II. A missile like the one envisioned by Marshall might work under laboratory conditions, but battlefield noises—artillery barrages, rocket blasts, gunfire—make acoustic homing impractical. Marshall's dream could be tricked with a pair of $100 speakers playing the taped sound of a Russian tank engine. "At the core of RMA is a radical hypothesis that would cause Sun Tzu, Clausewitz and George Patton to roll over in their graves," Chuck Spinney says of the doctrine. "That is, that technology will transform the fog and friction of combat—the uncertainty, fear, chaos, imperfect information which is a natural product of a clash between opposing wills—into clear, friction-free, predictable, mechanistic interaction."

RMA mania reached fever pitch in a 1998 *Newsweek* story, which predicted that "the computer chip and the robot will [soon] be mobilized as the military's shock troops." Here's the battlefield of the future, as described by the magazine:

High-endurance robot aircraft circle over remote terrain for days at a time. Their sensors spot a formation of enemy tanks. The information is radioed to a satellite, which distributes it to half a dozen designated receivers on the ground. Computers select the artillery battery best located to strike the new targets; they flash the coordinates to that battery and no other. Using signals from a constellation of global-positioning satellites overhead, chips in the battery's targeting computer calculate the precise location of the tanks in relation to the battery, thus working out the correct azimuth and elevation needed to hit the enemy. Computers orient the battery and fire its rockets. As they are across the thirty miles or so between the battery and its targets, the rockets spew a cluster of mini-projectiles. Each has a sensor in its nose and a computer inside, enabling the little projectiles to detect the characteristic heat signature of tank exhausts, ignoring the trucks that travel with the enemy squadron. In the last few seconds of flight, the projectiles use on-board rockets to accelerate, hurtling down onto the least protected part of the tank, its turret hatch. Robot craft circling tirelessly overhead—so high that soldiers on the ground never knew they were there—sense the explosions that mark the death of each tank. The news is flashed back, again by satellite, to the screen of the unit commander, telling him what has just happened.

It's doubtful that even Marshall himself would take this fantasy seriously. No sensor can tell the difference between a truck and a tank, even in peacetime—and certainly not in wartime, when an enemy would be deploying deceptive tactics. No robot craft can circle so high as to make its presence unknown to enemy troops. Such systems are visible on radar, and easier still to spot if actively transmitting information. Furthermore, in a full-scale war a savvy foe would take care to knock out highly vulnerable satellite systems.

"It's too much bullshit to be believed even in a George Lucas film," Pierre Sprey says of the *Newsweek* scenario. "Every step in that link is wrong and concocted by people who don't know what a tank looks like or what a sensor can do."

Mahnken is less extravagant in his assessments than the more wild-eyed RMA advocates. He concedes there is some hype associated with the RMA, but nonetheless insists that the "information revolution" is fundamentally changing the nature of combat. "History shows that having better knowledge is crucial in war," he argues. "We're never going to see 100 percent [of the battlefield], but if we're seeing seventy percent and an adversary is seeing fifty percent, that's a major advantage." He says enemy states can be expected to develop countermeasures to the Pentagon's high-tech weapons—"that's part of the game"—but that most will have a hard time competing. He points out that previous military revolutions have shown the importance of getting a jump on one's adversaries. For example, it was years before Hitler's enemies figured out how to counter the blitzkrieg, which combined tactical innovations with deployment of bigger and better armored vehicles, especially tanks. "We don't want to have [Nazi] Germany as our model, but we don't want to be France in 1940 either," says Mahnken. "RMAs don't last forever, but they can yield substantial benefits over a long period of time."

For RMA enthusiasts, the Persian Gulf War gave an early glimpse of the unfolding revolution. They pointed to video images—endlessly replayed by the media—of laser-guided bombs travelling down smokestacks of buildings in Baghdad and to a film shown by General Norman Schwartzkopf of a US plane destroying an Iraqi Scud launcher. Marshall himself suggested that "stealth" planes like the F-117 were especially important in defeating Saddam Hussein.

In fact, the baroque components of the American arsenal made only a partial contribution to the outcome of the Gulf War. More consequential were the greater numbers and training of the allied forces as well as the collapse of the Soviet Union, which had been Iraq's chief military supplier and political ally. Iraqi generals also made the fatal mistake of massing and exposing their armor in the open, where it could be easily picked out for destruction. (A task made easier by the fact that US planes were operating under optimal conditions of expansive, sunny, desert terrain with little vegetation to obscure targets.) Finally, Hussein's army suffered the largest mass desertions in history. Some 175,000 Iraqis fled the front before ground combat began, leaving 25,000 troops to confront 400,000 US-led soldiers. As Mahnken wrote in a 1998 article in the US Naval Institute's *Proceedings*, the Gulf War showed only "what the US armed forces can do if given the opportunity to deploy and to operate with impunity. It is unlikely, however, that future foes will grant us uncontested access to their regions."

Evidence that the effectiveness of high-tech weapons in the conflict was overblown is provided by a little noted General Accounting Office report that was declassified in 1997 (over the bitter objections of the military, especially the Air Force). One section of the report compared post-war claims made by the Pentagon and manufacturers with what occurred during combat. Whereas the Defense Department stated that eighty percent of the bombs dropped by F-

117s had hit their target—an accuracy rate characterized by the plane's primary contractor, Lockheed, as "unprecedented"—the GAO found that the actual rate was somewhere between forty and sixty percent. "No matter what the mission, air to air, air to ground. No matter what the weather, day or night," F-16 subcontractor General Dynamics eulogized about its plane. The GAO tersely noted that the F-16's "delivery of precision air to ground munitions . . . was impaired and sometimes made impossible by clouds, haze, humidity, smoke and dust. Only less accurate unguided munitions could be employed in adverse weather using radar." Martin Marietta (later bought by Lockheed), bragged that its LANTIRN system could "locate and attack targets at night and under conditions of poor visibility." The GAO found that LANTIRN was effectively "employed below clouds and weather," but its ability to operate under conditions of poor visibility "ranged from limited to no capability at all." Texas Instruments claimed that its Paveway laser guidance system had a "one target, one bomb" capability, a phrase swiftly picked up by Pentagon officials to demonstrate the value of advanced technology in Desert Storm. The GAO found that at least two laser-guided bombs were dropped on each target and that six or more were dropped on thirty-five percent of them.

The report further found that there was no significant difference in the effectiveness of high-tech versus low-tech weaponry. The Pentagon exalted the performance of the F-117, pointing out that the Iraqis had failed to shoot down a single one. True, said the GAO, but the F-117 flew fewer missions than any other plane and went into action exclusively at night and at medium altitudes. "The most probable number of losses for any aircraft, stealthy or conventional, flying the same number of missions as the F-117 would have been zero," the report stated. The A-10 attack plane, which entered service in 1977 and costs about one-fifth of the F-117, performed so spectacularly well in the Gulf that the Air Force pressured the GAO to delete much of the relevant data from its report. The Pentagon is currently phasing the A-10 out of service.

There *is* one substantial difference between "smart" and "dumb" weapons: the latter are a lot cheaper. Guided bombs cost about $30,000 each, versus $649 for unguided ones. The former made up just eight percent of the munitions used in the Gulf campaign, but accounted for eighty-four percent of total costs.

The war in Yugoslavia produced another wave of RMA fervor. Even as the fighting raged, Pentagon spokesman Kenneth Bacon told reporters that the RMA was the reason "we're making progress without forces on the ground." Afterwards, General Wesley Clark said that high-tech weapons associated with the RMA helped NATO carry out "the most accurate bombing campaign in history," while Major General Dennis Haines stated that while the nation's bomber force had been halved since 1990, the use of precision-guided munitions had resulted in a ten-fold increase in the bomber force's lethal power over the same period. The media joined the chorus as well, with the *Washington Post* stating that NATO's use of the RMA had "overwhelmed a large and capable military force."

Again, while there's no question that modern air power has become more effective, the Pentagon's claims of high-tech proficiency were considerably exaggerated. Unlike the friendly terrain of

Kuwait in 1990, pilots in Yugoslavia had to fly over mountains and hills, sometimes under heavy cloud cover. During the war's early days, many flights were grounded because targets could not be identified when it was raining. Even when the weather improved, NATO's high-tech surveillance systems were often unable to pick out enemy troops and equipment. Pilots interviewed by the *Post* after the war talked about seeing burning Kosovar villages from thousands of feet overhead, but having no way of finding the responsible Yugoslav army troops.

NATO did prove that it could inflict heavy damage on an enemy's civilian infrastructure and economy. That no doubt played a role in Milosevic's decision to surrender—though perhaps not as large a one as pressure from Russia, which threatened to cut off Belgrade's oil supply—but such devastation did not require RMA. "It was plain old random destruction," one Pentagon hand says of the Kosovo campaign. "The only thing we proved is that we're able to bomb the shit out of a little country."

Air power was most effective towards the end of the campaign, but only after the Kosovo Liberation Army had mustered 17,000 men and was able to force the Serbs to out into the open. Even then, it appears that the US-led campaign did little to harm Yugoslavia's war-fighting ability. When it came time for Milosevic's forces to pull out of Kosovo, 47,000 soldiers —more than NATO estimated had been there in the first place and a number that undermines the Pentagon's claim of 5,000 to 10,000 Yugoslav military casualties— staged an orderly withdrawal over a road and bridge network supposedly shattered by the bombing campaign.

Serb gunners were firing Russian surface-to-air missiles on the final day of fighting despite enormous efforts by NATO to destroy Yugoslavia's air defense system. After initially claiming that NATO forces had destroyed 120 tanks, about 220 armored personnel carriers and some 450 artillery pieces, Pentagon officials quietly conceded that the true numbers were far less than that. The climb down began when Yugoslav troops rolled out of Kosovo with huge quantities of heavy equipment, including about a score of MIG fighters that they'd successfully hidden from NATO's surveillance systems. NATO troops that subsequently entered Kosovo reported finding only three damaged tanks in the entire province. Belgrade admitted that ten more tanks were hit, but said they were still salvageable and were taken back for repair.

Just as embarrassing as the bogus equipment kill figures, and probably partly accounting for them, were reports that Yugoslavia had repeatedly duped NATO's high-tech arsenal with simple decoys. Among the "targets" destroyed by NATO pilots were dummy tanks, bridges and roads, some of the latter being no more than plastic tarp stretched across fields. All of which goes to show that "brilliant" weapons, like their precursors, are in large measure dependent on good old-fashioned intelligence. (An example: one reason that the Serbs managed to shoot down the F-117 was that a spy informed Belgrade of its departure from an air base in Italy.) The use of smart bombs did not prevent accidental attacks on refugee convoys and KLA posts, not to mention the precision-guided bomb strike that leveled the Chinese embassy in Belgrade.

As with the Gulf War, post-war claims from Kosovo about specific weapons programs are likely to have been greatly exaggerated.

According to the Pentagon, one of the heroes of the war was the JSTARS, a ground surveillance system built by Northrop Grumman that promised to provide a "God's eye view" of the battlefield. Lieutenant Colonel Clark Kelly told *Defense Week* that thanks to JSTARS, the Serbs were unable to mobilize their equipment to engage in an attack. "They realized that when they moved, they died," he said.

A retired Pentagon official who closely monitors new weapons development scoffs at the supposed super-capacity of Northrop's system. "JSTARS is pretty good at picking up a moving target and it can estimate its speed," he says. "But it can't tell you if it's a wheeled vehicle like a car or a tracked vehicle like a tank, so you won't know if you're looking at a civilian or a military target."

Certainly the war in Yugoslavia does not support RMA advocates' vision of future war by remote control. NATO's air campaign did little to stop Serb troops from targeting civilians in Kosovo. Indeed, President Clinton's announcement that he would not deploy ground troops meant that Milosevic was not compelled to put his troops on the border to protect against a possible attack. "If in a future war you want to end a conflict quickly and prevent violence, you're still going to need ground troops," says Michael O'Hanlon of the Brookings Institute.

There's nothing on the technological horizon that's likely to change any of this. Remote surveillance systems aren't able to identify targets that the military considers to be of real importance—such as where the leader of a country is sleeping on a given night or where a command post is located (which these days might be nothing more than a cell phone). They also can't find weapons of mass destruction and there's no technology that can find small arms in the back of a pick-up truck. "All sensors have limitations and to a large extent they are limitations imposed by the basic and immutable laws of physics," says O'Hanlon. "Visible-light and infrared detectors cannot see through heavy clouds. Radar tends to have mediocre resolution. None of these sensors can deeply penetrate metal, water, concrete or most soils."

Meanwhile, the Pentagon—and its bipartisan political supporters—are pressing ahead with the weapons systems they say are desperately needed to further the RMA. In July 1999, the Pentagon's acquisition chief, Jacques Gansler, said that Kosovo had demonstrated that the military's buying strategy was on the right track and that the US should speed the transition to the "digital battlefield." The following month, Kent Kresa, CEO of B-2 builder Northrop Grumman Corp., wrote an op-ed in *Defense News* lauding the "magnificent performance" of high-tech weapons in the Balkans and outlining the pressing need to invest in "technological solutions" that will "increase military effectiveness for the next conflict."

The services have already sunk more than $60 billion into stealth technologies that were supposed to eliminate the need for electronic jammers that suppress enemy radar. Meanwhile, stealth planes like the F-117 and the B-2 still must be escorted into battle by aircraft that are designed to blind enemy radar. The Pentagon has spent almost as much to acquire thirty-three different types of guided munitions, and wants to spend another $16.6 billion during the next five years to double its inventory to over 300,000 weapons. A GAO report from last December said that existing stockpiles were "suffi-cient to meet current national defense objectives" and questioned the effectiveness and reliability of the Pentagon's hardware. "It is dif-ficult to understand DoD's rationale for doubling its inventory ... in today's budgetary and security environment," the GAO concluded.

The great irony is that while the RMA foresees ever more techno-logically sophisticated weapons, a good chunk of the Pentagon's cur-rent systems are so complex as to render them nearly worthless. "Computers [in high-tech weapons] are ever more capable and advanced, and they can dump more data down the line," says the weapons development expert. "The problem is that testing shows that our people are already overloaded with information." In a 1998 speech to Army program officers, Brigadier General Russell Honore put the matter more bluntly, saying that much of the Pentagon's high-tech arsenal simply will not perform on the battlefield. "You are fielding pieces of crap," he said. "Is that clear enough for you?"

DESPITE THE PRODIGIOUS efforts of Marshall and other military-industrial complex stalwarts, the Pentagon's budget for new acqui-sitions is still insufficient from the point of view of private arms makers. Between 1979 and the mid-1990s, Lockheed Martin sold about 2,000 of its F-16 fighters to the Pentagon, helping make it (as a company spokesman told William Grieder) "the most prof-itable fighter in history." By 1999, Lockheed sold just a single F-16 to the Defense Department. To keep production lines open at the Ft. Worth, Texas factory that makes the plane—where employment fell from 31,000 to 13,000 between 1990 and 1994—Lockheed must find overseas customers. Other companies are in a similar predicament. The Boeing plant in St. Louis that makes the F-15 employs about 5,000 people. The company delivered its last domestic order to the Air Force in late 1999 and so was keenly seeking to sell the fighter to Israel, Greece, Turkey and Saudi Arabia. Exports are considered to be so important that in 1999, the Clinton administration blessed a proposal by Lockheed to sell the United Arab Emirates eighty F-16s that are more advanced than those flown by American pilots.

The government has greatly assisted the weapons companies in helping to expand their overseas markets. The bureaucracy that manages the arms trade consists of more than 6,000 government employees—at the Pentagon, the Commerce Department and the State Department—and has an operating budget of $500 million. Staffers at American embassies abroad are expected to do their part. "A big part of my job is to help put Americans to work by selling products overseas, and that definitely includes the arms industry," Raymond Mabus, a former ambassador to Saudi Arabia, told the *Boston Globe* in 1996. "It is our job to do everything possible, and legal, to make sure they buy American."

In 1997, the Clinton administration used billions in taxpayer money to underwrite foreign weapons sales, with the money used to provide the industry with subsidized loans and tax breaks, as well as to assist with marketing efforts and promotional activities. Government support has helped the US seize a fifty-five-percent share of the world arms market, with $23.5 billion in sales in 1996. Buyers range from Albania to Zimbabwe, with 165 countries in between. Only a handful of states—mostly official enemies like Somalia, North Korea and Cuba—are considered off limits to American exporters.

With huge stocks piling up from the Cold War, the US has even been giving away weapons, which the Pentagon sees as a cheap way of solidifying ties with allied governments. (Another advantage is that members of Congress aren't required to vote on giveaways, or even be informed about such packages.) A study by Lora Lumpe of the Federation of American Scientists found that the US shipped some $7 billion worth of free equipment abroad between 1990 and 1996, including 3,900 heavy tanks and 500 ground attack jets. Egypt, Turkey, and Morocco have all built modern tank armies with US giveaways.

Administration officials and arms exporters argue that military support for foreign armies gives the United States leverage that can be used to press recipients to improve their human rights records or resolve conflicts. This has rarely been born out in practice. In places ranging from Algeria, Indonesia, Uganda, and Turkey, recipients of US military support used US arms and training for internal conflicts and repression. Eritrea and Ethiopia, both non-democratic states, fought each other using American arms and training.

The heart of the official network is the Defense Security Cooperation Agency, the Pentagon bureau that manages the Foreign Military Sales program of government-to-government sales (as opposed to the Direct Commercial Sales program, in which defense contractors themselves negotiate private sales to foreign military and police forces). The DSCA—which until late-1998 was known as the Defense Security Assistance Agency—has a field staff of about 1,000 people working out of US embassies in some seventy-five countries. They offer everything from briefings on weapons systems to demonstrations of major aircraft, in addition to arranging the financing needed to close a deal. The DSCA receives a three percent commission per sale—an income that provides about eighty percent of its operating budget—and agency personnel are promoted on the basis of their ability to move weaponry. Due to this dynamic, says a 1991 report from Congress's now defunct Office of Technology Assessment, there is powerful incentive for DSCA staff to make as many sales as possible. By 1992, the DSCA had racked up so much money from the three percent kickback that Congress placed a $300 million cap on the funds the agency could accumulate in its account. As of 1998, the agency estimated that it had enough cash to stay in business until 2002 without any additional income.

Even with the US comfortably in first place as the world's Number One arms dealer, the Pentagon and industry are looking for ways to further increase American sales. In May of 1998, Deputy Defense Secretary John Hamre ordered a review of the Foreign Military Sales program with an eye towards cutting red tape. At an Institute of Aeronautics and Astronautics luncheon in Arlington that month, he said, "Our process today is still very much a restrictive Cold War mindset . . . Frankly, we ought to open up our thinking and say maybe there are new institutional arrangements for foreign military sales." He put together a study group on the subject that brought together military officials, industry leaders and foreign government customers.

By early 1999, the review was in high gear. A story in *Defense News* reported that the Pentagon hoped to "break down bureaucratic barriers that have prompted many US friends and allies to shop elsewhere for military goods and services . . . Officials at the Pentagon's DSCA have engaged in massive introspection with an eye toward reinventing its costly, cumbersome, and often condescending arms export system." The story explained that, with a glut of arms available on post-Cold War markets, "increasingly savvy and demanding international customers can often dictate the terms of a deal." Hence, an "attitudinal sea change" was needed at the Pentagon so customers were "treated as partners rather than aid recipients."

Soon, Hamre announced a number of changes to the Foreign Military Sales program, including more flexible prices and financing, and allowing customers and US industry greater participation in drawing up contract terms. In another important development, the Pentagon has formed an Arms Transfer Policy Review Group, which will seek to expedite decision-making time on proposed sales—especially controversial ones—and then lobby for their approval with the State and Commerce Departments, the CIA and the National Security Council.

Over at the State Department, which oversees the Direct Commercial Sales program, government bureaucrats set up the Defense Trade Advisory Group (DTAG) to review proposed foreign deals. Details about the DCS program are hard to come by, since only deals worth more than $14 million need to be reported to Congress. In theory, State allows the sale of weapons destined only for a "defensive" role. It will not vend arms to an "aggressor" nation.

In practice, it authorizes sales to virtually any nation capable of paying for its purchases. Of some 20,000 requests for licenses made by vendors in 1994, State rejected just 209.

That's hardly surprising if one examines the roster of DTAG, State's outside advisor. As of 1995, fifty-seven of the sixty panel members came from the arms industry. William Schneider, the group's head, served as undersecretary of state for security assistance during the Reagan/Bush years. Another enthusiastic DTAG member is Joel Johnson of the Aerospace Industries Association, who once said he "would feel more guilty selling sugar-coated breakfast cereal to kids" than he does about peddling weapons abroad. After the Chinese government carried out its crackdown at Tianamen Square, Johnson fretted that the US government might prevent arms companies from cutting new deals with Beijing. "If we get out of the Chinese market now, we could lose out on sales well into the next century," he told William Hartung, an analyst at the World Policy Institute. In any case, he added, Tiananmen was no big deal. "For the Chinese, whether it was 200 or 2,000 deaths, it's just a blip on the radar screen. It's like their version of Kent State." The three non-industry members of DTAG are two lawyers and Janne Nolan, a centrist from the Brookings Institute. When former Arkansas Senator David Pryor questioned State Department officials about the objectivity of the group, they pointed to Nolan as providing balance.

DTAG is not a policy-making body, but it has lobbied the Clinton administration on proposals it reviews, such as revisions in export regulations and conventional arms transfer policy. "DTAG has frequent, high-level access to the people who are making policy," says Lora Lumpe. "People from the arms control community are completely shut out of the loop."

ONE MEANS by which government supports the arms industry is to subsidize its participation in international exhibits like the Defentech show in Brazil. Until 1991, US companies participating in overseas exhibits had to lease military equipment for the shows and pay the Pentagon for transportation, insurance and personnel costs. Arguing that the shows promote national security, then-President George Bush permitted the Pentagon to cover those expenses. While on the campaign trail in 1992, Bill Clinton pledged to review arms sales policy and soon after taking office refused Pentagon participation in the 1993 Paris Air Show. Clinton subsequently reversed course and allowed Bush's original decision to stand. Since 1991, the Pentagon has, when required, provided companies with military equipment to display at the shows and subsidized exhibition costs. The Pentagon dispatched 200 support personnel to the Berlin Air Show in May 1998 while the "Golden Knights," the US Army's parachute demonstration team, were sent to perform at the arms exhibit in Santiago, Chile held two months earlier. The Pentagon also provides defense companies with on-site marketing and public relations assistance. At the 1999 Abu Dhabi show, American VIPs included General Anthony Zinni, commander of US forces in the Persian Gulf. At other events, US Air Force pilots have been deployed to take potential customers on test flights.

Government spending on arms shows amounts to only about $70 million a year, and the Pentagon sees it as a good return on the dollar. "The rationale is that it demonstrates US forward presence, the superiority of US equipment, and general goodwill," Clark Adams, a Defense Department spokesman, says in explaining official backing of the exhibits. Critics see it differently. In 1999, Representative Pete Stark of California introduced a bill that would ban Pentagon participation in weapons exhibitions unless contractors cover all the costs. "These shows serve the interests of the industry, but they certainly don't serve the national interest," he says. "The whole point is to proliferate weapons around the globe."

Until the past few years, the Middle East has been the arms makers' chief cash cow. Between 1987 and 1994, the United Arab Emirates spent $6 billion on new weapons. Saudi Arabia was an even bigger buyer, often spending several billion dollars for arms imports in a single year. (Latest estimates are that Saudi Arabia has 1,021 tanks in its arsenal compared with 906 held by France, one of the world's leading military powers.) However, plummeting oil prices have forced the region's countries to dramatically scale back on their purchases. Between 1993 and 1996, sales to Gulf nations plunged from $14.7 billion to $1.7 billion. The economic collapse in Asia, another big market, has further cut into arms makers' sales opportunities.

Latin America is in trouble, too, as a drop in commodity prices and the fall-out from the collapse of Asia's financial markets left governments with little money to spend on military hardware. The return of civilian rule to most countries during the 1980s has put a further damper on weapons purchases. "Things were different when the military ran things down here," a US official at Defentech said with a touch of melancholy. "Then they didn't have to go running to Congress for money."

Still, the arms makers have high hopes for the region. Chile has announced plans to buy twenty-four new fighter planes, though it postponed that decision in early-1999 due to a drop in the price of copper, its chief export. In 1995, Brazil bought sixty-one Leopard-1 tanks from Belgium and the following year Argentina spent $125 million on A-4 ground attack jets from the US. Overall, Latin counties imported $5 billion worth of arms between 1994 and 1997. That accounted for 6.9 percent of total purchases from developing countries, up from 4.4 percent during the previous three-year period.

An opportunity for further expansion came in 1997, when President Clinton—in response to a fierce industry lobbying campaign—lifted a two-decade old ban on the sale of high-tech weapons to Latin America. A report issued the following year by Forecast International/DMS, a defense marketing firm, said that the Latin market "finally shows signs of dynamism" and predicted that the region would purchase up to $80 billion worth of weapons in the following decade.

Such purchases do little to address the real problems faced by Latin nations. In response to questions posed by the Senate Intelligence Committee, the State Department in late-1997 categorized the leading threats to Latin stability as poverty, corruption, the lack of an independent judiciary, and poor education. A poll conducted the following year by the *Wall Street Journal* and sixteen Latin American newspapers found that sixty-five percent of respondents were opposed to the sale of advanced arms to the region.

The opening of Defentech in Rio coincided with a severe economic crisis in Brazil, leading to some questioning by the local press about the country's sponsorship of the show, and especially about the government's plan to spend billions of dollars on new military equipment. The general consensus was that the government's military spending plans are a sop to placate the armed forces, which ruled between 1964 and 1985, and remain powerful. Defentech was officially opened by Vice President Marco Maciel, who served as a government minister and leader of a rubber-stamp Congress during the dictatorship. "It might seem sad to someone who's not from the military area but if Brazil wants to gain more international prestige, the modernization of the armed forces is essential," an unnamed military specialist told the Rio daily *Jornal do Brasil* as the arms show got underway.

Brazil is one of just a few Third World nations with a sophisticated indigenous arms industry, manufacturing everything from bullets to planes. The country has found it hard to compete with First World nations following the end of the Cold War and has fallen from being the world's ninth biggest military exporter to a tiny player on the international scene. In discussing local industry's grim prospects, an official from arms maker Imbel noted with sadness that today one of the company's biggest customers for gunpowder are Brazil's *macumbistas*—practitioners of an African-based spirit religion who use it in their ceremonies.

Thirty-one Brazilian firms or organizations, including all branches of the armed services, were on hand at Rio Center. Like many companies, Condor, a Brazilian manufacturer of "non-lethal" weaponry such as tear gas launchers, pepper spray and rubber bullets, had hired a local woman to stand in front of its booth to draw in business. Wearing a sleeveless black minidress and high heels, she was attired in the unofficial uniform of the show's hostesses. The Condor stand was decorated with a poster showing urban rioters running amok and bearing the caption "Don't Lose Control." Another poster showed a protest by landless peasants with the caption "Shoot But Don't Kill." A Condor salesman showed me some of the company's merchandise, including what he called "a very special thing"—a police baton that fires rubber bullets, tear gas and plastic cartridges.

HeloPoint, an Israeli firm, drew crowds to watch demonstrations of its $200,000 video sniper system. The device, which is the size of a small suitcase, broadcasts the images from eight separate riflescopes on a video screen. "This allows a unit commander to decide which of his men has the best shot at the target," Mandy Rosenzweig, the company's vice president of engineering, explained. HeloPoint's overseas clients include Poland, Turkey and Greece. At Defentech, officers from police units in Rio and the northern state of Para expressed interest in purchasing the system, a chilling prospect considering that the Rio police killed 358 people in 1996, more than were killed by all police departments in the United States. Sixty-one percent of the victims had bullets in their heads. In Para, police have been repeatedly called out to attack rural unionists and break up demonstrations of peasants. In one 1996 incident, Para police shot dead nineteen peasants who were protesting the government's failure to carry out an agrarian reform program.

All the major arms exporting countries sent large contingents to Defentech. An exhibit sponsored by the British government sported a tropical theme. Every few hours, a group of soldiers—with experience in places such as Bosnia and Northern Ireland—staged the setup of a jungle base camp complete with anti-aircraft guns, mortars, and communications and surveillance systems. Twelve firms from Germany came to Rio, accompanied by the country's Deputy Minister of Defense, Walter Kolbow. South Africa, a leading Third World producer, was also well represented. At the spacious booth for Denel, the nation's leading arms manufacturer, uniformed help offered wine, cheese and assorted snacks. Moscow is still a player in the international trade, but its sales are significantly down from Cold War days, at just $2 billion for 1998. That was reflected by the forlorn booth mounted by the Russian state arms agency, Rosvooruzhenie, which was decorated with cheap model airplanes and tanks.

The French also had a strong presence, led by aircraft maker Dassault. The company heavily promoted its Mirage-2000, one of the top four competitors for the contract to supply Brazil's new fighter planes. (The other three are Boeing's F/A-18, Lockheed's F-16, and the Gripen, produced by a joint venture of Saab and British Aerospace.) Yves Robins, the company's stylishly dressed vice president of international relations, was one of the few salesmen on hand who seemed optimistic about future prospects. During the past few years, his firm has closed out major fighter plane deals in Taiwan, Qatar and the United Arab Emirates, the latter a $3.2 billion blockbuster that included the sale of thirty Mirage-2000s and the modernization of another three dozen fighters the company had previously peddled to the UAE. "We sign fewer contracts and sell fewer planes than we did [during the Cold War], but the aircraft are more advanced and they carry a wider array of weapons," he said. "In the end, the budgets can be just as big as they were in the past."

The single biggest contingent to Defentech, beating out even the locals, came from the United States, with thirty-four companies represented. In addition to Lockheed and United Technologies, Boeing, Raytheon, Pratt & Whitney, Northrop-Grumman, Fairchild Defense, and a host of others took part. When I made initial contact with Reed Exhibition Companies, the organizer of Defentech, I pretended that I represented a defense firm that intended to display its wares in Rio. Reed sent me an informational packet that included a letter of encouragement from the US Commerce Department. Coming to Defentech would allow my firm "to evaluate this growing market [and] expand your overseas sales," said the letter, which further promised that commercial staff from the US consulate in Rio would be on hand at the show "to facilitate contacts between exhibitors and Latin American business visitors."

On the first night of the exhibit, the US embassy hosted a dinner for hundreds of participants at Mario's, an upscale steak house on Copacabana beach. The crowd was briefed on the defense market in Brazil by a military attaché at the American consulate. The embassy had a spacious booth at Defentech, where potential customers were helpfully assisted by Commerce Department staffers down from the US as well as locals from the embassy in Brasilia.

The booth mounted by Sikorsky Aircraft, a division of United Technologies, offered glossy photos of the company's hardware, including a shot of the top selling Black Hawk attack helicopter flying past the Statue of Liberty. A video display showed off the helicopter in a variety of combat situations and boasted that it had been sold to eighteen foreign armies (including Turkey, where the government has made it a weapon of choice in its war on Kurdish separatists). Back in 1997, Sikorsky sold four Black Hawks to Brazil, breaking France's long-time stranglehold on the local helicopter market. "On that contract, the [US] ambassador became part of my team," Orlando Figueiredo, Sikorsky's director of international programs in Brazil, told me as we sat in the company's air-conditioned booth. "They gave us everything we asked for."

At the nearby Raytheon display, company sales reps were hawking such products as the TOW-2 anti-tank missile and the Stinger anti-aircraft missile. This booth also featured extensive displays of the company's Amazon Surveillance System, a $1.4 billion radar installation being built to monitor the vast rain forest. The deal that secured this was almost scuttled in 1996 when a major Brazilian newsweekly published transcripts of a phone conversation between Jose Afonso Assumpcao, a Raytheon sales representative, and a top presidential adviser named Julio Cesar Gomes dos Santos. "That son of a whore [Senator Gilberto] Miranda is fucking us over, screwing up everything," Assumpcao was recorded as saying. "He doesn't want the project to go forward, he's creating difficulties." To which dos Santos replied, "Shit, didn't you already pay that guy?" (After the transcripts surfaced, dos Santos said his suggestion of a bribe was only a joke and Raytheon dumped Assumpcao.)

Boeing sent at least half a dozen employees to Rio, where they talked up the firm's Harpoon anti-ship missile (a package deal for twenty, which included back-up spare parts, carried a price tag of $40 million) and Apache helicopters ($24 million apiece). The company's chief interest, though, was promoting its F/A-18 C/D fighter. One sales rep, who insisted on speaking off-the-record, enthused that Boeing's reputation had been bolstered by news from the Balkans, where its F-15 fighters had shot down four Yugoslav planes.

Boeing sells about twenty percent of its F/A-18 C/Ds abroad. The sales rep portrayed that as a "win-win" situation for US companies and taxpayers, since overseas sales create economies of scale that reduce per unit costs paid by the Pentagon. A second advantage is that selling US equipment allows for "interoperability" with foreign allies, here again pointing to the situation in Kosovo as an example. "When we go to these little dust-ups we don't go solo anymore," he said. "It helps if we go out with allies that have equipment that's just as good." (Exporting is win-win for the industry, too. In seeking to build congressional support for its F-22, a plane with soaring costs and dwindling promise, Lockheed put out a promotional brochure that laid out the top threats to American air supremacy, a list that included everything from Russian MIG-29s owned by nations such as Iraq and North Korea to Lockheed's own F-16s, which the company has sold to "hostile" nations like Israel, South Korea and Canada. Lockheed goes so far as to boast that the F-22 can stymie the air defense radar systems which it has installed on the planes it has previously exported abroad. "We can't predict the future thirty years from now," Jeff Rhodes, a Lockheed spokesman said in an interview. "A military dictator could take power in a country [that owns Lockheed aircraft] which is currently an ally.")

Like other US firms, Boeing brought consultants to Defentech, whose job is to open doors with the locals. Boeing's advisors included a retired Brazilian Air Force colonel and Langhorne Motley, a US ambassador to Brazil during the Reagan years. Dressed in slacks and a polo shirt, Motley conceded that there is no overwhelming need for Latin armies to upgrade their equipment. The threat of war in the region is low—Ecuador and Peru recently resolved the hottest problem, a half-century old border conflict—and only Colombia faces a major guerilla conflict. "There used to be a risk of conflicts between countries and internal threats from subversive elements associated with the Cold War situation," he said. "That shit's all gone."

The centerpiece of Lockheed's booth was its F-16 flight simulator. Ron Covais, a former Air Force lieutenant colonel and Lockheed executive who handles all business in the Americas, allowed me to take the plane out for a spin, but I performed far less capably than Commander Ruth Harkin. After crashing the F-16 into the desert terrain displayed on the video screen, I took off again only to be unceremoniously booted from the cockpit when two women from the Brazilian Justice Ministry stopped by and asked for a turn.

Covais later sat and chatted with me on a couch in the US embassy booth, located a few doors down from his company's display. Foreign sales are a prime growth area for Lockheed, he said, and praised the Clinton administration for overturning the ban on high-tech sales to Latin America. "We and the other countries worked two-and-a-half years to get that policy changed," he said. "Up until then, the Latin American governments didn't see the US as a reliable partner. It changed a lot of mindsets here and in the US, and created a lot of business opportunities."

Covais expressed optimism about his company winning Brazil's fighter jet contract. Like the Boeing rep, he believed that England's arrest of the former Chilean dictator Augusto Pinochet would kill the bid of Gripen because of that company's partnership with British Aerospace. Anti-European sentiment within the Chilean military would hurt the French firm Dassault as well, Covais suggested hopefully. Left unspoken was the thought that US firms would benefit from their government's long-time support for Pinochet and its refusal to cooperate with Spanish prosecutors seeking his extradition from England.

And so the arms industry prepares to face the new millenium, its chief strategy being to keep production lines open by selling expensive weapons to Third World countries that don't have the money or need to buy them. Two weeks before Defentech opened, President Fernando Henrique Cardoso announced that after having previously made deep budget cuts due to the country's economic crisis, he was restoring part of the lost funding for social programs "that have a fundamental importance for Brazil." Hence, the president came up with an additional $30 million for a program to reduce child labor. Two weeks after Defentech closed, the Swedish arms maker Celsius, which exhibited its wares in Rio, announced that Brazil had placed an order for the company's high-speed torpedoes. It was a small deal by the standards of the arms trade, just $59 million, but still nearly twice as much as Cardoso had committed to fight child labor.

In the months following the exhibit, other Defentech participants were also reported to have deals in the works. Meanwhile, the hunt to snare the Brazilian fighter deal intensified. Boeing and Lockheed's hopes soared with the successful US campaign in Yugoslavia, but Dassault countered by joining a French group that acquired a twenty percent share in Brazilian arms maker Embraer (a move seen within the industry as a means of strengthening its sway with government officials). There was more good news next door in Chile. As 1999 was coming to a close, President Eduardo Frei decreed that the economy had improved sufficiently and that the government could spare $500 million to revive its own fighter deal. The same four companies fighting for the Brazilian contract immediately sent proposals in the hopes of cashing in on the country's good fortune.

TWO

ARMS AND THE MAN

The Talented Mr. Glatt

"Vote! Bah! When you vote, you only change the names of the cabinet. When you shoot, you pull down governments, inaugurate new epochs, abolish old orders and set up new."

—Andrew Undershaft, the munitions magnate of George Bernard Shaw's *Major Barbara*

"Arms dealers provide the grease that makes foreign policy work. If you're going to have a covert war somewhere, somebody has to provide the bullets."

—John Miley, retired weapons dealer for the CIA and Army Intelligence

AT THE FOOTHILLS of the Blue Ridge Mountains about thirty miles south of Charlottesville sits Nelson County, Virginia, one of the state's loveliest and most bucolic corners. Unmarred by a single traffic light, the county is traversed by Highway 56, a two-lane country road that wends among vineyards, orchards and farms. The rich landscape draws plenty of tourists and weekend drivers. They come to take in Crabtree Falls, the highest waterfall east of the Mississippi, and to stop by the Walton Museum, which celebrates the series that brought John Boy and his family to millions of American TV viewers.

Nelson County is steeped in American history and boasts spectacular homes that date back to colonial times. There's Level Green, built in 1802 for the Revolutionary War leader Major Thomas Massie, and Bellevette (pronounced "belive it"), an estate constructed about a century earlier by Charles Rose on land granted to him by King George II. Across the Tye River from Bellevette lies MarkHam from, a plot of land once held by a granddaughter of Thomas Jefferson. MarkHam farm has changed hands many times over the years, most recently in 1980 when a German named Ernst Werner Glatt bought it. He subsequently purchased adjoining lands and turned the estate, which is valued at $2.4 million, into a modern sheep farm. One's imminent arrival at the farm is marked by a sign on Highway 56 that sports a crowned Black Eagle, the name of the property. The symbol hearkens back to Imperial Prussia and reflects the fiercely right-wing views of the estate's owner, who as a teenager fought in the Nazi army.

Nelson County is small enough for just about everyone to have heard of Glatt and his Black Eagle Farm, though it's doubtful that many draw the connection between the property's name and their neighbor's political ideology. It would surely come as a shock to most residents that Glatt, who spends most of his time in Europe, has had a long and spectacular career in the arms trade. Indeed, for many years he was the Pentagon's preferred gunrunner during the Cold War covertly funneled weapons to a number of American-backed guerilla forces and client regimes. Glatt was also the leading supplier for a still-active "black" operation called the Foreign Materiel Acquisition

Program (FMA) that secretly obtained huge amounts of weaponry from the former Soviet Bloc and other "enemy" states. Though health problems and age have slowed him down—he turned seventy-two in 2000—Glatt remains active in the arms trade and, at least until quite recently, still worked with the American government.

Nelson County residents aren't alone in being unfamiliar with Glatt's extraordinary past. Unlike most businessmen, arms dealers—at least those who support clandestine operations—try to keep their names out of the newspapers. Since their activities generally come to light only during periods of scandal—the Iran/contra affair served as a mass outing of brokers, as did the Lockheed bribery scandals of the 1970s and, further back, the huge uproar that followed revelations of arms makers' duplicity during World War I— many major arms dealers have come and gone without any public awareness of their actions. Glatt has been a player in the business for more than a quarter-century and has had a hand in some of the most sensational government operations of the post-war era. Yet he and his sponsors in government have so successfully hidden his activities that Glatt is barely known outside of intelligence circles.

I first came across Glatt when I learned, from the National Security News Service, of an unreported 1995 lawsuit between Glatt and another arms dealer, an American named Charles Petty. The lawsuit, filed at the Arlington County Courthouse in Virginia and settled on terms sealed from the public, stemmed from a botched effort to sell a Hungarian-made mortar to the US Army and in itself provided little useful information. However, during the discovery process, Petty asked Glatt to reveal his connections to dozens of people. In addition to many retired and active duty military officers, these ranged from the notorious—Oliver North and Ed Wilson, the former CIA agent now serving a lengthy term in prison for selling arms to Muammar Quaddafi—to the obscure—Loftur Johannesson "the Icelander" and "One Mr. Martin in Miami," both of whom I later discovered were arms dealers. Glatt v. Petty was settled before the plaintiff responded to the motion for discovery, but the list of names provided a useful guide to investigate Glatt's career. I tracked down most of the people named and the majority were willing to talk to me, though often only off the record.

Still, research proceeded at a snail's pace. Weapons dealers operate within a maze of front companies and intelligence agencies, fake names, and Swiss bank accounts. Charles Kerr, counsel for the Senate during the Iran/contra hearings, told me that one weapons broker he interviewed at the time had confessed to having "operated in a hall of mirrors for so long that he himself didn't know the difference between fact and fiction any more." Furthermore, Glatt's universe is a tiny one and before long I'd bumped up against its outer limits. One notable arms dealer called me, unsolicited, to offer information after he heard through the grapevine that I was working on Glatt's story. When I rang Michael Kokin, an American who brokered deals for the CIA during the 1980s and who knew Glatt, the first thing he said was, "I've been expecting your call." Glatt's activities on behalf of the United States are highly sensitive and remain classified, with the result that even friendly sources revealed only a fraction of what they knew. Not everyone was friendly. One person refused to help because, he said, there were people within the national security establishment who would prefer that I not write the story. The CIA, in response to a Freedom of Information request, would neither confirm nor deny a relationship with Glatt, but said if there was an association, the agency wasn't prepared to discuss it.

Glatt himself has never given an on-the-record interview, but after months of negotiations conducted through his US attorney, Lawrence Barcella, he agreed to a meeting in Frankfurt, where he had a scheduled business trip. Just days before I was to depart for Europe he cancelled, citing health problems. We did have several conversations by phone and Glatt responded to a list of questions that I sent him in a three-page letter. His replies were helpful but imprecise—he provided a date only once, saying that his military service in the German army ended "at the age of seventeen years and eleven days in April 1945"—and skirted many of my queries. (He declined to discuss at all his involvement in the FMA program.) Due to Glatt's limited cooperation, I had to rely, in part, on accounts provided by those who know him, which at times were confusing and contradictory. A number of the people I spoke with insisted that Glatt is Austrian, not German, a discrepancy that turns up in rare published accounts that name him. Some denounced Glatt as a Nazi while others said with equal certainty that he is secretly Jewish. One former business partner insisted that Glatt has a relative of the same name in New York City who is a rabbi. There is, in fact, a Rabbi Herman Glatt listed in Washington Heights, though his wife—the rabbi is sickly and unable to take calls — says she's never heard of anyone by the name of Ernst Werner Glatt. From his current home at the maximum-security Allenwood Federal Penitentiary in Pennsylvania, Ed Wilson offered the cryptic remark. "Yes, I knew Werner. But no one knew Werner well! He is a smooth character." Another source told me that Ernst Werner Glatt did not exist, that the name is merely an alias used by an asset of US intelligence.

What I finally discovered surely offers but a limited window on Glatt's life and prolific career in the arms trade. It's a remarkable and revealing story, none the less. Over the years, I learned, Glatt has expanded into more conventional forms of commerce. His business holdings, which include factories, farms, and real estate are spread across Europe, the Middle East and the United States. In addition to the Black Eagle, he owns three chalets in the Swiss Alps, an apartment in London two blocks from Harrods, an estate in Austria, and another in Luxembourg, his principal residence. Glatt's most lavish holding is a vast, forested estate near Edinburgh, Scotland, bought in the early 1980s from a former lord mayor of London and owned prior to that by Lord Balfour, the British diplomat who, early in the century, made the famous declaration which called for the creation of a Jewish state in Palestine. Glatt's contacts around the world are as diverse as his financial holdings. His friends and colleagues include European aristocrats, Middle Eastern government officials, and Third World defense ministers. In America, he helped fund the High Frontier, the "Star Wars" lobby headed, until his death, by Glatt's close friend General Daniel Graham. Glatt's ties to the American military run deep— which some of his competitors say explains how he got so much business from the Pentagon.

Combined with his appearance—military brush cut, dueling scar, expensive suits and (until recently), Coke-bottle glasses—Glatt's appetites for luxury and large-scale arms dealing makes it easy to cast him as the kind of shadowy villain that populate the James Bond genre. But the uncomfortable truth is that Glatt and his ilk are simultaneously 007 and Spectre's Ernst Stavro Blofeld, acting both as government agents and as mercenaries with only the "pure motive of pure profit" in mind. More than just a story of money and guns, Glatt's tale offers a virtual how-to guide of covert operations and reveals the synergistic relationship between governments and black market arms dealers. Because he was so often present when weapons were a component of US foreign policy, Glatt's career also serves as a prism through which to view American involvement abroad since World War II, when anti-Communism, national security, and other dogmas have been invoked as rationales for conducting secret wars, supporting dictators, and ignoring national and international laws—all in the name of democracy.

THE TERM "merchants of death" arose in the early part of this century, when the giant munitions makers of the day dispatched agents and salesmen around the globe to advance their commercial interests. Those agents sold to both sides, bought off government officials, and used their power to increase international tension, this always being the most practical means of generating demand. The spirit of the times was captured in a 1932 letter sent from an executive at Colt Firearms to a company representative in South America. "Dear Mr. Foster," the letter opens, "In view of the flare-up in some of the Latin American countries, it would be most advisable for you to keep closely in touch with the Colombian, Bolivian, and Peruvian consuls, advising them that we understand their respective countries may be in the market for munitions and it is our desire to extend them every cooperation. As you know, these ópera bouffe revolutions are usually short-lived, and we must make the most of the opportunity."

The most famous of all "merchants of death" was Basil Zaharoff, who represented several big Western munitions firms and was said to be the inspiration for Andrew Undershaft, the weapons magnate of George Bernard Shaw's *Major Barbara*. Undershaft's motto: "Give arms to all men who offer an honest price for them, without respect of persons or principles." Zaharoff pioneered the use of credit, thereby paving the way for arms races between cash-strapped nations, and was especially adept at fueling military insecurity. His most notable accomplishment came in the late 1800s when, as a salesman for the Swedish company Nordenfeldt, he sold a submarine to Greece, the country of his mother's birth. He explained to the official who approved the contract that he was "first a Greek, a patriot like yourself," and only second, a salesman. Whereupon Zaharoff immediately went to the Turks, the Greek military's most hated enemy, and terrified them so much with tales of the sinister new Greek submarine that they bought two of their own. Zaharoff was considered to be as influential as the industrial magnates of the time, and his knowledge of military affairs was so great that military officers reportedly consulted with him before planning major operations. The

Western powers were so enamored of Zaharoff that he was knighted by the British and twice awarded the French government's Legion of Honor.

Though not himself an arms salesman, Zaharoff's closest American counterpart was a one-time nightclub manager and fight promoter named William Shearer. Following World War I, he served as a covert propagandist for arms companies like American Brown Boveri. That firm paid him to defame as traitors prominent doves such as Charles Evans Hughes, later a chief justice of the Supreme Court. In an anonymous pamphlet, Shearer said Hughes had "betrayed America" by favoring arms control. "The shocked readers of Shearer's pamphlets did not realize, of course, that they had been paid for by armaments firms," Norman Cousins writes in *The Pathology of Power*, which contains a lively recounting of Shearer's career.

According to Cousins, the highlight of Shearer's career came in 1927 when shipbuilders Bethlehem Steel and Newport News sent him to that year's Naval Conference in Geneva. Fearing it would turn into an orgy of disarmament, the companies dispatched Shearer to do everything possible to sabotage the conference. "Nobody seemed quite sure who he was, but he entertained lavishly and was accepted as someone eminent because so many of the American officials present visibly deferred to him and recommended him to journalists as an expert on the problems of naval disarmament," writes Cousins. "Soon, newspapermen, statesmen and most of the US naval delegation were being 'posted' by Shearer on the sinister implications of arms limitation." Shearer succeeded in turning what promised to be a civil event into a diplomatic bloodbath and later boasted that he had wrecked the conference single-handed.

The activities of Zaharoff, Shearer, and other arms promoters outraged publics in Europe and America. By 1934, calls for legislation "to take the profit out of war" led the US Senate to create a Special Committee to Investigate the Munitions Industry. Known as the Nye hearings after its chairman, Senator Gerald Nye of North Dakota, the committee concluded that the effect of foreign arms sales "is to produce fear, hostility, and greater munitions orders on the part of neighboring countries, culminating in economic strain and collapse or war." (One aide to the committee was a young Congressional staffer named Alger Hiss.) The Nye hearings led to a number of reforms—henceforth all arms exporters had to seek a license from the new Office of Munitions Control, which was installed under the auspices of the State Department—but it wasn't public outrage that brought about the downfall of the "merchants of death." By World War II, governments had asserted control over the trade by requiring arms makers to export through official channels and otherwise regulating the industry. At the same time, weapons manufacturing became an ever more important component of modern economies. As George Thayer wrote in his 1969 book, *The War Business,* "Instead of operating at ten to twenty percent of capacity, as they had done in their prewar years of famine, the free-world's arms industries [began operating in] the late 1940s at eighty to ninety percent of capacity. With governments ensuring high production levels and buying nearly the entire output, arms industries have had no need of Zaharoff-type salesmen who roam the world in search of sales."

Government oversight has not served to restrain the arms trade, but to sanctify it (as reflected in the fate of the Office of Munitions Control, which in 1990 was replaced by the more precisely named Center for Defense Trade). American presidents have seen weapons transfers as a means of strengthening foreign alliances and propping up domestic manufacturers. Congress has the authority to oversee arms sales policy, but it effectively serves as a rubber stamp. Since 1986, the executive branch has approved the sale of almost $150 billion in weapons around the globe without Congress once exercising its lawful prerogative to vote on individual deals. Regulation also brought about the institutionalization of the arms trade within enormously powerful state bureaucracies. Today some 5,000 companies and individuals are registered with the government to sell weapons abroad, and their activities—46,000 separate transactions in 1997—are duly recorded in the State Department's annual report on commercial sales. As Thayer wrote, the government officials who supervise the trade "are subject to no specific recall. They are not elected to their posts. They control budgets that would stagger the imagination of Zaharoff, and they operate in bureaucracies that are so large, so Byzantine, so powerful that effectively they are beyond the control of elected representatives. However disruptive a Zaharoff in the past, he was in the last analysis subject to review by law: he could be subpoenaed, his records could be scrutinized, and he could be prosecuted. Today's bureaucrats are immune to this type of behavior . . . [T]heir behavior, if exposed, would reflect on the entire operations of government and not just one segment of it . . . The government officials who sell arms . . . have power that Zaharoff never dreamed of, they are protected to a degree that no private entrepreneur of old ever enjoyed, and they operate with less restraints on them than even those few imposed on the master arms merchant himself."

The bulk of the global weapons business is comprised of tanks, planes, ships and other big-ticket items sold by and to governments. Private arms dealers are still useful, especially when governments wish to ship materiel discreetly to controversial clients: guerilla armies that are not legally permitted to buy weapons, regimes facing international arms embargoes, and states that are notorious human rights abusers. In this regard, nothing has changed since 1934, when H.C. Engelbrecht and F.C. Hanighen wrote in their famous book, *Merchants of Death: A Study of the International Armaments Industry*, "The international sale of arms . . . has far deeper roots than the 'conscienceless greed' of the arms makers. If all private arms makers decided to discontinue their international traffic tomorrow, a world-wide protest of governments would not permit them to do it."

A 1997 article in *Jane's Intelligence Review* estimates that black market sales come to about $1 billion to $2 billion in bad years and up to five times that much in good ones. Because they primarily supply rifles, machine guns, mortars, grenade launchers, anti-tank rockets, and other materiel used in small-scale wars, private dealers play a more significant role than is reflected by the relatively small percentage of the global arms trade that they handle. Brokers break the paper trail by setting up shell companies and offshore bank accounts, secure vital documents such as end-user certificates—stating which nation the goods are headed to and serve as a pledge by purchasers not to re-export to third parties— and handle the delicate task of paying off government officials and customs agents. Most importantly, middlemen provide governments with "plausible deniability" if a deal is exposed or otherwise bungled. "That old opening to *Mission Impossible* is true," says one broker. "The Secretary really will disown any knowledge of you if things go wrong."

Buyers, especially pariah regimes, also employ brokers, as they often don't have the expertise needed to set up a deal. Identifying a source of merchandise, shopping for a good price, and arranging shipping and financing can be complicated, especially if the parties involved prefer to operate in the shadows. "Why do buyers use brokers?" Val Forgett, owner of Navy Arms Company in Ridgefield, New Jersey, repeats my question. "For the same reason you use one when you're looking to buy a house," he replied. A vigorous man of sixty-nine, Forgett has white hair and deep blue eyes, one hidden behind a cataract. We talked at Navy Arms Co., located in a modest building just across from Manhattan over the George Washington Bridge. A retail outlet offering assorted firearms occupies the ground floor and sits atop a basement stocked with crates of small arms bought from the Third World for resale. Forgett's office is on the third floor. It's decorated with an extensive collection of antique guns and presentation swords, including one given by Catherine the Great to her Russian field general/lover. There are also photographs of Forgett with arms industry luminaries such as Mikhail Kalashnikov, designer of the world's most popular assault rifle, the AK-47.

Forgett was determined to become a weapons trader ever since, as a teenager, he read about Zaharoff's exploits. During our interview, he pulled from a bookshelf his high school yearbook of 1948 and pointed to the words below his graduation photo: "Will design and export arms." Guns are still his passion. Though he now sells mainly to collectors, he has had plenty of controversial customers in the past, including the former Chilean dictator Augusto Pinochet. "Is there a regime you wouldn't sell to?" I asked. "There might be, but I can't think of one offhand," Forgett replied. "Our government is the biggest arms dealer in the world, and if they issue me a license, I'll sell." In Forgett's view, any decent spy agency can spot a deal in progress. Weapons move across borders on ships and planes, and transactions involve enormous bank transfers. Yet during the war in the Balkans, $2 billion worth of arms flowed to combatants despite the existence of a worldwide embargo. Germany helped arm Croatia, Russian entrepreneurs supplied Serbia, and Iran, with help from the United States, funneled weapons to Bosnia. "Ninety percent of the things that are said about the 'black market' in arms are the figment of writers' and politicians' imagination," Forgett says. "There are no secrets in this world. Everybody knows what you're doing. If weapons are being 'smuggled,' some government agency is behind it."

THERE ARE CERTAINLY modern arms dealers who have made more money than Glatt, among them Adnan Khashoggi, who for many years represented Lockheed and other US companies that sold weapons to Saudi Arabia, and Sarkis Soghanalian, the Armenian-born Lebanese dealer who got his start in the business by arming

Christian militias in Lebanon at the request of the CIA and who during the 1980s was the leading supplier of Saddam Hussein. In terms of mastery of the "black" world, though, Glatt may be to the last half of the twentieth century what Zaharoff was to the first half.

Like Zaharoff, who falsified his personal history so successfully that the dates given for his birth range from 1849 to 1851, Glatt appears to have deliberately obscured his past. A single sheet of paper released by the Army Intelligence Agency under the Freedom of Information Act—the only file I received from a variety of government agencies I petitioned—says he was born on April 13, 1928. Glatt was raised near the small German town of Lorrach, in the Black Forest directly across the border from Basel, Switzerland. His family grew prosperous, Glatt says, in textiles, tires, and real estate. They were also avidly pro-Nazi during Hitler's years in power. A retired army intelligence officer who has reviewed Glatt's CIA file said that his father, a colonel in the Nazi army, was badly wounded on the Russian front. Glatt himself joined the Hitler Youth—as did the great majority of young Germans at the time—and during the last year of the war was detailed to an Air Defense Unit and sent to occupied France. Allied forces captured his unit in the waning days of the war and Glatt spent a year in a French POW camp. His commander was accused of war crimes but was eventually absolved by an Allied military tribunal. "He grew up as a thoroughly indoctrinated young German," says the intelligence officer, who worked with Glatt and came to know him well. "Germany's defeat at the end of the war was crushing for him as was the fact that he lived in an occupied, divided country. He [became] an ardent nationalist with severe right-wing tendencies, but . . . he didn't do any stoking of the ovens." (To avoid confusion, the intelligence officer, who appears frequently in this story, will subsequently be identified as Col. Ryan.)

After returning to Germany, Glatt attended the University of Heidelberg, where he studied economics, political science, law, and history. In its pre-war incarnation, Heidelberg had been famously liberal, but most left-leaning professors sought exile abroad soon after the Nazis took power. Glatt was violently anti-Communist and joined one of the university's dueling societies, which were incubators of the German right wing. He sports a scar on his cheek from a match, considered a mark of honor.

Glatt's politics don't seem to have mellowed much with time. He clearly views Fascism—and Nazism—as being preferable to communism. As he wrote to me, "Since my early days in University, I wanted to know why there are still people who do not hate communism, for communism had killed until 1939 [the year Hitler invaded Poland, setting off World War II] forty million people. Until 1989, the communists killed approximately 180 million people . . . I wonder why the mass-medias keep the public in the dark, and a number of communists are back in power and politics, and I wonder even more why people ask me why I am anti-Communist."

Yet it's noteworthy that Glatt's German nationalism never—at least after WW II—took the form of anti-Semitism. He took as his bride Vera Gmelin, whom several of his former and current friends say is the daughter of an aristocratic Jewish family that fled Austria during the 1930s. (She later converted to Glatt's faith, Calvinism.) Friends and foes from later years recall him speaking of a desire to see Germany as a superpower again and of changing its border with Poland, but no one remembers him defending the Holocaust. Over the years, Glatt has made significant investments and established many friendships in Israel. (One casual acquaintance is said to be the hawkish former defense minister Ariel Sharon.) A retired American general says of Glatt, "He was a Deutschland *über alles* type of guy and would never apologize for what the Germans did. But if you asked him if it was a good idea to weed out the Jews, I presume he'd say no." Glatt himself told me that "the anti-Semitic stuff [said about me] is bullshit."

After working in a German bank following his graduation from Heidelberg, Glatt "decided that I needed to study languages if I wanted to succeed in international business." He went to the University of Geneva, and there an English friend introduced him to Sam Cummings, the most famous arms dealer of his time, who was then seeking to open a Swiss office. Cummings served as a gun instructor for the US Army during World War II, and in the early 1950s went to work for a CIA-linked company called Western Arms Corporation. He was sent to Europe with a cover story of purchasing weapons on behalf of a Hollywood studio; Cummings's real task was to buy up surplus wartime stocks that the CIA then funneled to organizations and governments friendly to American interests.

In 1953, Cummings went into business on his own, forming the company that later became known as Interarms. Cummings had no helpers but—"to give the impression that there was at least one more employee," he said later—bestowed himself with the title of "vice president." He wrote to embassies, chiefs of police, and defense ministers, asking to buy up obsolete equipment for cash or in trade for more modern equipment. He then resold the materiel to Third World countries and to collectors. By the end of the decade, Cummings was a very rich man—to burnish his image, he bought a penthouse in Monte Carlo virtually next door to where Zaharoff resided during his gun-running heyday—and dominated the private weapons market. Cummings set up warehouses in Alexandria, Virginia, and Manchester, England, the latter a five-story building that housed huge amounts of weapons. For many years, Cummings worked in collaboration with the US government. He supplied arms for the 1954 CIA-led coup in Guatemala and sold weapons to American allies in the Third World, such as Anastasio Somoza in Nicaragua and Rafael Trujillo in the Dominican Republic. (Dictators "have a sense of order and they pay their bills on time," Cummings once said.)

Cummings had a network of agents around the world. Their job was to ingratiate themselves with locals and buy up surplus arms before the competition did. According to Anthony Sampson's *The Arms Bazaar*, Cummings's helpers in Finland included Major Kurt Touri, a hero of the Finno-Russian Winter War; in Thailand, David Cumberland, a retired American military man who had advised the government on arms purchases; and in Iran, Ali Dadshaw, a close associate of the Shah.

Glatt signed on with Cummings in 1959. As a European who spoke six languages and who moved easily in the East Bloc, Glatt proved a useful acquisition and rose quickly within company ranks. By 1961, he held the title of vice president and for the next decade, when Cummings reigned supreme as the world's biggest private arms broker, Glatt was a vital part of Interarms's success, especially in the Middle East and Eastern Europe.

Of course, business didn't always run smoothly. During one trip to Saudi Arabia, Glatt found himself detained by security agents after landing at the airport. He soon learned that a competitor in the arms trade—Gerhard Mertins, another German and the subject of the following chapter—had learned of his impending arrival in the country and informed the secret service that Glatt was married to a Jewish woman. Glatt spent a day in detention before he being freed on the orders of his Saudi contact, who was a relative of King Faisal.

Glatt left Cummings employ in the early 1970s, but they continued to collaborate until late in the decade. Then, a bitter feud erupted when Cummings accused Glatt of cheating him out of a major deal. "In my personal view, he wouldn't steal a red hot stove," Cummings said of Glatt in a CNN documentary on the arms trade in 1984. (CNN secretly filmed Glatt, and though he's but a passing figure in the documentary, it is, to my knowledge, the only time that his image has appeared in the American media.) For his part, Glatt told me that he cut ties with Cummings when the latter became persona non grata at the Pentagon and was effectively banned from participating in "black" operations. Cummings's loss of official status was primarily caused by what Glatt called "his love for stupid publicity," by which he meant Cummings' eagerness to talk to the press about the arms business. "This caused all sorts of difficulties with the competent authorities in the trade, and affected my income," Glatt says.

(Another reason for Cummings's diminished stature with the US military, Glatt told me, was that the Interarms chieftain renounced his citizenship in the early 1970s for tax purposes. Given that the CIA has worked with everyone from well-known Nazi war criminals to Guatemalan death squad members, I at first found it hard to believe that being a tax evader could get one blacklisted by the agency. However, I was told by several intelligence sources that Cummings's renunciation of his citizenship did in fact stick in someone's political craw.)

It's just as likely that the Cummings-Glatt feud was fueled by simple professional rivalry. Arms dealers are among the most ruthless of businessmen and love to expose competitors' dirty laundry to intelligence agencies and otherwise seek to destroy their commercial foes. One famous story has Cummings on a plane to an arms auction in Europe, where he spotted a competitor heading for the same event. Upon deplaning, Cummings told customs officials that the man was seeking to acquire weapons for terrorist groups. The authorities promptly detained his business foe.

Whatever the circumstances, the split coincided with Cummings's eclipse in the arms world. From the mid-1970s until his death in 1997, Cummings sold mostly to collectors, though journalists continued to trot him out as the consummate arms dealer well after his time had passed. Dick Winter, who worked for Cummings for more than three decades, burst out laughing when I asked him about some of his boss's more sensational claims to the press, such as a boast that he kept enough weapons on hand at his warehouses to equip forty army divisions. "That may have been embellished a bit," he said between guffaws. Col. Ryan, who after retiring from the military opened a boutique weapons firm in the Washington suburbs, was more scathing: "Cummings was the P.T. Barnum of the gun business. He had a warehouse full of junk—old, antiquated arms and there were probably enough rifles to outfit a division. But there's no magic in having a warehouse. I could buy rifles in lots of 1,000 today without blinking an eye. All he did was every once in awhile dump a few thousand rifles into some African countries that nobody gave a flying fuck about."

IN HIS POST-Cummings career, Glatt was obsessed with outdoing his former employer. Like Cummings, Glatt got into the business of refurbishing used weapons and for a time was a co-owner of a company called Collector's Armoury in suburban Virginia. Cummings had a huge farm in Middleburg—Glatt bought the Black Eagle. "He often said he wanted above all else to be bigger in the arms business than anyone else, particularly Sam Cummings, that one day the West German government would call him to Bonn and offer him the position of Defense Minister," says a former friend who knew him at the time. The call from Bonn never came, but by the late 1970s Glatt was known as one of the top international arms dealers, an exclusive club with generally no more than a dozen members at any time.

All in all, it was a marvelous time to be in the arms business. After a long period selling almost exclusively to NATO allies and a few other close partners, the United States had begun offering sophisticated arms to Third World countries as a means of buying support in the Cold War. Suddenly, high-tech fighter planes and other high-priced items from the American armory were being shipped to favored clients such as the Shah of Iran, the Saudi monarchy, and other friendly regimes. (Nixon's national security advisor Henry Kissinger believed that selling the Shah any weapon system he wanted would win his support for holding down oil prices. The strategy failed miserably. Not only was the Shah an OPEC hawk, but his entire arsenal would soon fall into the hands of the Ayatollah Khomeini.) The policy shift, known as the "Nixon doctrine," was expounded by the president's Deputy Secretary of Defense David Packard: "The best hope of reducing our overseas involvements and expenditures lies in getting allied and friendly nations to do even more in their own defense. To realize that hope, however, requires that we must continue, if requested, to give or sell them the tools they need for this bigger load we are urging them to assume."

Meanwhile, buyers were plentiful. Decolonization resulted in new countries in Africa and the Persian Gulf taking on security responsibilities previously assumed by the British, French, and Portuguese. With the creation of OPEC, a number of once poor countries were awash in "petrodollars," of which great quantities were recycled back to Western countries via arms purchases. All this caused an explosion in the international arms market. The American government's sales soared from less than $5 billion in 1970 to more than $27 billion in 1982.

A proliferation of US covert operations in support of anti-Soviet guerilla groups brought about a simultaneous boom in the black market. Private weapons brokers were in great demand— all the more so after CIA director Stansfield Turner began dismissing some 800 agents in mid-1977. The firings—which came in response to revelations about the agency's involvement in the coup that brought

Pinochet to power in Chile, its attempt to assassinate Fidel Castro, and other embarrassments—left the CIA badly uninformed about the international arms market. "Turner fired the old boys and they were the memory bank," says John Miley, who in 1978 became a junior partner to Loftur Johannesson—"The Icelander" from Petty's list —following a tour of duty in Vietnam and a stint as assistant military attaché at the American embassy in London. "The new boys couldn't find their names in a telephone book."

Miley, who now lives in suburban Tampa, greatly enjoys reminiscing about his days in the arms trade. We spent the better part of two days going through old files behind the closed doors of his small study, where a solitary air purifier was hopelessly overwhelmed by the smoke from Miley's cigarettes, which he lit one after another. Johannesson, a former commercial pilot and Red Cross flyer, ran a Panamanian-registered shell company called Techaid out of a tenth-floor office at London's Roebuck House. He sometimes teamed up with Glatt, who Miley once met over drinks at a London flat. "He starts off on this Nazi routine, that the one thing he'd like to see before he dies is the resurrection of the Third Reich," Miley says of the encounter. "He didn't care about a nuclear exchange between the US and the Soviet Union because it would create a power void that Germany would fill. My own sense is that this posturing is too straight out of central casting to be taken very seriously. Certainly Glatt likes getting under people's skin, and he displays the exceedingly black humor common is these circles.

One of Techaid's most profitable operations came in 1979, when Miley and Johannesson supplied the CIA with rifles and other weapons for anti-Communist guerillas in Afghanistan. Their contact at the CIA was "Joe Ryan" of Hackman, Inc., a front company headquartered at a post office box in Merrifield, Virginia. The partition between arms dealers and intelligence agencies—the ambiguous space that allows for "plausible deniability"—was thin indeed. "You're a private businessman and you don't want to alienate your best customer, which in our case was the US government," said Miley. "But arms dealers are aggressive. When people are shooting at each other, they are consuming small arms and ammunition, ergo any civil war is a business possibility."

Techaid bought weapons for the *mujahedin* from China, a pipeline that Miley had a significant hand in opening. Through his embassy duties, Miley had met Wu Chu-ling, the deputy Chinese army attaché in London. Over lunch at an Indian restaurant, he politely inquired about the possibility of Chinese support for the guerillas. The Chinese hated the Russians as much as the Americans did, but Miley was still surprised when Wu called a few days later and agreed to put him in touch with Communist Party superiors in Beijing. (Unbeknownst to Miley, the Carter administration dispatched Defense Secretary Harold Brown to Beijing at roughly the same time for identical purposes.) During a series of subsequent trips to Beijing for meetings with officials from NORINCO, the state arms company, Miley was assigned a translator named Gua Fongwei. "Before market reforms, some of the young fellows liked to get their hands on the most current *Playboy* or *Penthouse* and, along with everyone else who was trying to do business in China in those days, I used to smuggle in a couple of hot copies for Gua," he recalled. "Quite a few bottles of Tsing Tao beer were consumed in my hotel room discussing the degenerate ways of the West." Whether it was the centerfolds or, more likely, a need for hard currency, the Chinese agreed to provide weapons to the *mujahedin*, as well as to other American client regimes. "I do not exaggerate when I say we have moved light years in our relationship with NORINCO," Miley was reporting to Army intelligence in the fall of 1980. "[I] can assure you that not only are we now all very cozy, but more importantly we are wired in to a very—very—high level in the CCP."

The CIA and other US intelligence agencies could, of course, acquire as much American-made equipment they desired. But for covert operations, they preferred "enemy" materiel, especially Soviet-made. Not only was it cheap and of high quality, but its use obscured American fingerprints. Carrying Russian equipment also allowed US-backed groups to re-arm themselves on the battlefield with weapons captured from Soviet-supplied opponents. "You're not sending FedEx," a US Special Forces veteran patiently explained to me. "Shipping routes are often difficult and you might not be able to send in American weapons whenever you want."

One of the little-known secrets of the Cold War was that East Bloc officials, if greased with enough bribe money, were more than willing to sell their Russian equipment to arms dealers working with the West. Russia's allies were so desperate for hard currency that such sales were frequently approved at the highest levels of government, even when it was obvious that the materiel would end up in the hands of anti-Communist armies. Miley, Johannesson and a number of other American suppliers had contacts of various stripes in the East, but no one was better at quietly tapping into Soviet Bloc armories than Glatt, who had worked extensively in Eastern Europe during his years with Cummings. "He liked the idea of bribing communist officials to sell us communist weapons that could be used to kill communists," retired General John Singlaub, who worked with Glatt in the 1980s, told me. "He thought that was neat."

Glatt's ready access to Soviet equipment also made him a valuable source to the officials in charge of the Foreign Materiel Acquisition Program, a "black" operation run by the three military services and the Defense Intelligence Agency. Unlike the CIA, which passed Russian materiel on to its Third World allies, the services used East Bloc equipment to test against their own equipment and to take apart in order to design countermeasures. The FMA's origins date to 1973, when the Israelis captured large quantities of Soviet equipment from Egypt and Syria during the Yom Kippur war. Golda Meir was so grateful for the help President Nixon provided to Israel during the conflict that she decided to share part of the captured treasure with the United States. The Pentagon concluded that it should seek out its own supplies of Russian arms and the FMA came on line a few years later. "What Glatt [and other US-linked dealers] was able to do just boggles the mind," says a former CIA official who was familiar with the FMA. "They were dealing with communist officials at the highest levels and getting factory-fresh weapons out of the East Bloc. There was nothing money couldn't buy."

Indeed, it was Glatt's great wealth—which grew by leaps and bounds as he prospered in the arms trade—which often gave him a leg up on his rivals. Col. Ryan recalls that he and Glatt were once competing to buy a quantity of Russian-made equipment. Col. Ryan had a jump on the deal, but didn't have sufficient funds to secure the $7 million letter of credit needed to close it. As he began the process of arranging a bank loan, Glatt used personal funds to secure a letter of credit and the equipment in question disappeared from the market.

Money was also essential in obtaining an end-user certificate showing a false destination—a piece of paper essential to any secret weapons transaction. Heinz Baumann, a Viennese arms dealer whom I interviewed, said the going rate for a certificate was around $50,000 and spoke highly of the flexibility displayed by Peruvian officials in supplying this vital document. "If all the end-users issued over the years by Peru were legitimate, the country would have a bigger army than the United States," he said. A retired CIA agent waxed nostalgic for Chad in the same regard. "The country was poor, the government corrupt, communications almost non-existent, and for a long time the Soviets didn't have representation there," he said. "It was an ideal situation." Glatt himself is said to have secured end-users from a variety of Third World countries, including the Gulf States, Syria, and Nigeria.

Beyond that, Glatt's success in the trade stemmed from a keen intellect, a powerful personality, and a fiercely competitive business drive. Several arms dealers I spoke with used the same term to describe a final strength of Glatt's, this being a highly prized quality in the macho world of gunrunning: "Steel nuts."

SHORTLY AFTER RESIGNING from Interarms, Glatt received an invitation to lunch from a man that he had once met at Cummings's office in Monte Carlo. The man, who worked for American intelligence, asked if he would continue to work the East Bloc arms market, only now on behalf of the United States. Hence, was born a relationship that was to span four decades.

Glatt's initial deals for the US were small transactions for low-end equipment. His first major operation, and one that made him a small fortune, involved a 1977 deal to arm Somali dictator Siad Barre. That year, Somalia and Ethiopia went to war over the disputed Ogaden region, a desolate stretch of desert lying between the two countries. Barre had been the Soviet Union's closest client in Africa, but Moscow decided to back Ethiopia—which had been in the American orbit until a 1974 left-wing military coup—in the Ogaden conflict. The official posture of the Carter administration was that the United States would play no part in the war. "Although this is a very important, strategic part of the world, we see no reason why we should intervene militarily," General George S. Brown, chairman of the Joint Chiefs of Staff, told *Newsweek* at the time. Meanwhile, the Pentagon quietly encouraged Barre to break with the Soviets with promises of infusions of weaponry and economic aid. "The Carter government clearly understood that the Horn of Africa was endangered," Glatt told me in explaining how he became involved in the affair. "The situation in Iran had just started to worsen as well, and the support of Somalia became a necessity."

The Carter administration feared that that lingering "Vietnam Shock" might provoke political and public opposition if American involvement was exposed. Hence, a web of foreign players handled the deal. The Saudis, who frequently supported American covert activities, picked up the tab for the operation. Glatt and several men from a Lichtenstein-based arms brokerage firm called ICW were in charge of securing the needed weapons. They turned up 580 tons of assault rifles and assorted other small arms at Technika, Hungary's state-owned arms company. Glatt, who had somehow established a relationship with Major General Mohammed Ali Samantar, the Somali defense minister, also secured a fake end-user certificate showing that the arms were destined for Nigeria.

Loftur Johannesson was in charge of moving the arms to Africa. To accomplish that goal, he hired his friend Hank Warton, a free-lance adventurer who owned three Boeing 707s that carried the weapons from Hungary to Somalia. A German Jew, Warton fled the Nazi regime and made his way to the United States, where he joined the army as a volunteer during World War II. After the fighting ended, he briefly worked a series of odd jobs before obtaining a pilot's license under the G.I. bill. For the next two decades, until his doctor grounded him following a heart attack, Warton was almost always in the air. He carefully concealed his Jewish background, which allowed him to work all over the Arab world. He flew Moslem pilgrims to Mecca for Ramadan, worked as a commercial pilot for Syrian Airways, and moved cattle between Sudan and Yemen. Warton's military exploits included transporting United Nations forces during the civil war in the Congo in the mid-1960s. In 1967, he gained a certain notoriety when he ferried food and weapons to the Ibo tribe after it seceded and declared the independent state of Biafra. The Nigerian government ended the rebellion by cutting Biafra's links to the outside world—it put a $250,000 bounty on Warton's head for running the blockade—with the result that a million people died from starvation and disease.

Now eighty-two, Warton recounted his role in the Somalia episode as we sat in the living room of his apartment in a high-rise building overlooking Miami Beach. In addition to supplying the planes, Warton rounded up crew members to fly them, among them Larry Raab, a retired US airman, Alberto Alberty, a Cuban exile who helped lead the Bay of Pigs operation, and John Lear Jr., son of the inventor of the Lear Jet. Between runs from Budapest to Jeddah—the Saudis granted stopover rights for refueling—to Mogadishu, the pilots stayed in Salzburg, where Glatt put them up at the Hotel Vollerhof, just outside of town, and less than a block from his house. "The crews were mostly Americans and they weren't allowed to go to Budapest, which was behind the Iron Curtain and off-limits," Warton recalls. "Glatt said not to worry because it was all sanctioned by the CIA and was basically a CIA operation." Between August and December 1977, Warton's crews hauled the weaponry on twenty-eight separate flights to Mogadishu.

All went smoothly until a feud erupted between ICW and Glatt over dividing the profits. Like his old boss Cummings, Glatt was an ardent practitioner of what one broker calls the gun trade's First Commandment: Fuck Thy Neighbor. When ICW tried to squeeze him out, Glatt leaked details of the airlift to newspapers in Switzerland and England. The ensuing publicity shut down the operation and prompted Lichtenstein to revoke ICW's corporate charter. (I told Glatt that several of his competitors described him as being a ferocious businessman. To which he replied, "I think [they] are basically right, for at least I am able to protect my interests at any time they are threatened.")

Still, from the US perspective, the operation was a rousing success. Somalia was now squarely in the Western camp and Siad Barre soon gave the US rights to highly desirous naval and air bases on the Horn of Africa. Things didn't turn out as well for Somalia itself. Ethiopian troops decimated Siad Barre's forces, with civilian and military casualties running to about 100,000. The defeat led to a military rebellion, which Siad Barre suppressed by executing some eighty officers who criticized his handling of the campaign.

Things also turned out badly for Hank Warton. When he returned to Miami, where he rented a hangar for his aircraft, US Customs officials seized one of his planes when an inspection of flight logs revealed that it had flown behind the Iron Curtain to Hungary. Warton provided the names of several officials at the Pentagon who knew about the Somali operation, but they denied all knowledge of the affair. According to Warton, those officials told him that the government could not afford to be tied to the weapons airlift and convinced him to plead guilty, suggesting that future contracts from the CIA would be his reward for cooperation. Warton was sentenced to a one-year suspended sentence and fined $110,000. The promised future contracts from the government never materialized.

GLATT ALSO WORKED with Johannesson in putting together his early deals with the Foreign Materiel Acquisition Program. Their secretary at Techaid's London office was Nini Baring, the estranged wife of an heir to the Baring Bank (which collapsed in 1995 after a young broker based in Singapore lost $1.4 billion on Asian stock markets). For transportation, Techaid sometimes turned to Farhad Azima, an Iranian exile who ran a CIA-linked airline out of Kansas City. (In later years, Azima became a large donor to the Democratic Party, thereby winning himself three White House coffee klatsches in 1995 and 1996.)

Anthony Sykes, who ran in royal circles, thanks to his marriage to the sister of a duke, sometimes traveled abroad to meet with potential Techaid customers. So, too, did Clyde Ferguson, who'd served as a deputy assistant secretary of state for African affairs during the Nixon years and, following his brief career in the arms trade, later became a law professor at Harvard specializing in international human rights. Another Techaid associate was Sir William Lindsay-Hogg, a heavy-drinking baronet who had squandered a large inheritance. On one occasion, Hogg was stopped at Heathrow airport when authorities there discovered a Soviet-made rocket that Techaid had obtained from the *mujahedin* and was attempting to deliver to the US Army. The affair caused a minor row between the US and Britain because there is an unwritten rule that neither side is to conduct covert operations on the other's soil without alerting the proper parties.

An equally exotic cast of characters occasionally dropped by Roebuck House in hopes of drumming up interest in deals of one sort or another, not all of them involving arms. Of particular note was Sheila Petrie, a one-time burlesque dancer, who had access to a small cargo plane and was running whiskey to Idi Amin, to whose regime she also sold a French-made locomotive. "Do you have a good impression or a bad impression of Idi Amin?" she asked when I called her, "because my experience with him was very good."

The first FMA deal I learned of took place in 1977, when Johannesson arranged for the purchase of small arms from Bulgaria. Hank Warton flew into a military airport in Sofia to pick up the weapons, and delivered them to the Army's Aberdeen Proving Grounds in Maryland. Two years later, Glatt and Johannesson set up the first FMA purchase from Romania, a deal that involved Russian armored personnel carriers. Transactions out of Romania generally required payment to at least one of two men, both brothers of the country's dictator, Nicolae Ceausescu: Marin, who headed the Romanian trade mission in Vienna until 1989, when he committed suicide after Nicolae was overthrown and murdered; or Ilie, who served as deputy defense minister and is now incarcerated in Bucharest. Nicolae, the East Bloc's most hard-line Communist leader, took a cut as well. As a result, millions of Pentagon dollars found their way into Swiss bank accounts controlled by the Ceausescu family.

A senior military official who read intelligence reports about the affair says Glatt set up the 1979 deal with the assistance of Marin Ceausescu, who was duly compensated for his services. So, too, was the Peruvian general that supplied a bogus end-user certificate, and officials aboard the Klek, the passenger-carrying Yugoslav freighter that picked up the vehicles at a port in Romania. The Klek was supposed to head for a southern port, where the passengers would disembark and the vehicles would disappear into the Army's hands and make their way to a military base in Charlottesville. For unknown reasons, the vessel stopped first at a Navy facility in Earle, New Jersey, where the armored personnel carriers were unloaded. This took place before the gaping eyes of passengers, who were furious about being delayed. Some talked to the press, leading to an *Associated Press* story that ran on the wires on August 2: "In a move tinged with mystery, the US Army has obtained some new Communist Warsaw Pact military equipment through a private company whose name is being kept secret," the story said, adding that the Pentagon was refusing "to answer some key questions" about the episode. Even worse, one passenger took a picture of the Russian vehicles, which somehow got into the hands of officials in the East Bloc. "Heads probably rolled in Romania but the vehicles finally ended up in Charlottesville," recalls the military official. The foul-up created a flap at the Pentagon—the White House raised hell with the Army—and led to the bitter split-up of Johannesson and Glatt when the inevitable dispute arose over the division of spoils. (With millions of dollars sometimes riding on a single transaction, an atmosphere of paranoia and greed marks the arms trade. As a result, business partnerships are frequently short-lived. "There are a lot of bribes paid so it's hard for one partner to know the real expenses being paid by the other partner," says Miley. "You may say you paid $250,000 in bribes, and you may even have a check stub to prove it, but the guy you wrote it to gave you a kickback of $100,000.") Even so, the operation was considered important because it led to Romania becoming one of the biggest sources of weaponry to the FMA.

At about the same time, Glatt had a series of largely unsatisfactory dealings with Ed Wilson. A former employee of the CIA and Naval Intelligence, Wilson and another retired agency man, Frank Terpil, signed a multi-million dollar deal with Muammar Qaddafi's government in 1976 to arm Libya and train its agents in everything from piloting helicopters to terrorist tactics. Six years later, the Justice Department used an informant to lure Wilson from his villa in Tripoli to the Dominican Republic. There he was arrested and flown to the United States, where he was convicted in three separate trials and sentenced to a total of fifty-two years in prison for, among other things, supplying Libya with twenty tons of plastic explosives.

I drove up to see Wilson at Allenwood penitentiary, where fellow prisoners include another notorious ex-CIA employee, Aldrich Ames, the Soviet spy, as well as several of the World Trade Center bombers. Wilson today bears little resemblance to the tall, brawny figure I remembered from photographs taken during his trial. Now seventy-one, white-haired and slightly stooped from age, he was accompanied to the prison's visitors area by his case officer, Mark Tanner. We sat and talked at one of two dozen or so tables; the rest sat empty during my four hours at Allenwood. The fresh paint and bright lights do little to diminish the room's inherent gloominess, which is heightened by a small area with books and toys for inmate's kids, and the dark screen along the wall where prisoners and loved ones can pose for photographs.

Wilson calls Glatt "one of the smartest operators I've ever been around," and says he "liked him a lot." He was first introduced to Glatt by Dick Woods, a retired American military man who ran an office for Wilson in Geneva. On several occasions, Wilson tried to interest the German in selling arms to Libya, and once traveled to Salzburg, where he stayed as Glatt's guest at the Vollerhof. Nothing ever came of his overtures though, because Glatt showed no interest in dealing with Qaddafi. "He wanted nothing to do with the Libyans," Wilson said. "I wish I'd had the same attitude." (Wilson claimed to have worked on one FMA deal with Glatt, though I was unable to confirm that independently. His admiration for Glatt was apparently not reciprocated. Lawrence Barcella—who in addition to being Glatt's attorney, is also the assistant US attorney who led the prosecution of Wilson—says Glatt provided the Justice Department with important information that aided the government's case against Wilson.)

A still-classified Justice Department memorandum indicates that Glatt's contacts with Wilson did indirectly lead to business with the Pentagon. The document, written in 1982 as the government was preparing to try Wilson on the plastic explosives charge, cites information provided to the Justice Department by Douglas Schlachter, one of Wilson's employees in Libya. According to the memorandum, Schlachter told government investigators that Thomas Clines, a CIA officer who was friendly with Wilson, contacted him in 1977 and asked for help in obtaining Russian-made "small arms, cannons, grenades and ammunition from Eastern Bloc countries. Supposedly, these weapons were destined for South America and Africa for unspppecified [sic] purposes." Schlachter turned to Glatt for help, but the deal fell through when Pentagon officials learned of the involvement of Wilson, who was not yet indicted but already highly controversial within the defense establishment. Some time later, Clines—who after retiring from the CIA in 1978 worked as a private supplier to the FMA and later played an important role as a freelancer in the Iran/contra affair—informed Schlachter that Glatt

had subsequently "traveled to Washington, D.C., and met personally with various Pentagon and CIA officials . . . [They] arrived at an
agreement and Glott [sic] furnished the required weapons to the
CIA and DIA." Goulding, the second Wilson employee, told the
Justice Department of a 1978 deal in which Glatt delivered two
Russian ZPU anti-aircraft guns to the CIA, along with "20,000
rounds of Soviet high explosive ammunition and 20,000 rounds
of their armor-piercing ammunition." (Neither Goulding or
Schlachter seem to have provided information about where or how
Glatt obtained the equipment in question.)

GLATT WAS NOT universally admired within the American military,
where in certain circles he was categorized as a Neo-Nazi. "I'm no
Pollyanna," says one former military officer. "You've got to deal with
people you wouldn't want as friends. I've done a lot of work in intelligence, and I accept that. But Glatt's political views were repugnant to
any decent human being." Another person familiar with Glatt says,
"Arrogant. Dictatorial. Stubborn. Go down the list of all the endearing
qualities of the German people and Glatt has them."

Such people were in a distinct minority. Glatt established close personal friendships with a number of high-ranking military officials,
some whom he played host to at the Black Eagle or at one of his
European estates. Over the years, Glatt conducted business of one sort
or another with a number of retired military officers and spooks,
among them General Singlaub and General Ed Soyster, a former
director of the DIA. One former intelligence officer's daughter
became the godmother to a grandchild of Glatt's. Through his friend-

ship with General Graham, Glatt helped the daughter of a retired general get a job at the High Frontier.

By the time Ronald Reagan took office in 1981, US intelligence agencies were fighting to court Glatt. (Army intelligence won out and became his main handler.) That year, the Pentagon threw a birthday party for Glatt at Washington's Georgetown Club, an exclusive private club where government insiders and prominent locals gather to discreetly discuss affairs of state. Located in a three-story brownstone on Wisconsin Street, the Georgetown Club was founded in 1966 by Washington powerbrokers such as Robert Gray, the PR man who later headed Hill & Knowlton, Thomas Corcoran, the aide to President Franklin Roosevelt known as "Tommy the Cork," and Milton Nottingham, a prominent Washington-based businessman. Tongsun Park, another founder and the club's chief financier, hosted numerous gatherings at the club. That proved embarrassing when a government investigation during the Carter years revealed Park to be an agent of the South Korean CIA and found he had made hundreds of thousands of dollars in payoffs to members of Congress in order to influence policy on Korea.

The Pentagon's birthday party was hosted by Nottingham—a friend and sometimes shipping agent of Glatt's—and was held on the same night that then-Vice President George Bush was feted in another part of the club. Glatt's well-wishers included a number of senior intelligence officials, general officers, and several bankers who washed money for the Pentagon's black programs. The Georgetown Club is secretive—membership status seems to be most commonly revealed in one's obituary—and Nottingham, still a higher-up there, politely declined my request for a tour. Col. Ryan, who attended the birthday party, describes the Club as elegant yet reserved, with antique furniture arranged in small clusters to facilitate intimate discussion. "It bespeaks good taste, power, and sophistication," he says. "It's not ostentatious. There are no Robert Hall suits to be found anywhere."

On several occasions I spoke with Col. Ryan at his firm's nondescript office, which is notable only for a sign-in sheet that asks visitors to note if their appointment is of a classified nature. "There were some people [in government] who felt Glatt was not a nice man, but who cares," he told me when I asked if he had any trouble with Glatt's hardline politics. "Western civilization required his services." Didn't anyone object to his choice of the Black Eagle—a symbol of Nazi Germany—as a name for his Virginia property, I asked? Not at all, he replied: "Glatt was viewed as a source, potentially our most lucrative source of Russian arms. We weren't considering him for citizenship, we were hunting for Soviet weapons that had great military value to the United States. The more virulently right-wing he was, the more we felt comfortable with him because we knew he wouldn't deal with the Russians. We weren't running a de-Nazification program. If he wanted to call his farm the Black Eagle, that was his business. We weren't going to tell him what to name his property."

GLATT WAS PRIMARILY an "asset" of US intelligence, but as a private businessmen he also worked with other governments. Among those he supplied with weapons were the apartheid regime in South Africa and the monarchy in Oman. In the latter he established a personal friendship with Sultan Qabus bin Said, who after overthrowing his father in a British-backed coup in 1970, turned his country into a base for Western intelligence operations and military maneuvers. Glatt was also tight with a small coterie of British advisers who exercised enormous influence on the Sultan. Among his contacts was a retired brigadier general named Timothy Landon, who served as the rough equivalent of the Sultan's national security advisor. When the Sultan visited the United States in 1984, Landon alone accompanied him to a private meeting with President Reagan. (During the Arab oil embargo against the United States and other countries friendly with Israel, Ashland Oil made millions of dollars of illegal payments—some which went to Landon—to secure business in Oman. The Securities and Exchange Commission and the Justice Department both launched investigations but neither aggressively pursued the matter. Eventually, the whole thing "went away," as one well placed source put it, in thanks to Oman's support for American covert activities. Landon now lives in London. Through his secretary, he said he knew of Glatt but otherwise refused comment.)

Glatt's overseas connections proved fruitful when Reagan's CIA director William Casey greatly expanded the scope of government-run covert actions. The agency's support for the *mujaheddin* rebels in Afghanistan, which started under Jimmy Carter, grew to become a multibillion dollar effort and the CIA's biggest operation since World War II. The US also ran huge programs in support of forces seeking to topple left-wing governments in Nicaragua and Angola. Directly or indirectly, Glatt had a hand in arming all three of those guerilla groups. "I realized that the monolithic bloc of the Soviet empire showed big cracks which were beyond repair and as a student of history who knew what communism means, I decided that it would be worthwhile to help widen these cracks," he told me of his business efforts during the period.

In the case of Angola, Glatt purchased Soviet weapons for South African military officials. According to several sources, they in turn passed the materiel on to UNITA, a right-wing guerilla group led by Jonas Savimbi. The CIA, which also supplied Savimbi, was surely aware of Glatt's activities.

Glatt insisted to me that he did not arm the Afghan rebels, who were fighting a pro-Soviet regime as well as Russian troops Moscow sent to support it. "With the *mujahedin* I never had any dealings," he said. "It is my understanding that this . . . was done by professionals in this special type of business." While technically correct, I later learned that the reply was a feint. According to at least three intelligence sources, Glatt bought huge quantities of weapons for the *mujahedin*—land mines, grenades, rifles, machine guns and other small arms—from CENZIN, the Polish state arms agency. However, his client was not the *mujahedin* but Army Intelligence. Its officers turned the material over to the CIA, which transported the weapons to depots the agency set up in Pakistan. From there, the local intelligence service sent Glatt's provisions across the border into Afghanistan for distribution to the guerillas.

Glatt's biggest find for the *mujahedin* was hundreds of Russian-made Strela-1 shoulder-launched anti-aircraft missiles. As arranged by Glatt, a Polish plane carried the Strelas to a military airstrip in Oman. An American plane was there to meet it, then departed for a US naval base at Diego Garcia in the Indian Ocean. From there, the Strelas were shipped to the CIA's depots in Pakistan. The *mujahedin* used the Strelas against helicopter gunships flown by Soviet pilots. They weren't nearly as effective as the American-made Stingers the CIA began sending in 1986, but they did bring down a few Soviet craft and, more importantly, prevented helicopter pilots from acting imperviously. "We wanted to see the Russians get their asses kicked, and it was demoralizing as shit to have your own weapons fired at you," a person directly involved in the Strela deal says of its significance.

Glatt also played a role in the chief scandal of the Reagan years, the Iran/contra affair, though his name was barely mentioned in news accounts as the intelligence community went to great lengths to protect him. So sensitive was his relationship with the US that the FBI took his testimony in secret and had it permanently classified. Glatt's involvement in Iran/contra came about through his association with Barbara Studley, a right-wing radio show host in Miami. An eccentric former beauty queen, Studley forged close ties with a group of arch-conservative military and political leaders and set up a Washington-based arms company called GeoMilTech Consultants Corporation (GMT). Her board members and employees included General Singlaub, head of the World Anti-Communist League; John Carbaugh, a top aide to Senator Helms; and Robert Schweitzer, an army general who supervised Oliver North at the National Security Council until being fired in 1982 after declaring to a reporter that the Russians were preparing to invade Poland. In his deposition to the Iran/contra committee,

Schweitzer said the real meaning of GMT's initials were "God's Mighty Team."

Studley was known within GMT by the code name "Cleo," as in Cleopatra, and Glatt—"The Baron"—was her arms dealer of choice. (The company also used codes for its merchandise. In internal memos I obtained, rocket launchers were dubbed "mothers" and rockets "children.") Through Glatt's Swiss banker and financial advisor, Eddy Maissoneuve, then of the Banque Nationale du Paris in Geneva, Studley set up a Swiss account to handle GMT's overseas funds.

(What exactly was taking place at the offices of GMT was never fully explored by the Iran/contra committee. A wealth of information can be found in a 1992 deposition given by Ron Harel—a former Israeli air force officer who ran a GMT office in Tel Aviv—in an unrelated lawsuit that involved Studley. Harel, who submitted dozens of internal company documents in support of his account, claims that GMT was seeking to sell weapons to Indonesia, South Africa, Peru, Venezuela, Iran, and numerous other destinations. One 1984 memorandum discusses a series of meetings that Singlaub arranged between American officials—including William Casey and Oliver North—and Shapoor Ardalan, an opposition leader whom the CIA hoped to enlist to overthrow the Ayatollah Khomeini and put the former Shah's son in power. During one of the meetings, a CIA official is described as having pulled out a briefcase full of money and offered it to Ardalan. Either an honest man or embarrassed to be receiving so public a bribe, Ardalan asked that any funding for his group be routed through its Swiss bank account.)

GMT was one of the three important suppliers to the Nicaraguan contras, the other two being "The Enterprise" of Oliver North and retired Air Force Major General Richard Secord, and the Honduras-based "Arms Supermarket" run by a CIA-linked arms dealer based in Miami, Ronald Martin. Studley declined a request for an interview, but I did manage to speak with Singlaub as he signed copies of his autobiography, *Hazardous Duty*, at the 1998 convention of *Soldier of Fortune* magazine in Las Vegas. (See Chapter Four for a broader description of the convention.) I had read Singlaub's book, which mentions a certain German arms dealer who is referred to only as "Sam." Yes, he conceded, Sam was a pseudonym for Glatt, who came to GMT on the recommendation of two old friends, General Daniel Graham, who had held top positions at both the CIA and the DIA, and CIA director Casey. (Singlaub also sought to protect Glatt during his testimony before the Iran/contra committee. Asked by House investigator Kenneth Ballen to identify his arms dealer, Singlaub spells out his name as C-L-O-T-S. A confused Ballen replies that he knows the dealer in question as Werner L-O-T-T. Minutes later, Singlaub is again asked to identify his friend, whose name he now spells out as K-L-O-T-S. Neither Ballen nor anyone else noticed the blunder.)

Singlaub first met Glatt in early 1985, at the Palm Court of the Sheraton Carlton Hotel in downtown Washington. According to *Hazardous Duty*, Studley and a top contra official, Adolfo Calero, were also in attendence:

> As he perused the shopping list I had drawn up with [contra leader] Enrique Bermudez, Sam nodded calmly and made notes on a pad

with a gold mechanical pencil. He might as well have been pricing out a plumbing job. Sam looked up and said he could procure brand-new Polish AKMS-47 assault rifles in quantity for only $135 each.

Barbara and I looked at each other. We had learned that AK-47s normally retailed for between $200 and $300 on the retail arms market. These were the lowest prices that we had ever heard quoted.

"This is new equipment?" I asked.

"New from the factory," Sam assured us. "This is even better than Soviet manufacture."

"Why are the prices so low?" Barbara asked.

Sam shrugged, "I'm a good client."

The deal under discussion came together in May 1985, ten months after Congress had cut off aid to the contras. Glatt obtained a fake end-user certificate—from Syria, Singlaub recalled—and a Greek freighter docked in Gdansk to pick up the materiel. From there, the weapons—the AK-47s, as well as machine guns, grenade launchers, shoulder-fired anti-aircraft rockets—were delivered to contra bases in Honduras. Calero subsequently called the shipment the "biggest and best" deal arranged for the contras by the private arms suppliers. The transaction violated the spirit if not the letter of the Congressional ban on military aid to the contras. Barcella, who was still an assistant US attorney at the time, told me that a government official he would not identify came to him for a legal opinion about the deal. He insisted then, and now, that it broke no laws. "They were foreign arms from a foreign port sent on a foreign ship to a foreign group and Glatt himself was a foreigner. It was not illegal."

Oliver North saw Glatt's low prices as a threat to the profit-making activities of The Enterprise. He immediately went to Casey and blackballed Glatt with a bogus story that the German was a Soviet double agent. (North told me he'd never heard of Glatt, which is hard to fathom given all of this. Furthermore, Glatt's name appears several times in the diaries North kept while at the National Security Council.) Ron Martin was also displeased. He learned about the transfer and swiftly dispatched one of his employees, a Cuban-American named Mario Del'Amico, to make an unannounced call at the Polish embassy in Washington. To the horror of officials there, he demanded that the Arms Supermarket be offered weapons at the same prices. "It took all of Sam's considerable diplomatic finesse (and probably a fair amount of hush money) to calm down the offended officials," Singlaub writes in *Hazardous Duty*.

The following August, Glatt had a hand in a surprising offer Singlaub made to Casey. This was a point when Congress had restored funding for the CIA's contra effort, but the appropriated monies would not be available for several months. Therefore, Glatt would not only sell the CIA $10 million worth of Soviet arms out of Poland but float the agency money to pay for the merchandise as well. "Our banker [the unidentified Maissoneuve] is prepared to fly to Washington and take care of the Letter of Credit directly with your designated bank," Singlaub informed the CIA chief in a confidential memorandum. "This eliminates all bank tested telexes or paper trails. The loan can be in the name of a corporation of your choice. It is not necessary for our bank to know your identity, only your banker. Our bank has been exceptionally discreet in processing our transactions in the past. At the close of the transactions, the bank file will only show corporations, numbered items and amounts. No reference will be made of . . . the individuals or actual organizations involved." Alas, Casey turned down the offer—perhaps due to North's efforts to discredit Glatt—and GMT's trail in the Iran/contra affair disappears at this juncture.

However, GMT's gun running activites later played a largely unnoticed role in yet another huge scandal, the Savings and Loan debacle. Whereas Maissoneuve controlled GMT's Swiss accounts, Louis Petrillo, director of international finance at the Florida National Bank in Miami, handled the company's domestic funds. Petrillo, who was also a high-ranking officer at the American Banker's Association, admits to having helped obscure GMT's activities by keeping loans and other transactions off the books. By 1986, Petrillo had moved on to become president of Miami's Bayshore bank, from where he made an unauthorized $2 million loan to GMT. The money was never paid back and Bayshore went under the following year. In 1994, Petrillo pleaded guilty to bank fraud and was sentenced to one year in prison and ordered to pay back the $2 million. The Judge in the case, Clyde Atkins, ordered the Justice Department to "pursue diligently" action against Studley and GMT. No action was ever taken, and one can only wonder if this act of government kindness was in some way tied to the services Studley rendered in support of the Reagan administration's overseas adventures. Studley had signed an agreement with Bayshore, in which she pledged as collateral, properties in Virginia and Tennessee, as well as all of her company's assets, none of which were ever seized. Rubens Oliva, Petrillo's attorney, says he never got a straight answer from officials at the Justice Department when he asked why Studley was not held accountable. "It's like you take out a mortgage and stop paying, and the bank let's you keep the house," he says. "Lou's no saint but it's not right that he gets whacked and she walks off untouched."

IF GLATT WAS an important supplier of weapons to Reagan's "freedom fighters," he was more vital yet in securing Russian weapons for the Foreign Material Acquisition program. Other than a few excellent stories in the *Washington Post*—which didn't mention the name of Glatt or any other weapons dealer who supplied the Pentagon—the program's history is all but unknown.

The Pentagon considered the program to be hugely important because it was the only way of testing its weapons against those of America's opponents. The DIA and the military services drew up their own shopping lists, but a small group of beltway firms with strong ties to intelligence agencies handled the job of obtaining the weaponry: BDM, headed by former Defense Secretary Frank Carlucci; Vector Microwave Research Corp., whose executives included Leonard Perroots, a former director of the Defense Intelligence Agency; and Electronic Warfare Associates, whose board of directors included, until his death in 1997, former CIA director William E. Colby. The American companies relied in turn on a cabal of European-based arms brokers to buy the desired goods in the East Bloc, a strategy that allowed for the skirting of the Foreign Corrupt Practices Act, which prohibits Americans from bribing foreign officials. In addition to Glatt, those dealers included Heinz Baumann; a German named Gunther Leinhauser; Manny Weigensberg, a Canadian who helped "The Enterprise" arrange the first shipment of arms to the contras; and Johannesson, who after splitting with Glatt developed excellent contacts to the East German Stasi. (Johannesson's biggest FMA deal came in 1987 when he arranged, through East German and Czech sources, to buy a dozen T-72 tanks for the CIA. The tanks were shipped to Qatar—the East Germans were told that the purchaser was the presidential guard in that country—where they sat for three days before being sent on to the United States. With his earnings from the Pentagon, Johannesson bought a home in Barbados, vineyards in the south of France, and an estate on Maryland's Eastern Shore formerly owned by a member of the Dupont family.)

The FMA's precise budget is impossible to determine because it was hidden in the Pentagon's "black" account ("It's a democracy but there are ways of being creative," one of the players told me). However, it's a safe guess, based on information I obtained, that over $100 million per year was allocated to the program throughout much of the 1980s. The FMA's black dollars were turned white at a Washington branch of the American Security Bank (now owned by Bank of America), where the Pentagon and the beltway firms set up accounts for their respective dummy corporations. "We were asked to do it as a favor to the US government, to do our patriotic duty," says James Kliendienst, an executive at America Security who helped handle the money. "We didn't know what the hell they were buying, and we didn't want to know. What made me feel damn good was that after the Gulf War I got a call from somebody—I won't mention who—at the big house there in Virgina saying that thanks to all your work we knew what that bastard Saddam Hussein had."

By all accounts, Glatt was far and away the program's biggest single supplier. During the lawsuit with Petty, he revealed that he handled between $150 million and $200 million worth of contracts between 1983 and 1993. A person with direct knowledge of the program says that's considerably low, estimating that Glatt did up to $500 million worth of business for the Pentagon. Glatt made so much money that competitors complained he exercised undue influence on the FMA through his ties to military officials. Of particular concern was his relationship with Lieutenant Colonel Larry Caylor, who headed the Army FMA office from 1985 to 1991, and then swiftly went to work as Glatt's assistant in the arms business after retiring.

Russia was not a direct source for FMA materiel, but a flood of arms from its East Bloc allies found their way to the Pentagon: tanks from Czechoslovakia; armored personnel carriers out of Bulgaria; anti-aircraft systems from Hungary; mobile rocket launchers and radar systems from Romania; air defense systems and helicopters from Poland. Further materiel was secured from friendly Third World regimes. In 1988, for example, Chad turned over to the Pentagon a coveted Russian MI-25 helicopter that it had captured during fighting with Libyan forces.

(In his interviews with Justice Department officials, Douglas Schlachter said that in 1977, Clines instructed him to try to bribe Libyan officials in exchange for help securing Soviet military equipment. As summarized in the classified Justice Department document, "Clines told Schlachter he could offer any Libyan at least $7 million if he could supply the MIG-25 airplane. Clines also told Schlachter that if any Libyan official would cooperate, the CIA was prepared to promise United States citizenship, transportation out of Libya, and a new identity in the United States. Clines also gave Schlacter the names of Libyan officials the Agency thought were approachable and why the Agency thought they were . . . susceptible to taking bribes from the United States." Schlachter succeeded in developing friendships with a number of high-ranking Libyan officials, but stated that he was unable to arrange any deals.)

The FMA sometimes revealed enormous problems with the Pentagon's weapons systems. In 1984, the Army FMA office, with help from an Israeli arms dealer, obtained a Soviet-made attack helicopter and delivered it to Fort Rucker in Alabama. The helicopter was subsequently matched against a hugely expensive anti-aircraft gun called the DIVAD, which was made by a subsidiary of Ford Motor Company and consisted of two radar-aimed guns mounted on the chassis of a tank and designed to home in on the sound of helicopter blades. The demonstration showed that the lethal range of the attack helicopter was greater than the range of the DIVAD, and that the weapon would be unable to protect ground troops from enemy aircraft. Even worse, the test revealed in embarrassing fashion that the DIVAD's homing mechanism was fatally flawed. Since a number of military poobahs were due to attend the demonstration, a portable toilet was installed near the testing ground, complete with a fan to ensure that no unpleasant aromas wafted towards the generals. In the midst of the test, the DIVAD's guns mistook the sound of the fan for helicopter blades, swiveled on its chassis, and blew the empty outhouse to smithereens. Then-defense secretary Caspar Weinberger soon killed the program.

Like any program run by the Pentagon, the FMA had its share of boondoggles. In one case, an American arms broker tried to sell the Army FMA—for $2 million—a can of Russian "stealth paint" he had bought from an East European country. Before sealing the deal, the Army sent the can's contents to a laboratory for analysis. It turned out that the "stealth paint" was nothing more than mercury. In another case, BDM once was burned by a European middleman who sold the company Russian-made sea mines. The mines turned out to be filled with concrete. Beyond such individual foul-ups, FMA officials didn't pay much attention to program costs. Arms dealers were richly rewarded with profit margins of ten to twenty percent, all courtesy of the US taxpayer.

Heinz Baumann, who brokered deals on behalf of BDM and Electronic Warfare Associates, is now retired and resides in Bad Fischau, a spa town in the hills outside of Vienna. His one-time partner John Miley put me in touch with Baumann and sent me an e-mail before I departed for Austria to interview him. "Heinz is one helluva nice guy," he wrote. "[S]uspect you'll be expected to partake of a healthy ration of schnapps. Might be useful to go with the flow and then do the necessary penitence on return home." This advice proved prescient. Wearing a leather jacket and jeans, Baumann was waiting at the international arrivals area at 11 A.M. and immediately took me to an airport bar for three rounds of beer with a schnapps chaser.

Vienna has been a crossroads between East and West for over 1,000 years, and so it was only natural that it emerged as a center for the FMA business. In addition to geography, Austria's strict bank secrecy laws proved alluring to arms traders. Even today, it's the only country in the world that offers totally anonymous accounts, which can be opened without identification. To transfer funds in or out, the bearer need only provide a password provided at the time the account is opened. Business negotiations were frequently conducted within the cozy confines of Vienna's coffee shops, including the Café Landtman, which sits across from the Burgtheater, the Café Europa, just off the Karntnerstrasse, and the spectacular Café Central, where during the early 1900s. Stalin and Trotsky played chess.

As Baumann recounted over glasses of beer in the den of his comfortable home, the key to success in the FMA was establishing mutually beneficial relationships with officials in the satellite countries. "You couldn't get a screw out of the Eastern Bloc without bribes," he said, hastening to add that "extra payments" are an accepted means of business in many parts of the world. Initially, "extra payments" took the form of a VCR, a small television set, a tape recorder. Later, East Bloc officials preferred hard cash. "You can't run a business, especially a secret one, without such things," Baumann says. "I wouldn't call it a bribe, it was a reimbursement for services. If they did a good job, they deserved the money." Baumann was always looking for ways to win favor with Communist officials. After concluding one deal for the Pentagon with the Ceausescu regime in Romania, he delivered a train car full of chocolate bars for distribution to orphanages, to his contact in the military. As a result of such courtesies, Baumann never saw the airport terminal in Bucharest, though he flew into the city dozens of times; the military always had a chauffeured limousine waiting for him on the runway.

In his biggest coup, Baumann made a $1.8 million purchase for infrared-seeking missile heads out of the Ukraine in the early 1990s. But like the arms trade in general, the FMA is a feast or famine business. For every deal that was successfully concluded—and the process could take up to a year from start to finish—many more fell by the wayside. "There was no steady income," Baumann laments. "In this business you have to be a dreamer."

Baumann didn't know Glatt personally but he was well aware of the German's many FMA successes. According to him and others, Glatt had contacts across Eastern Europe, but his main venue was Poland, where he had a virtual open door at the state arms company, CENZIN. Glatt became close friends with CENZIN's head, General Bolesaw Lukavski, a man known affectionately as "Bolo." "Bolo was the key at CENZIN, but he was also the managing director for all FMA business in Europe," Baumann says. "When he told you that a piece from Bulgaria will arrive at 3 o'clock tomorrow, it was there—at five to three. He knew about all the deliveries, who was involved, and who to call if there was trouble." In the late-1980s, Lukavski died in a car crash but Glatt remained in good standing at CENZIN through his ties to two other key officials, Zbigniew Tarka and Tadeusz Koperwas.

Over the years, Glatt's purchases from Warsaw included assault weapons, air defense equipment, and attack helicopters. In 1992, he and several partners purchased three Russian-made torpedoes from CENZIN for $3.5 million. The torpedoes were picked up at an airfield near Gdansk and flown to Andrews Air Force Base by Kaliha, a commercial freight shipper. The same year, Tarka and Koperwas were arrested in a sting operation conducted by US Customs agents in Frankfurt and were accused of attempting to sell illegally $15 million worth of weapons to Iraq. Charges were later dropped, reportedly in response to a request from the CIA, which remained grateful for past services the pair rendered on behalf of the United States.

During the course of his career, Glatt's purchases from other East Bloc countries covered the full range of the Soviet arsenal. According to several knowledgeable people I spoke with, Glatt long ago purchased virtually every weapon fielded by the Yugoslav army NATO confronted in 1999.

WITH THE END of the Cold War, the world of gunrunning has been radically transformed. The CIA still stages covert operations but nothing on the scale of the huge Reagan-era programs, and now that the conflict in the Balkans is relatively contained, there are no decent wars to speak of. The Russian Army has dumped huge quantities of small arms on the international market in the course of its brutal downsizing and China, which is in the process of rearming its troops, recently added two million old rifles to the global arms pile. Combine all that with growing production from countries such as the Czech Republic, Pakistan and Israel, and the end result is a textbook case of oversupply and underdemand.

The players have changed, too. In place of the few mega-brokers that once held sway, hundreds of small-time niche operators have emerged. "The old guys could get a pistol or a tank," says Keith Prager, a weapons trade specialist with US Customs in Miami. "The new guys can get one or the other, but not both. They're the kindergarten class compared to the old Ph.D.s." At the same time, the old-timers look like veritable gentlemen next to the kindergartners, whose ranks include Russian and Balkan mobsters and who are likely to be trafficking drugs and prostitutes as well as arms.

Some former Communist states, most notably Bulgaria, have begun selling arms directly to embargoed regimes and controversial clients without the help of middlemen. That's further narrowed the domain of Glatt and other brokers who made money by exploiting their contacts in the Soviet Bloc. "Ten years ago, if you wanted to get something out of CENZIN you had to go through Glatt," says an arms broker based at a big firm outside of Washington. "Now anyone can show up in Eastern Europe with an end-user certificate and buy whatever he wants."

Glatt himself has been slowed in recent years by a heart operation and a bout with cancer. He spends more time with his family and is a generous donor to a variety of charitable causes. He built an irrigation system for farmers in Switzerland and paid for incubators for newborn babies at a hospital in Poland. In Germany, he is a large donor to his old alma mater at Heidelberg. At the behest of an American friend, the eminent cardiologist Dr. Robert Matthews, Glatt met with the cardinal of Hungary and offered to put up $1.5 million to help finance a heart laboratory for a Catholic hospital in Budapest. "My charitable activities are my tribute for having had a wonderful and interesting life," Glatt wrote me. "But I do not want to talk about it. I am not a Pharisee!"

If arms now comprise a much smaller part of his business activities, Glatt remains a player in the field. "[P]olitical events in the Soviet Union and Eastern Europe have significantly reduced the perceived threat to the US and the West," reads a 1993–1996 strategic plan for a company he was involved with, "[but] there is strong growth potential for our business for the next five to ten years." Still, the plan's overall tone is rather sullen and, along with a host of other internal memos, reflects the lackluster realities of the current market. There's talk of doing business in military spare parts and hopes of expanding the company's "client base" to include China, Thailand, Singapore, Taiwan, Turkey and a few other Third World countries. Other internal documents I acquired mentioned sales possibilities such as Czech-made battlefield radars for Sierra Leone, armored personnel carriers to Turkey, Russian radars for Saudi Arabia, and Russian helicopters to Peru. During the past few years, Glatt has also turned up in Hungary, where he has been attempting to buy an idled mortar factory in Budapest. "The idea was to keep these factories going," he told me on the phone. "It was a country with terrible economic problems. This would give a few hundred people in Hungary good jobs. Of course, I wanted to make money. I don't claim to be a do-gooder."

Since 1996, Glatt has worked at least three deals for the FMA, which is still up and running though on a greatly reduced budget. China and North Korea are currently targets, as is Russia, which no longer is an official "enemy" but sells to countries that are. Now, materiel comes straight out of Moscow, where the government is so broke that it is willing to sell virtually anything—short of nuclear, chemical and biological weapons—to the United States. In one of those bizarre twists of the arms world, the Russian military uses the Pentagon's money to finance its next generation of weaponry. Rosvoorouzhenie, the Russian state arms agency, publishes a glossy seven-volume sales catalog that offers information and prices on everything from small arms to submarines, planes and even warheads. Such an atlas would have constituted the single biggest intelligence find of the Cold War; now it's available for $1,500 and can be found in the libraries of all the beltway companies still working the trade. Secrecy has become less important than it was during the Cold War, but Moscow and Washington still insist on the use of middlemen who can play the enduring role of scapegoat in the event that things go sour. As always, Glatt has positioned himself well. Some years ago a Russian general was in need of a hip replacement. The general—now in a position of some power—couldn't afford the operation so Glatt paid for it himself.

Russian weapons are still popular on world markets, especially in the Third World, and Glatt's contacts in Eastern Europe remain valuable. In 1997, a private company was seeking to curry favor in Azerbaijan, where it was competing for a deal. A company consultant came up with four options, one of which was to broker a $20 million arms deal for the Azeri government. The firm ultimately opted for another course of action, but it had identified Glatt as the preferred supplier if the arms plan were to move forward. "There are a lot of fly-by-nights in the private arms business," says a person familiar with the details. "Glatt has been around and he's trustworthy. He's one of only four or five men in the world who can quickly obtain and transport large quantities of Russian equipment."

IN THE MIDST of researching Glatt's story, I was given a letter that a European arms dealer sent to an American colleague in the early 1990s. It opened by lamenting a spate of anti-American bombings in the Middle East and then, without missing a beat, turned to the immediate business at hand: closing a deal for land-mines.

The government bureaucrats who manage the global weapons trade seem equally incapable of self-reflection. During the Cold War, they saw countries as pawns in the holy war against communism and sent arms to any government willing to sign up. More often than not, that simply allowed authoritarian regimes to occupy their own countries by force. The consequences are now on display across the globe. The enormous amounts of weapons that the US poured into Somalia completely destabilized the country, which has had no real central government since Siad Barre was overthrown by tribal militias in 1991. That coincided with the end of the Cold War and, after the Bush administration's brief and disastrous intervention there the following year, the country now holds no interest for the United States. "The thing about Somalia," an unnamed "regional analyst" told the *Washington Post* last year, "is they really don't get the fact that nobody gives a shit about them any more." The CIA considers Afghanistan to be one of its greatest success stories as the *mujahedin*'s defeat of the Red Army accelerated the Soviet break-up. Between 1979 and 1991, the agency shipped huge amounts of weaponry into the country, including some 400,000 AK-47s and more than 100 million rounds of ammunition. Like Somalia, Afghanistan is in a state of anarchy with the fundamentalist Taleban militia fighting a number of other armed groups for control of the government. Last year, President Clinton ordered cruise missile attacks on what he described as a terrorist training camp run by Osama bin Laden in a remote corner of the country. It was the very same spot the CIA had used a decade earlier as a staging area to supply the *mujahedin*. Meanwhile, the CIA has been desperately seeking to get back the Stinger missiles that it sent the *mujahedin* for fear that our former friends might use them to shoot down a civilian jetliner or carry out similar acts of terrorism. In Angola, the CIA's old ally Jonas Savimbi was defeated in presidential elections, but refused to honor the results and later took up arms against the country's government. The US-sponsored contra war in Nicaragua succeeded in destroying that country's economy, leading to the Sandinistas being ousted in elections in 1990. Nine years later, the country has yet to recover. It is the second poorest nation in the Western hemisphere, ahead only of Haiti, and its current president is an old crony of the Somoza dictatorship.

Meanwhile, Glatt and other arms dealers who supplied Cold War combatants continue to profit from the war business. Barbara Studley and John Singlaub turned up in Washington in late-1998 trying to sell an Israeli missile guidance system to the American government. Ron Martin heads R/M Equipment in Miami, which advertises itself on the worldwide web as "The #1 Supplier of 40 mm Grenade Launchers." Richard Secord was seen not long ago in Azerbaijan, where he was attempting to sell the armed forces a package of military training and equipment. Sarkis Soghanalian, who now has offices on the Champs Elysées and works closely with French intelligence, helped funnel weapons to the military officers who overthrew the democratically-elected leader of the Congo Republic in 1997. "There's nothing as big as the Iran-Iraq War, but there's still a lot going on," he told me from Paris during a phone interview. "The countries change, but there's always business." (A few months after our conversation, Soghanalian was arrested in Miami after arriving on a flight from Paris. As this book is being completed, he is being held in federal detention on bank fraud and money laundering charges.) Gunther Leinhauser, working in conjunction with a weapons company in Chile, was implicated in 1995 in the illegal arming of Croatia during the Balkans war. Even Oliver North, the would-be senator and talk show host, heads a floundering body-armor company called Guardian Technologies International. "Every time you think one of these guys has died he turns up somewhere peddling arms," says an American weapons broker who still dabbles in the field. "Once you're in the business, you're in the business."

THREE

ARMS AND THE MAN (II)

The Shady Mr. Mertins

"He's on our side and that's all that matters."

—CIA director Allen Dulles, speaking of Reinhard Gehlen, spy
chief for Hitler and, following the war, the West

GERHARD GEORG MERTINS, another important German arms dealer,
competed and occasionally collaborated with Ernst Werner Glatt and
his one-time boss, Sam Cummings. A war hero of the Third Reich,
Mertins's business contacts over the years included prominent Nazis
such as Otto Skorzeny, the SS commando who rescued Mussolini
from an Allied prison in 1943, and Klaus Barbie, the Gestapo chief
who escaped to South America after WWII before finally being extra-
dited to France, where he died in prison after being convicted of
crimes against humanity. Mertins's governmental clients ranged
from Chile's Augusto Pinochet to Iraq's Saddam Hussein.

Mertins's company, Merex, was headquartered in Bonn and had subsidiaries around the world, including an important branch in the United States. That was not by chance. While by no means as integral to US agencies as Glatt, Mertins, who died in 1993, had a four-decade long relationship with American intelligence and sometimes worked in conjunction with government operations. Like Glatt, he procured Russian-made arms for the secret Foreign Materiel Acquisition Program. He was also involved in arming the "freedom fighters," including a controversial deal Oliver North's Enterprise arranged for the contras. As one retired intelligence officer said of Mertins's role as an American asset, which until now has never been disclosed, "You were either so high up that you didn't say anything about him or too low to know."

Born in 1919 and raised in Berlin, Mertins served as a paratrooper during the war. He was a brave soldier—US Army Intelligence files obtained under the Freedom of Information Act show he was hospitalized with wounds five times between 1940 and 1943—and rose to the rank of major. He took part in the Balkans campaign of 1941 and the same year was awarded the Iron Cross when as a platoon leader he parachuted into Crete during the German invasion. After serving several years on the Eastern Front, Mertins was sent West in 1944 with his Wehrmacht unit (Fallschirm-Pionier-Bataillon 5). The unit was decimated while fighting Allied troops that swarmed into France after the D-Day invasion, but Mertins's actions brought him the Knight's Cross, or Ritterkreuz, the Third Reich's highest war decoration and an honor bestowed by Hitler's government on only about 7,000 soldiers.

After the war, Mertins held an administrative job with Volkswagen, then opened a company that operated buses between Bremen and Berlin. Army Intelligence files show that he was active in neo-Nazi movements of the early 1950s. Mertins was a leader of the Bremen branch of the "Green Devils," an organization of former paratroopers whose primary political cause was a remilitarized Germany. Its members included a number of suspected war criminals as well as General Kurt Student, the brilliant military strategist who led the 1940 assault on Holland, Belgium and Luxembourg, and the glider-and-paratroop invasion of Crete.

On one occasion, Mertins invited members of the Hilfsgemeinschaft auf Gegenseitigkeit (Mutual Aid Society), an association of former Waffen SS men, to accompany the Devils on a boat trip to Helgoland, a North Sea island that the British seized during the war and which the Royal Air Force used for bombing practice afterwards. (Reclaiming Helgoland became a rallying cry for the German right; the British returned it in 1952.) The Devils also hosted a guest lecturer series. Among the speakers invited to address the group was Otto-Ernst Remer, commander of the Grossdeutschland battalion that in July 1944 put down an attempt to overthrow the Third Reich. A fanatical Hitler admirer, Remer called the anti-Nazi resistance "a stain on the shield of honor of the German officers' corps" and dismissed the holocaust as a creation of Allied propaganda. In 1950, he founded the Socialist Reich Party (SRP), the successor to the Nazis. According to a 1951 Army report, Mertins himself "is considered to be an important SRP sympathizer and it is believed he will aid the party financially." The United States closely monitored the SRP,

which that same year caused an uproar when it obtained eleven percent of the votes in state elections in Lower Saxony. In October 1952,
German courts banned the party as a subversive organization.

By then, Mertins had moved to Egypt as part of a German advisory group sent to supervise the training of King Farouk's troops, who
had been humiliated by Israel during the 1948 war. The delegation
was led by Navy Captain Theodor von Mauchenhein, Panzer General
Oskar Munzel, and Wehrmacht General Wilhelm Fahrmbacher,
another Knight's Cross recipient. Mertins, who arrived in Cairo in
September 1951 and served as one of Fahrmbacher's top aides, led
the training of an elite Egyptian parachute regiment. Mertins also
helped train parachutists in Syria, where another German advisory
team, this one run by Colonel Rainer Kriebel, had arrived about the
same time.

The Fahrmbacher mission had at least the tacit blessing of both
the CIA and German intelligence, then known as the "Gehlen Org"
after its head, Reinhard Gehlen. A Gestapo general who oversaw military intelligence programs throughout Eastern Europe for Hitler,
Gehlen surrendered to US troops in 1945 and offered to provide intelligence on Russia in return for light treatment at the hands of the
Allies. A deal was swiftly cut. Gehlen was flown to Washington (disguised as an American general) for interrogation and training. In the
summer of 1946—when the policy of denazification was already
being supplanted by anti-communism—he was allowed to return to
Germany to set up the country's new intelligence agency. Christopher
Simpson, author of the book *Blowback*, estimates that during the next
decade the United States spent some $200 million and employed at

least 4,000 people to construct the Gehlen Org. "I don't know if he's a rascal," Simpson quotes CIA director Allen Dulles saying of Gehlen. "There are few archbishops in espionage . . . Besides, one needn't ask him to one's club."

Former US intelligence officer Miles Copeland says the CIA had a direct role in implementing the German mission in Egypt. Fahrmbacher was, he writes in *The Game of Nations*, one of a number of Germans the Pentagon had on its hands "who were not—or in some cases not quite—war criminals, and whom it was to our advantage to have absorbed, with a minimum of fuss and embarrassment, by various countries of the world where they could live inconspicuously and earn a living." Copeland says that an American military attaché suggested that Fahrmbacher—"eminently available as his Nazi standing was well enough known to make him unwelcome in Germany"—was the perfect man to handle the Egyptian job.

Gerhard Bauch, a former Wehrmacht captain and one of Gehlen's intelligence operatives in the Middle East (and, as we shall see, later went to work for Mertins) says the Vatican secretly helped install the German programs in Syria and Egypt. Bauch now lives in suburban Maryland, where he keeps on a dining room end table a silver salver that Gehlen gave him after he returned from one trip to Egypt (inscribed "Be wise as the serpent and harmless as the dove"). By his account, the German delegation to Syria, which included his friend, the fighter pilot Karl Romain, first traveled to Rome. A Vatican official received the group, which stayed in housing provided by the Church. A few days later, the delegation traveled by boat to Damascus. (Vatican involvement would hardly be a surprise. The

Church despised atheistic communism and was deeply involved in the post-war "ratlines" that funneled Nazis out of Eastern Europe and Germany. In a speech in 1970, Nazi war hero Hans-Ulrich Rudel thanked the Vatican for its assistance: "One may otherwise view Catholicism as one wishes. But what the Church, especially certain towering personalities within the Church, undertook in those years [following the war] to save the best of our nation, often from certain death, must never be forgotten. With its own immense resources, the Church helped many of us to go overseas. In this manner, in quiet and secrecy, the demented victors' mad craving for revenge and retribution could be effectively counteracted.")

In 1952, young officers led by Gamal Abdel Nasser staged a coup against King Farouk Fahrmbacher's men; they didn't initiate the uprising but did provide the plotters with advice. Nasser needed help building up his new regime's intelligence and police apparatus and, once again, the United States and the Gehlen Org were eager to lend a hand. After consulting with Dulles, Gehlen recruited SS Sturmbannfuhrer Otto Skorzeny to work with Nasser.

Skorzeny had escaped from a US prison camp in Germany in 1948 and moved to Franco's Spain, where he worked as an arms salesmen for several Spanish and German firms. While there, US intelligence officials established a cordial relationship with Skorzeny—even though he was technically a fugitive on an American arrest warrant, still faced potential prosecution for war crimes and was known to be a central player in neo-Nazi movements. A June 28, 1948 US Air Intelligence Report (obtained under FOIA) reports on a meeting in Madrid between an unnamed US operative and Skorzeny, alias Rolf Steinbauer. "Skorzeny appears to be very friendly and affable with the reporting officer," the report opens. "Customary greeting is not unlike being welcomed by a huge bear or engulfed by a huge Saint Bernard dog." Skorzeny warned the reporting officer that Germany "once had a tremendous Communist party before the war and could easily fall prey once again." He offered to help the United States in whatever way he could, though not openly as "he fears a loss of face in his followers who purport to be violently anti-US."

Quietly giving a hand in Egypt seems to have been one way for Skorzeny to help out his American friends. According to Copeland, Skorzeny used CIA money to hand pick and pay about 100 German veterans, including a number of unrepentant war criminals, to train Egyptian security forces. These included Hermann Lauterbacher, an ex-SS officer and leader of Hitler Youth, who served as the liaison between the Gehlen Org and the German delegation in Cairo. (Bauch portrays Lauterbacher as an inept bungler who suggested that German companies be encouraged to advertise on billboards along the Suez Canal. Bauch pointed out that great quantities of cargo but very few passengers moved through the canal, and the idea was dropped. Bauch denies that the Gehlen Org employed other prominent Nazis in Egypt. He specifically disputes accounts saying that Alois Brunner—an aide to Adolf Eichmann, who the Simon Wiesenthal Center estimates is responsible for the murder of more than 100,000 people—worked for the Org in Egypt or Syria. Bauch does say that he met Brunner socially in Damascus— where the Nazi war criminal was living under the name of Georg

Fischer—but that he didn't know who he was at the time. The most important Nazi now at large, Brunner still lives in Syria. The French have repeatedly requested his extradition, most recently in 1999, but the Syrian government pretends that it has no knowledge of Brunner's presence in the country.)

Skorzeny's assistance endeared him to the Egyptian government. At the half-year celebration of the Nasser regime in January 1953, he was seen inspecting a military parade from a grandstand seat usually reserved for foreign dignitaries. By then, Egypt was literally crawling with Nazis, who were welcomed with open arms by the government. "Hitler is the man of my life," enthused health minister Dr. Noureddine Tarraf. "[He was] an ideal leader who dedicated his life to the realization of his noble ambition." Wilhelm Voss, a manager of the Hermann Goering Works—a huge wartime industrial web that oversaw vast properties in occupied territories—became an economic adviser to Nasser in 1952. Johann Von Leers, a viciously anti-Semitic propagandist who openly called for the extermination of the Jews—his Nazi-era works included *Fourteen Years of the Jew Republic* and *The Criminality of Jewry*—also took up residence in Cairo at around this time. He worked for Nasser's foreign propaganda service and later converted to Islam, taking the name of Omar Amin von Leers. The German colony also included dozens of scientists hired by Nasser to lead an Egyptian missile program.

Mertins was on cordial terms with some of the more extreme Nazi elements. A US Army intelligence report from December 1954 notes that Skorzeny—in his role as a representative of the Spanish weapons manufacturer ALFA—had been in contact with Mertins about an arms deal he was negotiating with Nasser's regime. An American embassy dispatch out of Cairo two years later said Mertins was "closely cooperating"—in what fashion is not spelled out—with Skorzeny and Voss.

Bauch says Mertins was also friendly with Rolf Engel, one of Nasser's missile helpers. As described by Bauch, Engel was "a scientist who worked for France after the war." Engel's background was actually more interesting than that, as detailed in Tom Bower's book *The Paperclip Conspiracy*, which describes the secret operation by which American intelligence shipped hundreds of Nazi scientists to the United States after the war to work on industrial and military projects. During World War II, Engel worked at Peenemunde, the huge rocket weapons project on the Baltic coast run by Wernher von Braun, designer of the V-2s which terrorized English cities during the final nine months of the war. Von Braun and Engel could easily have been tried for war crimes—the V-2 project was served by slave laborers at the adjoining Dora concentration camp, who were starved, beaten, and worked to death. Instead, von Braun was brought to the United States under the "Paperclip" program. He went on to design the army's Jupiter rocket and in 1970 was appointed deputy assistant director of planning for NASA. (Harvard mathematics professor turned musician Tom Lehrer sang of NASA's man: "Don't say that he is hypocritical, say rather that he is apolitical, 'Once the rockets are up, who cares where they come down, that's not my department,' says Wernher von Braun.")

Engel, an SS officer, was stationed in Strasbourg, France before being posted to Peenemunde. His Nazi Party files show he was commended by his superiors for his "intelligence, hard work, and competence" in suppressing the French resistance. That didn't stop the French from taking him straight from a POW camp to a rocket center in Paris, where, Bauch says, he helped design the Gabriel missile. From Paris, Engel briefly returned to Germany before moving on to Cairo to work for Nasser.

Mertins worked in the Middle East until the late-1950s, by which time Nasser had moved into the Soviet camp. In addition to his work as a trainer, Mertins brokered deals for German companies seeking to export to the Middle East. He sold 500 wine-red Mercedes-Benz to Saudi Arabia for the Kingdom's top officer corps and peddled everything from parachutes to steel helmets to Egypt and Syria. At some point in the mid-1950s, the US military attaché at the Cairo embassy recruited Mertins and put him on the payroll of Army Intelligence. "The United States wanted to know as much as possible about Arab military activities," Bauch says in explaining Mertins's usefulness to American intelligence. "Mertins traveled to many of the major countries and learned a lot through his contacts [with government and military officials]."

IN THE LATE-1950S, Mertins decided to return home and rejoin the German Army. "The screening committee included a German who had spent the war in London and another who had spent the war in Moscow," Mertins later told Russell Howe, author of the book *Weapons*. "I decided the odds were stacked against me, so I withdrew my application."

After a brief return to the Middle East—he led a German team from his days in Cairo to train paratroopers in Saudi Arabia—Mertins established Merex in Vevey, Switzerland in 1963. He intended for the firm to be a general exporter but, according to the German writer Heinz Vielain, who authored a vanity biography of Mertins, became engaged in the weapons business at the request of Reinhard Gehlen. Vielain says that Gehlen wanted to secretly arm selected Third World nations as a means of keeping them in the Western camp but—due to political sensitivities and the need to evade arms export laws that banned sales to regions of conflict—needed a cut out to carry out the transactions. In addition, the West German government was then under great pressure from the United States to modernize its military hardware—with American-made weaponry, needless to say. Selling off its excess stocks of old weapons to the Third World would allow Bonn to pay for the new equipment.

Mertins was already well known in ruling Christian Democrat circles—it helped that he hired Fritz Westrick, son of then Secretary of State Ludger Westrick—and he and Gehlen soon cut a deal. German intelligence would provide Merex with information about which Third World countries were looking to buy arms, and the company would sell them what they needed, using false end-user certificates when necessary. "Any complications that arose for Merex were taken care of by [German intelligence]," Vielain wrote. "The most important thing was secrecy, that no one discover the real destination for the weapons."

Mertins's role as West Germany's unofficial weapons dealer quickly helped establish him as a major player in the international arms trade. By 1965, Sam Cummings and Ernst Werner Glatt had hired Merex as their purchasing agent in Germany for Interarms. The two firms teamed up that same year to sell Venezuela 74 F-86 fighter planes.

In 1966, Merex sold ninety F-86s to Pakistan, which along with India, was under a NATO arms embargo after the two countries had fought a brief war the prior year. Since Pakistan could not make the purchase legally, the Shah of Iran agreed to have his nation stand in as the supposed buyer. Mertins arranged for Luftwaffe officers to fly the planes to Teheran, where Iranian pilots dressed in Pakistani military uniforms secretly delivered them to Islamabad. Mertins always claimed that the United States—which favored Pakistan against left-leaning India—signed off on the transfer, and of this there can be little doubt. Congressman Stuart Symington, who later led an US investigation of the deal, concluded that "Our own intelligence services knew exactly at the time that these F-86s were meant for Pakistan."

The Indian government learned of the F-86 operation and was understandably furious. To appease New Delhi, Mertins—in a move that Basil Zaharoff would have admired—immediately sold India several dozen Seahawk fighter-bombers. Here, too, a cutout was used. The Seahawks were to be shipped—according to loading documents, anyway—to an Italian firm called Tirenna. A freighter Mertins leased in Nordenham set sail for Naples, then changed course en route and made its way to Kotchin, where the Indians took possession of the planes.

The India-Pakistan conflict made Mertins a very rich man. He used part of the estimated $10 million in proceeds from the aircraft deals to buy two estates in Switzerland—one in the Alps, about 300 yards from a villa owned by Cummings—and a third on the Rhine near

Bonn. He also bought a home in Bethesda, Maryland, where he established a US branch of Merex at offices on upper Wisconsin Avenue.

Mertins hired Gerhard Bauch, the German intelligence operative, to run his US subsidiary. In 1962, Gehlen had named Bauch to be his station chief in Cairo, where a company owned by banker Herbert Quandt provided his cover. In addition to being a friend of Gehlen's, Quandt happened to be the stepson of Nazi propaganda chief Josef Goebbels. (Quandt's mother, Magda, divorced his father to marry Goebbels, with whom she had six children. The entire family joined Hitler in the Fuhrerbunker in Berlin, where the Nazi leader committed suicide in 1945 as Russian troops closed in on his compound. Hitler picked Goebbels to succeed him as Reich Chancellor, but he refused the fuhrer's final order. Instead, Goebbels had his six children poisoned by a lethal injection administered by an SS doctor and than himself and his wife shot by an SS orderly.)

By the time Bauch arrived in Egypt, Nasser had moved into the Soviet camp and Germany had established diplomatic relations with Israel. Unbeknownst to Bauch, Israeli intelligence, apparently with the secret collaboration of Gehlen, had smuggled an agent—Major Ze'ev Lotz, son of a German father and a Jewish mother—into Egypt the year before he became station chief. "Wolfgang" Lotz, an accomplished horseman, opened a riding school that was frequented by top Egyptian officers, who provided him with a great deal of information useful to the Mossad. Lotz also kept an eye on Egypt's ongoing missile program, which the Israelis deemed to be a serious threat. The Mossad first tried to shut the program down by leaking details about it to the international press and by mailing threatening notes to the

German scientists working for Nasser. When those tactics failed, Lotz began sending letter bombs to the scientists, several whom were badly injured.

In 1965, the Egyptians uncovered Lotz and threw him in jail. Bauch, who the Egyptians believed to be his collaborator, was also taken into custody. There he remained until Hans-Heinrich Worgitzky, vice president of German intelligence and Bauch's close friend, made three separate trips to Cairo to arrange his release. (Lotz was tried and sentenced to twenty-five years in prison; several of his Egyptian accomplices were executed. In 1968, Lotz was released to Israel in exchange for nine Egyptian generals and thousands of soldiers captured during the Six Day War.)

Being exposed as a German agent put an end to Bauch's career in intelligence. He returned to Germany and took a job with the Bonn office of a locomotive company called Henschel. He claims, somewhat implausibly, that he had never met Mertins when the latter was involved with the Fahrmbacher military mission in Egypt, but now looked him up at the suggestion of their mutual friend, the German rocket scientist Rolf Engel. In any event, Mertins offered Bauch a job and he agreed to move to the United States.

If the Pakistan deal brought riches to Mertins, it also created some difficulties. When his role in the affair leaked out and hit world newspapers, the Swiss government barred him from working out of the country. The deal received widespread attention in the United States as well, prompting the *Washington Post* to send a reporter to visit Mertins at his home in Maryland. Sitting on a silk upholstered Louis XV couch "in his Mittel-Europa living room,"

Mertins told the *Post* that he was different "from the 'bad Germans' of World War II." Furthermore, he was no more accountable for what his clients did with Merex-supplied guns, he said, than was an automobile dealer responsible for the death of someone run down by a car he sold.

The "Pakiscam" uproar also led to hearings before the US Congress in the spring of 1967. Mertins was not called to testify, but he met privately with two key figures from the hearings, Representative Symington and Senator J. William Fulbright. Meanwhile, the Justice Department asked J. Edgar Hoover at the FBI to investigate Mertins and determine whether he should be required to register as a foreign agent of West German intelligence. The Bureau concluded that "Mertins does maintain and promote contacts with agencies of the Defense and State departments, as well as with various congressional offices, [but] it is believed these are legitimate business contacts designed solely to serve Merex's business interests and not those of the West German government."

Despite the unwanted publicity, Merex continued to thrive. Partially censored FBI and Army Intelligence files obtained under the FOIA show that Mertins's firm had subsidiaries or representatives in Iran, Saudi Arabia, North Africa and South America. Much of Merex's supplies came from West German stocks, the reports state, but the company also bought surplus military hardware from France, Italy, Britain and Holland. Merex's clients were said to be spread across the Middle East, Africa and South America. Among the few specific names not redacted by FOIA officers were Chad, Greece and Turkey. The German government apparently used

Merex to funnel weapons to the last two at the request of the United States. One of the FBI reports also states that Merex had made a number of proposals—to a country whose identity was censored—"for projects such as organizing and training police forces [and] designing and equipping explosives factories."

Bauch, who worked with Merex until 1972, told me of several other deals that took place while he was with the firm, including the sale of radar stations to Pakistan and police handguns to the Saudis. One of the bigger transactions he remembers took place in the mid-1960s, when hostilities erupted between Egypt and North Yemen. The Saudis supported the conservative rulers in Yemen, and paid Merex to ship vast supplies to its ally. Bauch says the weapons came out of West Germany's surplus US stocks, and that both governments approved the deal.

I learned about a more unsavory side of Mertins's commercial dealings from the files of Fritz Schwend, which were found by authorities in Peru after Schwend's companion, Klaus Barbie, was apprehended in neighboring Bolivia. (Barbie was returned to France in 1983, shortly after a civilian government took power in Lima. Schwend had died in Lima in 1980.) Schwend, one of Mertins's primary business contacts in South America, joined the Nazi Party in 1932 and went on to serve as a purchasing agent for the SS and the Wehrmacht. In 1944, he was put in charge of Operation Bernhardt, a counterfeiting scheme intended to enrich the Third Reich and undermine Britain's economy by massive forging of sterling. Schwend acted under orders of the Austrian Nazi Ernst Kaltenbrunner, head of the Reich Main Security Office, which controlled the Gestapo and the concentration camp network. (Kaltenbrunner was hanged at Nuremberg.) Schwend was taken into custody by American counterintelligence agents in 1945, but escaped being jailed by becoming an informant. He was later released by American troops—the precise circumstances are redacted in Army Intelligence records obtained under the FOIA—whereupon he slipped out of Europe on a false passport and settled in Lima.

Schwend remained deeply involved in worldwide neo-Nazi movements. His personal phone list, a copy of which I found in his files, contained the names of Otto Skorzeny, Walter Rauff—a sadistic killer who administered a gas truck execution program used to kill approximately 250,000 people, and who fled to Chile after the war—and Hans Ulrich-Rudel, Hitler's most decorated airman. Rudel lived in South America between 1948 and 1953, and became a confidant to a number of fascist rulers. He personally convinced Paraguayan dictator Alfredo Stroessner to grant citizenship to Dr. Josef Mengele, the notorious "Angel of Death" of Auschwitz. Thanks to help from Rudel and other neo-Nazis, various Nazi hunters who sought to track him down never apprehended Mengele. In 1979, he drowned while swimming in the ocean near his home in Brazil, where he had moved in 1960.

But Schwend's best friend was Klaus Barbie, the Gestapo chief in occupied France who is best known for torturing to death resistance leader Jean Moulin and sending Jewish children to Auschwitz. Like Schwend, Barbie worked for US Army Intelligence after the war. The Army helped him flee Europe when the French learned of his whereabouts and demanded that he be turned over for prosecution. Schwend and Barbie became advisors to right-wing generals in their adopted South American homelands, and jointly acted as arms purchasing agents for the Peruvian and Bolivian governments. With the help of their friends Rudel and Skorzeny, they also arranged sales to right-wing regimes in Paraguay, Chile and Spain.

In 1966, the same year he was opening his office in Bethesda, Mertins was in regular touch with Schwend about possible arms deals. In one letter he sent the former SS man a list of all of Merex's "possible exports," which ranged from rockets to spy equipment (such as microphones concealed in fountain pens and tie clips). Schwend was highly impressed by Mertins, who, he wrote in a letter to a friend, "has good connections to [Germany's] armed forces. If the Peruvian government writes to Bonn, he has a copy of the letter the following day." In September 1967, Merex wrote to a Peruvian military official to say that it had appointed one of Schwend's firms, Commercial Agricola, as its local representative.

Schwend's files include dozens of letters he exchanged with Mertins and other Merex officials. In one, Schwend asked for pricing information and availability of American-made M-14 tanks for the Peruvian Army. Mertins cabled back with the desired information and told Schwend to reply via "Our common friend Colonel R [Hans-Ulrich Rudel], who also works for us." In another letter, Mertins informed Schwend that Skorzeny had contacted Merex in the hopes of purchasing pistols, machine guns, and tanks for a Peruvian general. In February 1968, Schwend informed Merex that a Bolivian firm called Transmaritima, owned by a certain "Herr Altmann"—Barbie's alias—was looking to buy used ships for the Bolivian navy. (Barbie's board of directors at Transmaritima, which shipped coffee and tin as well as weapons, included the head of the Bolivian joint chiefs of staff and the director of the secret police, General Alfredo Ovando Candia). Mertins soon informed Schwend that "your request that we talk to Altmann was passed on to our Naval Department and is in the hands of Herr Hansen."

Other Merex clients were less sinister, if only slightly, than the Nazi mob. In 1971, two years before General Augusto Pinochet seized power in a coup d'etat against elected president Salvador Allende, Bauch traveled to Chile to negotiate an $800,000 deal for bridles and saddles for the mounted police. Pinochet was then the Army's purchasing chief; he and Bauch were the signers on the deal, which included the sale of 40,000 steel helmets and 20,000 rounds of ammunition. "Pinochet was very happy with the agreement," Bauch recalled. "He said, 'You have done us a favor, now what can we do for you?' I asked to go to their Calvary School [south of Valparaiso] and ride their best horse. The next day, Pinochet had arranged everything."

The deal led to Bauch's resignation from Merex—he felt that Mertins stiffed him on the commission—but it seems to have led to a long and fruitful relationship between the company and authorities in Chile. Mertins became a regular visitor to the country, where he sometimes stayed at Colonia Dignidad, a right-wing agricultural community near Parral, at the foot of the southern Andes. Dignidad's founder was Paul Schafer, a renegade Baptist pastor who fled Germany in the 1960s after being accused of sexually abusing children. At Dignidad, he established a closely guarded, cult-like society of German immigrants. According to accounts given to Amnesty International by a few escapees, the colonists at Dignidad worked up to thirteen hours a day, contact between the sexes was banned and parents and children were separated. Meanwhile, the Chilean military maintained close ties to Dignidad, which was visited by Pinochet and his intelligence chieftain, the dreaded Manuel Contreras of DINA.

In Germany, Mertins created a "Circle of Friends" of Colonia Dignidad that supported the community financially. In 1979, he gave a deposition in a lawsuit brought in Europe by escapees from the colony. He denied that Chilean police or intelligence agents ever entered the colony, which he portrayed as an idyllic farm settlement. "The mass of the population is content that the Allende-Castro show came to a close," he wrote in his statement. "General Pinochet and members of the junta are great patriots." Dignidad was shut down at gunpoint by the civilian government of Patricio Aylwin, who was elected in 1989. A Commission for Truth and Reconciliation appointed by Aylwin concluded that during the Pinochet dictatorship, DINA agents used Dignidad as a torture center and training camp.

Mertins also helped broker agreements for private arms manufacturers. His German clients included the arms giant Messerschmitt-Boelkow Blohm; while in America he represented Fairchild Weston Systems (later bought by Loral, which in turn was purchased by Lockheed Martin). That latter relationship ended with an ugly lawsuit over a deal Mertins helped set up for the company in the People's Republic of China. (The precise circumstances of the lawsuit will be explained later in this chapter.) Mertins's attorney in the case submitted papers to the court which said that beginning in 1972, Merex had "performed substantial work and services and maintained a substantial business relationship on behalf of Western companies and other Western entities" in China. Mertins was said to be especially well-connected to Poly Technologies and the China International Trust and Investment, both companies that are linked to the People's Liberation Army. Zhao Fei, the third ranking executive at state arms company NORINCO, was another crucial contact.

I spoke to a number of major Cold War-era arms dealers and all were well-acquainted with Mertins. Arif Durrani, a Pakistani arms dealer, moved to the United States in the early 1970s and set up shop in Spring Valley, New York. He and a partner had a contract to supply spare parts for the Pakistani Air Force's F-86 planes—the ones Merex had supplied back in 1966. Mertins, meanwhile, was supplying F-86 spares to the apartheid government in South Africa. "I bought truckloads and trainloads of spares from Canada," Durrani recalls. "Mertins was buying them from me until I left Spring Valley in 1979." According to Durrani, Mertins had substantial business of his own in Pakistan, where he retained as his agent an important general.

From Paris, Sarkis Soghanalian said he met Mertins in 1969 when they were both sales representatives for Colt Industries. "We did light business together on the side, rifles and pistols," he recalled. "Our buyers were police and internal security in Saudi Arabia, Abu Dhabi, and Qatar." What about Mertins's political views, I asked? Soghanalian was aware of Mertins's Nazi past and links—he erroneously believed that Mertins had been a Waffen SS officer—but said, "In this business, you don't ask about politics or religion."

AS HE PROFITED by selling arms to his dubious client list, Mertins maintained a well-rounded relationship with American intelligence agencies. In addition to moving arms discreetly to countries allied with the United States, he also spied on his clients (buyers and sellers) for the Army. Mertins's primary targets, says one of his case officers, were Eastern Europe, China, and the Middle East, where he frequently traveled in the course of peddling arms. When the FBI was investigating Merex in the aftermath of the 1966 Pakistan deal, Army Intelligence intervened to protect Mertins's status as an asset. "The Army has opposed registration of Merex or Mertins [as a foreign agent] on any basis which could jeopardize [their] continued use," reads an internal FBI memo prepared as the investigation was underway. Another Bureau memo from the same period states, "Whatever the outcome of this investigation may be, we will not solicit [Mertins's] registration without first ascertaining the views of the Department of the Army."

Mertins's relationship with intelligence agencies gave him an open door at American embassies abroad, and with military attachés who tracked the armaments needs of their hosts. It also bolstered his credibility with his corporate clients and foreign military officials, the latter whom no doubt assumed that a weapons deal brokered by Mertins must have the US seal of approval. Most importantly, Mertins was allowed to conduct his business activities with little oversight from US authorities charged with monitoring the arms trade. "The government turned its head to his activities, even when his clients were highly sensitive," says the former case officer.

Like Ernst Werner Glatt, Mertins helped cement his ties to the United States defense establishment by offering employment to American military officials. In 1970, he hired Colonel Richard Amity, a recently retired Army Intelligence officer, to be president of Merex's American subsidiary. The two men had met in the early 1960s, when Amity was the assistant Army attaché at the American embassy in Germany and Mertins was emerging as an important private arms broker. Unaware that he was already on the American payroll, Amity cabled home to say he'd met Mertins at a local arms exhibition. "He was already a source," Amity recalls. "I got a twix from the CIA saying not to contact him again," Amity recalls. At about the same time, Mertins hired as Merex's vice president Lieutenant Colonel Helmut Huber (now deceased), another Army Intelligence official who for many years had been Mertins's case officer.

Both Bauch and Amity had fond memories of Mertins returning to Merex's Maryland office after visiting with his intelligence handlers. "Every time he came to Washington he met with people at the Defense Intelligence Agency, and they paid him cash," says the former. "He'd come back and hand out $500 to whoever happened to be around." Amity attested to the government's generosity as well, saying Mertins "always came back from the DIA with money to spread around."

In the early 1970s, Mertins worked as an agent for a top secret Army espionage unit called the Field Activities Command. USAFAC, as the unit was known, operated out of the Hoffman

Building in Alexandria, Virginia, across from Washington over the Woodrow Wilson Bridge. Essentially a microcosm of the CIA, USAFAC collected human intelligence worldwide for the Army.

Mertins's relationship with USAFAC wasn't always smooth. He angered his handlers by selling inflatable rubber boats to Egypt— illegally, since they came out of West Germany's surplus stocks from the US, which did not authorize of the transfer. The boats were later used by the Egyptians to cross the Sinai Peninsula during the 1973 Yom Kippur War with Israel. Mertins was also considered to be "uncontrollable," says his handler. "He once walked into US military headquarters in Saigon [during the Vietnam War], announced he was with American intelligence, and demanded to see the officer in charge," this person recalls. "He didn't care if it was a Prince or a Prime Minister or a private, he'd demand to see the person on the spot."

The episode in Vietnam led military officials there to complain to the Army about Mertins's lack of discretion. Similar objections came in from American embassies abroad, leading USAFAC to terminate its relationship with Mertins in 1972. "This was clandestine espionage, and Mertins was too much of a loose cannon to use," says his handler. Mertins was furious and, to the horror of intelligence officials, took the Army to court. He sought a large cash settlement, charging that his dismissal had been unjust and caused him to lose his access to the Pentagon and his credibility with clients. The CIA hired a lawyer to assist the Army and succeeded in having the proceedings classified by arguing that disclosures about the case could damage national security.

The government prevailed in court, but the whole episode scared Army officials, who feared that USAFAC's operations would ultimately be exposed. Hence, the unit was disbanded a short while later, though most of its agents were picked up by the CIA. "The generals were afraid that one of our guys would get caught with a phony passport somewhere, and the authorities there would discover that there was no record of that person coming into country," says Mertins's former case officer. "We got out of the business and the books were closed."

MERTINS SUFFERED a series of other setbacks during the following years. The moderately leftist Social Democrats took power in Germany in 1969, and its leaders were far less friendly to Mertins than the right-wing Christian Democrats. For his part, Mertins considered the Social Democrats to be stooges of worldwide Communism. This was consistent with his view that Moscow's agents were covertly manipulating worldwide public opinion. Mertins told Russell Howe that the Soviet Union was the secret force behind the US peace movement and even the push for gun control.

The end result was that Merex lost its status as the government's weapons disposal agency. Then in 1974, the government of Helmut Schmidt announced that it would prosecute Merex for its now deemed-to-be illegal sale of warplanes to Pakistan nine years earlier. A federal court agreed that the deal had violated Germany's arms export laws, but the judge acquitted Mertins on the grounds that the government in power at the time had sanctioned it. Still, the case generated a wave of bad publicity that damaged Mertins's arms business and earnings. By the late 1970s, Mertins's financial problems were so serious that bank creditors took possession of his lavish estate on the Rhine, which until not long before had been the scene of glamorous parties attended by prominent politicians and businessmen.

Mertins encountered more difficulties in Mexico, where in 1978 he bought a forty-nine percent share in a silver mine near Durango. He also purchased a ranch in the area, located near a home owned by John Wayne. Four years later, the newspaper *Excelsior* published an article raising questions about Mertins's links to Nazis and suggesting that he was selling arms out of the country. Mexican authorities soon expelled him on the grounds that he had violated immigration and investment laws.

Yet another blow came in the mid-1980s, with the previously mentioned lawsuit between Merex and Fairchild Weston Systems. In 1982, the company had engaged Merex to help it sell military surveillance systems to China, where it had never before done business. Mertins set up a series of business meetings between Fairchild and NORINCO; two years later, China bought two of Fairchild's Long-Range Aerial Panoramic Cameras for $20 million. (The deal was approved by the Reagan administration, over the objections of some at the Pentagon. The Defense Department officials who reviewed the sale application said that the LORAP cameras represented "an advanced engineering application of most current technology . . . Forty-mile range results in quantum increase in strategic imagery and intelligence capability. Can provide photo reconnaissance of Taiwan without flyover. Therefore, due to technology involved, advance in intelligence-gathering capability and resultant threat to US allies, we would recommend denial.")

Mertins had spent heavily to advance the deal and went to court when Fairchild refused to pay a commission. The company claimed that the sale came despite, not because, of Mertins's efforts. It charged specifically that Mertins had failed to come to China for several crucial meetings. The jury sided with Mertins, but the company won on appeal.

All was not lost, however. Following his firing by the Army, the CIA picked up Mertins as an asset. That allowed him to get a piece of the pie from the Reagan-funded programs in support of anti-Communist guerilla movements. "The CIA is always looking for guys who can get small arms, and Mertins was perfect," says a former US military official. "He supplied weapons for a variety of groups." Among them says this and several other sources (including Durrani, who did substantial business with Mertins in the 1980s), were the *mujahedin* in Afghanistan and the contras in Nicaragua. In the case of the latter, I found evidence of Mertins's involvement in the files of Judge Lawrence Walsh, the independent counsel in the Iran/contra affair.

One of Mertins's partners on the deal in question was his great friend Colonel James Atwood, an eccentric Georgian who served, at one time or another, in the Army, Navy, and Marine Corps. Atwood, who died in 1997 and is buried at Arlington National Cemetery, served with US forces who reached Berlin as Hitler committed suicide and the Nazi regime collapsed. He married a German woman and seems to have become obsessed with all things German, especially the Third Reich. As told by John Berendt, author of *Midnight in the Garden of Good and Evil*—which takes place in Atwood's home town of Savannah, and in which he is a minor character—Atwood bought sixty German arms factories together with their stocks of abandoned Nazi weapons at the end of the war. He later wrote a book called *The Daggers and Edged Weapons of Hitler's Germany*, which made him something of a cult figure in certain Neo-Nazi circles. "I once went with him to a World War II paraphernalia show in Baltimore, and when the convention hall found out he was there, business just stopped," says a former CIA man who knew Atwood well. "They rearranged everything so he could speak to the crowd." Atwood owned Hitler's personal silverware—"heavy oversized pieces with AH engraved in a slender sans-serif," writes Berendt—and, according to the CIA officer, a large collection of porcelain figurines made in the concentration camps.

From his base in Savannah, Atwood traveled the world buying and selling everything from sports cars to water chestnuts to arms, which he peddled to personal collectors as well as government clients, including the United States. He had plenty of friends at the CIA, where he curried favor by presenting procurement officers with gifts such as buckets of shrimp, watches and chrome-barreled Chinese assault rifles.

In September 1986, Atwood and Mertins helped work a deal involving weapons for the Nicaraguan contras. Oliver North's Enterprise had used $2.2 million in proceeds from secret sales to Iran to buy from Poland twenty-seven containers of mines, grenades, assault rifles, mortars, and plastic explosives. The Enterprise intended to resell the weapons—purchased with the help of Mansur al Kassar, an arms dealer, suspected drug kingpin and known associate of the terrorist Abu Nidal, architect of the 1985 Christmas massacres in Rome and Vienna, among other notorious attacks—to the Nicaraguan rebels. The Erria, a Danish freighter chartered by the Enterprise, picked up the weapons in Poland and set sail for Portugal to pick up additional cargo. From there, it would deliver its treasure to contra camps in Honduras.

As the deal was unfolding, Congress lifted the ban on military aid to the contras, who no longer wanted the Erria's overpriced cargo. That left the Enterprise stuck with a boat-load of weapons and no buyer. At this point, Mertins and Atwood stepped in on the Enterprise's behalf and convinced the CIA to buy the weapons. Helmut Mertins—Gerhard's son and an officer of Overseas Trading and Consulting, the Merex shell company that handled the deal—was dispatched to Portugal and arranged to have the Erria sail to Cherbourg. There, the weapons were transferred to another ship, the Iceland Saga, which in October 1986 docked at a CIA depot at Sunny Point, North Carolina. Later still, the agency apparently sent the weapons on to the contras. (The final desti-nation of the weapons is not known for certain because much about the deal remains classified, including Atwood's lengthy interview with Congressional investigators. FBI agents tried to depose Gerhard Mertins, but could never find him at his home. They did interview Helmut Mertins, whose deposition is the source for part of the information above. Helmut was never charged, but as a precaution he retained the attorney Plato Cacheris, whose clients over the years have included Oliver

North's secretary, Fawn Hall, Soviet spy Aldrich Ames, and Monica Lewinsky.)

During the Iran-Iraq war of the early-1980s, Mertins also helped move weapons to Saddam Hussein. I learned of the relationship because Fairchild Weston had sought to embarrass Mertins by submitting to the court a 1984 letter he wrote to Zhao Fei in which he boasted of having Iraq as a client and saying he was trying to convince Baghdad to buy Chinese weapons. "Negotiations are carried on with the [Iraqi] Military Attaché in Paris, Mr. Mohammed Younis, who keeps the largest Procurement Office abroad," Mertins wrote. "At the same time, we have contacted Saddam Hussein and pointed out again the quality of Chinese military production."

The United States would surely not have objected to Mertins's business with Hussein. The Reagan administration professed to be neutral in the Iran-Iraq conflict but tilted towards Hussein, who was viewed as a bulwark against the Ayatollah Khomeini. The official thinking at the time was summed up in a 1984 report by the Congressional Research Service: "Some observers consider that Iraq is important to short-term US interest in that it protects the vulnerable oil-producing Gulf Arab States from Iranian military power and coercion . . . The installation of a [Pro-Iranian] government in Baghdad, should Iraq collapse, would raise the potential of the formation of an Iranian-Syrian axis which would threaten not only the Gulf region but also Israel, Jordan and Lebanon, and US interests in the eastern Mediterranean."

A number of sources, among them arms dealers and former intelligence officials, told me that Mertins was also a CIA supplier to the secret Foreign Materiel Acquisition (FMA) program. He is said to have had good contacts in a variety of Eastern European countries, including the former Yugoslavia, Romania and Bulgaria. Heinz Baumann, the Viennese arms dealer, says Mertins's purchases for the CIA included anti-personnel carriers that came from Romania and T-72 tank rounds bought from Bulgaria. Mertins had the tank rounds delivered to the airport in Frankfurt, where they were transferred to the US Air Force base operating at the same site.

Mertins was active in the arms trade until he died in March 1993, felled by a heart attack during a trip to Florida. His legacy, however, lived on. Helmut Mertins took up the Merex banner for a time and later formed a firm called United International Supplies, Inc. An Internet listing says the company's product line includes—in addition to office supplies, automobiles, and boats—police and military equipment such as body armor, riot control gear, firearms, ammunition, night vision equipment, and spare parts.

During the 1980s, Arif Durrani formed an American company called Merex. He told me that he had no formal connection to Mertins, but picked the name to take advantage of the instant recognition it provided within arms business circles. In 1987, Durrani was sentenced to a 10-year jail term for selling anti-aircraft missile parts to Iran. Durrani was released after serving half his term, and now lives in Mexico. In 1998, federal agents raided Signal Aerospace, a Ventura, California company they charged with selling counterfeit jet parts to banned countries. Signal's president is Susanne Stehr, Durrani's wife, who authorities claim is simply a front for her husband. (In regard to Iran, Durrani claims, with a fair amount of evidence to back him, that he was merely an agent for the Reagan administration, which at precisely the same time was secretly supplying the Ayatollah's regime. He dismisses the Ventura raid as a case of government harassment.)

Another of Mertins's spawns is Joseph Housepian, a former military officer in Lebanon and Merex's long-time agent in that country. Housepian moved to Germany in the late 1980s and became partners with Mertins in a new company called Merex, which sold arms and industrial equipment. That Merex went out of business after Mertins's death, but as this book goes to press, Housepian is under investigation, according to German sources, for arms deals he allegedly made in South Africa during the apartheid years.

FOUR

MERCENARY, INC.

"The modern mercenary firm is increasingly corporate. Instead of organizing clandestinely, they now operate out of office suites, have public affairs staffs and Web sites, and offer marketing literature."

—from a 1997 report by the Center for Defense Information

"Why not, when nations have already lost the monopoly on violence, consider creating volunteer mercenary forces organized by private corporations to fight wars on a contract-fee basis for the United Nations—the condottieri of yesterday armed with some of the weapons, including non-lethal weapons, of tomorrow?"

—Alvin and Heidi Toffler, *War and Anti-War*

TEAM LEADER

Successful experience in force management and leadership positions. Able to develop and implement a system for force integration for a foreign nation that is tailored to that nation's unique requirements. Able to interact effectively with US and foreign officials. Able to build credibility and trust with foreign military leaders. Preference is for a former Colonel experienced in armor and artillery systems.

TRAINER

Requirement for former US Army personnel to support training of African forces in peace operations and humanitarian assistance operations. This program places importance on experience and training in battalion and brigade level operations and staff procedures to include: Rapid Deployment, Combined Joint Operations, Peacekeeping Operations, Humanitarian Operations, and Training Management. Additionally experience in Africa useful.

SENIOR TRAINER

Advises, trains, and evaluates organizational supply and personnel functions in mechanized and/or light armored vehicle (LAV) infantry battalions. Coordinates and supervises planning and preparation for LAV equipment and supply. Provides advice and assistance to the battalion S1/S4 and staff. Knowledge of US and Saudi Arabian National Guard supply, maintenance and personnel policies, procedure and doctrines.

NO, THESE AREN'T the usual job offers you come across in the morning newspaper. These classified ads were posted on the Web sites of two private American firms—Military Professional Resources, Inc. and Vinnell, both of Virginia—that provide military and police training to foreign regimes allied with the United States.

Like other companies that offer similar services, MPRI and Vinnell are staffed by retired armed forces personnel and maintain tight links to the Pentagon and intelligence agencies. A decade ago, the men running these firms would have been called mercenaries. Today, they're merely the foot soldiers of privatization, by which the responsibilities of government are transferred to corporate hands— a process that now occupies the halls of war-making.

The Pentagon and CIA have long used private contractors for a variety of tasks, from building base infrastructure to assisting with covert operations. The current situation differs in both scope and size from past practice, most famously revealed in the Iran/contra scandal. Today, the firms most heavily involved are not CIA cut-outs but multimillion-dollar corporations with diverse interests. Their work is implemented not by foreign locals trained by the CIA but by high-ranking US military officers fresh out of the armed forces.

The Mercenary Inc. companies operate across the globe. Some of their activities seem mostly innocuous, such as supporting United Nations peacekeeping operations by providing convoy protection and guarding refugee camps. Other aspects of their work are more controversial. MPRI is training two Balkan armies and has won contracts in Africa and Eastern Europe. Vinnell trains the Saudi Arabian National Guard. Other private contractors support the Pentagon's own overseas military operations. DynCorp, a billion-dollar company based in Virginia, has been especially active in supporting top-secret anti-drug actions in Latin America. A Florida firm called Betac works closely with the Pentagon's Special Operations Command, which engages in covert activities in the Third World.

All of this helps supplement a web of official government-run training programs, such as the Pentagon's International Military and Education Training Program (IMET) and the School of the Americas at Fort Benning, Georgia, where thousands of Latin American soldiers received training (and frequently went on to launch careers as war criminals once they returned home). A chief factor driving the proliferation of corporate mercenary firms is huge cutbacks in the number of US armed forces personnel. Between 1985—the peak of the Reagan-era arms and military build-up—and 1999, the Army's troop levels fell from 800,000 to 480,000. Cuts were less severe in the other services, but military manpower overall is off by an average of thirty percent. Meanwhile, the US has greatly reduced its overseas presence, with military bases abroad declining from a peak of 115 in 1956 to just 27 in 1995. "Private companies augment our ability to provide foreign training," says retired Lieutenant General Lawrence Skibbie of the National Defense Industrial Association. "We'll see more and more of this as we continue to cut back on our uniformed forces."

Indeed, the private military firms are effectively an arm of foreign policy. Before offering military assistance to foreign governments, corporations must first apply for a license from the State Department's Office of Defense Trade Controls (DTC), which oversees the emerging field. "The [private training] programs are designed to further our foreign policy objectives," says a former top official at the Defense Intelligence Agency (DIA). "If the government doesn't sanction it, the companies don't do it."

The firms themselves are not eager to discuss their activities. Nor is the DTC, which rejected a request for an on-the-record interview.

An official there said he could provide very little information even on background because of the need to protect the "proprietary information" of the companies involved (a loophole that makes the Freedom of Information Act all but useless in this area). However, the official defended the use of private firms and said the government would never allow the companies to directly dispatch soldiers in support of a foreign government. "Training a military is a lot more than teaching guys how to shoot guns straight," he said. "The companies offer instruction in how to run a military in a democracy, subordination to civilian control and respect for human rights."

For the government, privatization offers a number of distinct advantages. Primary among them is that the use of private military contractors allows the United States to pursue its geopolitical interests without deploying its own army, this being especially useful in cases where training is provided to regimes with horrendous human rights records. "It's foreign policy by proxy," says Dan Nelson, a defense expert at the George C. Marshall European Center for Security Studies. "Corporate entities are used to perform tasks that the government, for budgetary reasons or political sensitivities, cannot carry out."

MERCENARIES ARE ONE of the world's oldest professions and have existed ever since war began. As a 1997 report from the Center for Defense Information points out, the Carthagian armies were mercenary, as was that of Hannibal when he invaded Italy. Alexander the great employed some 50,000 mercenaries in 329. "Throughout much of human history it was considered the order of things that the destruction of war should be left to needy foreigners so citizens of rich states could go on making their fortunes," the CDI report states.

Mercenaries have played a role in American history ever since the founding of the Republic. During the revolutionary war, the British feared that the Colonists could field a 50,000-man citizen militia. The Crown's Army was only 30,000 strong and at least half of those troops were tied down in garrison duty in Ireland. In 1775, with news of British military disasters making their way across the Atlantic, King George III urgently requested 20,000 Russian soldiers from Catherine the Great. (Thereby prompting the drafters of the Declaration of Independence to scornfully write that George III was seeking to transport "large armies of foreign mercenaries to complete the works of death, desolation, and tyranny already begun, with circumstances of cruelty and perfidy scarcely paralleled in the most barbarous ages, totally unworthy of the head of a civilized nation.") Catherine snubbed the British, replying that she could not accept such an offer "simply to calm a rebellion which is not supported by any foreign power."

After a similarly unsuccessful effort with the Dutch, the British turned to His Most Serene Highness the Landgrave of Hesse Cassel, whose troops were among the best disciplined in Europe. His Most Serene Highness agreed to provide, for a steep cost, thirteen Hessian battalions. Many thought the fate of the Revolution was now sealed. That proved short-sighted, as Britain's use of mercenaries only further inflamed the passion of the revolutionaries.

During the latter half of the twentieth century, mercenaries were a common sight on Cold War battlefields. Take, for instance, Britain's "Mad Mike" Hoare, who during the 1960s headed a mer-

cenary group called the Fifth Commando. Dubbed "les affreux"—
the frightful ones—for their murderous rampages, Hoare's men
were best known for their exploits in the Belgian Congo (later Zaire),
where they served a secessionist regime headed by Moise Tshombe.
Hoare's last crusade came in 1981 in the Seychelles, where he and
other mercenaries traveled to support a South African-organized
coup attempt. Disguised as a rugby fan, Hoare was arrested at the
airport when customs officials discovered he and his companions
had stored guns in a false-bottom suitcase.

Bob Denard, a Frenchman, served with Hoare in the Congo and
went on to fight in Biafra, Chad, Morroco, and Rhodesia, among
other places. In 1967, Denard mounted a coup in Benin with just
sixty paratroopers. Eleven years later, he took over the Comoros
Islands in the Indian Ocean and installed a puppet regime. In 1995,
Denard, then sixty-six, attempted another coup in the Comoros.
This time French troops intervened on the government's side, and
Denard ended up in prison.

As the US emerged as a superpower, it produced a glut of well-
trained, experienced men who were eager to rent out their services
as soldiers of fortune. (Though never in numbers as great as those
exported by colonial powers like Britain and France, or from highly militarized societies such as Israel and South Africa.) A few hundred Americans took up arms in support of white-ruled Rhodesia
during the 1960s; the following decade, a somewhat smaller number joined up with anti-communist guerillas in Angola.

Bob MacKenzie, the son-in-law of one-time CIA deputy director
Ray Kline, was amongst the better known American mercenaries.

After being wounded in Vietnam, MacKenzie served with Rhodesian forces against guerilla leader Robert Mugabe, who went on to become president of black-ruled Zimbabwe. MacKenzie fought leftist rebels in El Salvador and trained Muslim Special Forces units in Bosnia. He met his end in Sierra Leone, where he headed a group of sixty mercenaries sent to help government forces fighting the vicious Revolutionary United Front, a rebel group whose tactics include chopping off the hands of "enemy" children (as well as adults). MacKenzie and his men were supposed to be limited to a training role, but they soon became involved in combat operations. In February of 1995, RUF soldiers killed and ate MacKenzie and several other mercenaries.

The CIA also found a steady pool of American "mercs" to draw from when planning its covert operations. For the 1954 agency-sponsored coup in Guatemala, the CIA hired Al Haney, a retired Army colonel, to help draw up military plans. Another American, William "Rip" Robertson, trained the Guatemalan rebel army on a plantation owned by Nicaraguan dictator Anastasio Somoza. During the fighting, Robertson bombed and sank a British freighter that he mistakenly believed was delivering fuel to the Guatemalan government.

The agency has employed foreign mercenaries as well. After Cuban troops landed in Angola in the spring of 1975, the Ford administration committed about $32 million to subvert the left-wing regime in Luanda. Because of the contemporaneous Vietnam failure, sending American military trainers to support Jonas Savimbi and his UNITA army was politically impossible. Hence, the CIA turned to Bob Denard—recommended by the French secret service—who was paid $425,000 to send a team of twenty men to support UNITA.

The Reagan years gave rise to a host of mercenary-style adventures. Some were quite comical, none more so than Oliver North's use of three Long Island men—Kevin Kattke, an engineer at Macy's, Roy Harris, an unemployed carpenter who had once trained television star Zippy the Chimp, and Sal Imburglio, a building inspector—to subvert the left-wing government of Maurice Bishop, leader of the tiny Caribbean island of Grenada. The chief mission of Ollie's Army was to organize a Grenadian exile movement in the United States. In 1983, when radicals within his own regime murdered Bishop, North tasked Kattke with forming a Grenadian government in exile. He managed to drum up a rally of about 100 people in Brooklyn, but the only thing the protesters could agree on was that Bishop's death was a tragedy. That same year, Kattke and his pals traveled to the Dominican Republic to represent the United States at the inauguration of the new president. Ollie's emissaries created a minor scandal when they heckled Nicaraguan President Daniel Ortega, who was also in attendance. "We weren't so much like [a] secret army," Kattke later confessed to *New York* magazine. "It was more like the Three Stooges."

North and the CIA made more deadly use of freelancers during the Iran/contra operation. Then, a number of former pilots for Air America—the CIA's airline in Indochina during the 1960s—were hired to make covert airdrops to the contras in Nicaragua. The men were paid in cash, which they picked up from the Miami offices of Southern Air Transport, a CIA front company. One of the pilots, John

McRainey, dubbed the group the "over-the-hill gang" because all but one was over fifty years of age. The operation came to a halt after the Sandinistas shot down William Cooper's C-123K on October 5 1986. Cooper and two other men were killed, while Eugene Hasenfus was captured and tried in Managua on charges of terrorism. The disaster prompted North to begin shredding documents about the CIA's activities in Central America. Despite his efforts, the shoot-down soon led to the unraveling of the whole Iran/contra network.

John Piowaty, a member of the "over-the-hill gang," now lives in Ft. Walton Beach, Florida—home of MacDill Air Force Base, headquarters to US Special Forces and a favorite spot for American military men to retire. He says contractors looking to hire military freelancers never have much trouble meeting their quotas. "The network is just a matter of people. If you wanted to put together a camping trip, you'd call people you'd been camping with before. As best as I can tell, that's the way it goes. People know who they want to fly with, and I'm sure the people on the ground know who they want to fight with. They know who they can trust, they know who's dependable. In combat, that's more important than mom, home, apple pie, the Constitution, and all the rest." (Piowaty said that he still carried out some "unconventional flying," though he wouldn't say where. He did volunteer that between 1989 and 1991, he flew C-123s in government anti-drug operations in Peru and Colombia. His employer was a private company called National Air Transport Inc., which Dyncorp later replaced as the firm of choice for official US actions in Latin America.)

To learn more about the world of mercenaries, I attended the September 1998 *Soldier of Fortune* magazine convention in Las

Vegas. Conventioneers were encamped at the Continental Hotel ("Come in and Win! Cash your paycheck at the Continental!" read a gigantic neon sign out front), located not far from the famous strip but a world away from the new family-oriented Las Vegas with its Disneyland-style themes and attractions. The Continental's facilities were so modest that some conventioneers complained they'd had better accommodations in the Third World bush.

Robert Brown, a one-time lieutenant colonel who led a Special Forces unit in Vietnam, runs *SOF*. Brown, who is nearly deaf in one ear due to gunfire and mortar explosions on the battlefield, founded the magazine in 1975. The first issue featured a bush-hatted mercenary on the cover and inside a gruesome photo of an African man who had been shot in the head. *SOF*'s circulation climbed steadily over the next decade, peaking at about 150,000 subscribers during the mid-1980s. The end of the Cold War brought about a thirty-five percent circulation drop, but the magazine is still read by about 110,000 in the US and Canada. In 1997, Brown launched a wildly popular Russian edition.

At least half dozen *SOF* staffers have been killed in battle. Editor George Bacon, a former CIA agent, was executed in 1976 when he and a group of nine mercenaries were captured in Angola. Another editor, Vietnam veteran Michael Echanis, served as a trainer and de facto commander of Somoza's Nicaraguan National Guard. When the Sandinistas seized the National Palace in the summer of 1978, Echanis and hard-liners in the Nicaraguan military wanted to blast the rebels out. Somoza overruled them and the siege ended when the Sandinistas negotiated the release of a number of political prisoners in exchange for sixty hostages they were holding. Soon afterwards, Echanis spearheaded a National Guard campaign against Sandinista-held cities. On September 8, 1978, a plane containing Echanis, fellow American Charles Sanders, and a number of native Guardsmen exploded over Lake Nicaragua. It was never determined who or what brought the plane down.

Brown himself frequently visits global battlefields and has been pictured in his magazine waving an AK-47 in Afghanistan and posing at a Laotian resistance camp. The Gulf War proved to be a frustrating time for *SOF*'s leader. He traveled to Saudi Arabia hoping to see frontline action, but the Pentagon kept him penned up in Riyadh along with other news representatives. "I thought I'd be leading the first tank into Baghdad," Brown told the *Wall Street Journal* as he stewed in Riyadh. "Instead, I'm stuck in a briefing room with the biggest bunch of boobs and dorks I've ever met."

SOF was long considered to be a soapbox for ultra-conservatives. Today, as the extreme right heads off into the netherworld of black helicopters and New World Order conspiracies, some in conservative circles believe *SOF* has gone soft. Brown criticizes the militia movement and right-wing conspiracy theories, charging that Zionist powerbrokers control American politics. He also encourages readers to vote, and his magazine has published a number of stories on racism at federal law enforcement agencies such as the ATF. History professor Jeffrey Kaplan compares Brown to Hugh Hefner, the *Playboy* founder, whose magazine used to be considered bold and daring but today is seen as tame. "Yesterday's radicals are today's statesmen," Kaplan told the London *Independent*.

Indeed, I was surprised at the conference when the magazine's Africa correspondent, Al Venter, used his podium time to mount an appeal on behalf of the dwindling wildebeest population of Tanzania. I was more startled still when he referred to South African president Nelson Mandela as "one of the most honorable men I've ever known" (a pronouncement greeted with almost tomb-like silence by the audience of about seventy-five).

Still, for the non-initiated, the *SOF* convention is pretty rough stuff. On the convention's opening day, Bob Brown held a press conference to announce that *SOF* was bestowing its first ever Humanitarian Award on the pilot of the Enola Gay, retired Air Force General Paul Tibbets, who dropped the atomic bomb on Hiroshima. Brown conceded that the award might seem inappropriate—after all, the bomb had "devastated a major city and killed scores of hundreds of people"—but said Tibbet's act had saved many more lives, American and Japanese, by hastening Japan's surrender.

A trade show held in conjunction with the convention was mounted at the Sands Expo and Convention Center, a vast hall about a mile from the Continental. Groups on hand included Marathon USA, which was distributing a flyer attacking Sarah Brady—wife of former Reagan administration aide James Brady, who was wounded when John Hinckley tried to kill the president in 1982—for using the "Big Lie" to promote gun control. The flyer quoted Sarah Brady as saying, "Our main agenda is to have ALL guns banned. We must use whatever means possible. It doesn't matter if you have to distort facts or even lie. Our task of creating a Socialist America can only succeed when those who would resist us have been totally disarmed."

Another hand-out from Marathon USA said that according to a "reliable, confidential informant," certain members of the New World Order, including President Bill Clinton, would soon launch a plot for "the actual takeover of the United States of America" (a seemingly unnecessary step with Clinton already the nation's chief-of-state). At a nearby booth a man named Ted Gunderson was offering for sale an eclectic assortment of items ranging from the Paula Jones deposition to "Conversations with Nostradamus: His Prophecies Explained" to Subliminal Mind Control (the latter details "how the masses are controlled through advertising. Includes the 666 connection"). At another exhibition booth, a cannon was for sale. "Is that legal to own?" I asked. "It might not be in the People's Republic of California," came the gruff reply from the vendor. "It's gotten to the point where in some parts of the country it's illegal to carry a stick."

Panel discussions at the Sands were equally spirited. At one, Harry Humphries, a former Navy Seal who heads GSI, a firm providing security for corporations working in the Third World, defined "home invasion" as "nothing more than a bunch of thugs realizing that nobody's got a weapon on the inside of a house—thank you very much for our gun laws." Before offering a demonstration of self-protection on the battlefield known as America's streets, Humphries cautioned that he didn't want to make people paranoid. However, he said, "threat recognition" is the key to avoiding becoming prey to street thugs. And what constitutes a clear and present danger? "Anybody coming up to you and saying, 'Sir, have you got the time?'" Humphries replied. "Walking up to you, violating your space, your defensive perimeter that you should always maintain around yourself, violating that space, coming in for such idiotic statements as 'What time is it?' Who cares what time it is?"

The culmination of the *SOF* event came at a shooting range on the outskirts of Las Vegas, when a dozen men armed with machine guns and dynamite blew to smithereens a white van with the words "Bin Laden's Explosives Express/Worldwide Deliveries" painted on its side. The affair was emceed by Peter Kokalis, an *SOF* editor, who lovingly described the machine guns used in the assault on the ter-rormobile between telling jokes (What do you get when you cross a bisexual communist with a congenital liar? Chelsea Clinton. Why aren't they prosecuting Bill Clinton? Because Monica Lewinsky swallowed all the evidence) and berating reporters in attendance for being a bunch of pansy-assed liberals.

While there were plenty of colorful people and action at the convention, I was disappointed to discover that groupies outnumbered real soldiers of fortune by a comfortable margin. "The vast majority of people here are fans of the magazine who share common goals," Brown told me as we sat and chatted near a registration desk at the Sands. In fact, bullshit artists outnumbered combat vets by a wide margin. One ominous looking fellow dressed entirely in black—military-style pants, vest and boots—claimed to be a veteran of the French Foreign Legion and told one and all of his hair-raising combat adventures. Convention regulars said the man, who spoke not a word of French, comes to the Las Vegas affair every year and that his war stories have become more epic over time. "You'll meet a lot more mercenaries here as liquor is consumed," one person told me as a group of conventioneers had drinks around the Continental's pool one night.

There were, however, a few battle-hardened mercs on hand. Ralph Edens fought alongside government troops in El Salvador during its civil war with leftist guerillas in the 1980s. He dressed daily in battle fatigues, a style that seemed somehow inappropriate when he was working as an isometric foot massage salesman at a convention booth. Seventy-three-year-old Mike Williams traveled to Las Vegas from his current home in Houston. A US army veteran, he signed up with the Congolese armed forces in 1964 and went on to command an elite unit in the former Rhodesia. Williams was thrown out of that country when his unit was accused of torturing prisoners, a charge he insists is untrue (though his name tag identified him as "War Criminal" Williams). While at the convention, Williams tried to pick up a woman less than half his age, using a come-on line—"I think I've known you in a previous life"—that I never would have expected from a seasoned soldier of fortune.

Among those who'd seen more recent action was Rob Krott, a stocky, blonde-haired *SOF* editor. Krott has worked in war zones from Central America to Africa and has lived with a number of guerilla groups. During the convention, a colleague approached him to see if he'd be interested in a mercenary posting in the Congo. Tom Reisinger, another *SOF* editor, served as a medic with US Special Forces units in Vietnam. In 1994, he was one of about three dozen Americans recruited to go to Azerbaijan—then involved in a bloody war with Armenia over the disputed province of Nagorno-Karabakh—and help train Army medics. "Ninety percent of the casualties were bleeding to death," Reisinger recalled. "When they got wounded, they'd throw them on the trucks and say 'If he lives it's

God's will.'" Reisinger wouldn't say who recruited him for the job in Azerbaijan, but he worked under a retired American military man named Gary Best, head of a murky Marietta, Georgia-based firm called MEGA Oil. Best didn't know much about the oil industry, and it's likely that MEGA was fronting for a legitimate company that hoped to curry favor with authorities in Azerbaijan—which sits atop some of the world's largest petroleum and natural gas reserves—by assisting the country's war effort. If that was the plan, it didn't work. "Once we got over there, there was no support in terms of medical supplies or teaching aids," says Reisinger. "We sat on our asses for a few months, and then I headed back."

Rusty Rossey, a Vietnam veteran, saw more substantial action during the 1980s and early 1990s, mostly in Latin America. He bristles at the term "mercenary," saying he acted out of patriotism and would never have worked for a Marxist regime. "When people hear the word mercenary, they think of a guy running around with a machine gun who gets paid a lot of money," says Rossey, an amiable man with neatly trimmed hair and dressed in blue jeans and a polo shirt. "A lot of these jobs only pay $100 to $200 a day. I'm no mercenary, I'm a professional soldier and businessman—a concerned, patriotic American."

Rossey went to Central America in 1983 with Civilian Military Assistance, a group based in Madison, Alabama and founded—with encouragement from the Reagan administration—by Tom Posey. An American colleague who went by the name of "Tirador," or "Shooter" in Spanish, recruited Rossey, who himself used the code name of "Ramos." (Rossey declined to disclose Tirador's real name, but in his book *Disposable Patriot*, Jack Terrell, another

Civilian Military Assistance veteran, identifies him as Joe Sam Adams, a former Marine from St. Louis. According to Terrell, Rossey and a number of other CMA cadres were trained at "Recondo," a "mercenary" school run by Frank Camper, a Vietnam veteran and "Defense Intelligence Agency snitch.")

CMA funneled military aid to the contras at a time when Congress had banned such assistance. CMA's fighters were sheltered in Honduras, but frequently made cross-border raids to confront Sandinista forces. In 1984, two of its members were killed when their helicopter was shot down during an attack against an army school inside Nicaragua. Posey and five others were later indicted for violating the Neutrality Act. The charges were dismissed when a judge pointed out that their activities were taking place at the same time that the Reagan administration was running its secret war on Nicaragua.

Rossey led a team of nine Americans who staged thirty to ninety day missions inside Nicaragua with Miskito Indian troops. "At one point we didn't have much chow, and we killed a couple of deer," he recalls. "We were eating in a wide open frontier and saw a twinkling of lights coming toward us [from a Sandinista unit]. We ran just about all night to get back to Honduras."

Rossey later carried out a "small job" in El Salvador training paramilitary forces, then in 1989 was recruited by Tirador, now using the nom de guerre "Colonel Blue," to go to Burma. Rossey arrived in Burma shortly after the military massacred more than 3,000 students and pro-democracy demonstrators, and installed the State Law and Order Council, affectionately known as the SLORC. He was deployed with a Karen guerilla unit that carried out a number of sabotage operations, including the destruction of six bridges. However, his stint came to an end after only a few months when he fell ill with malaria. Rossey spent three weeks in a hammock fighting for his life, then was put in a dug-out canoe and taken to a Karen outpost where he received quinine. After his condition improved, he traveled on to Bangkok and returned home. Rossey vowed never to go abroad again, but he carried out a final mission in 1992 when he was hired to train Guatemalan Special Forces units.

Rossey now works for an Alabama company that manufactures high-quality sniper rifles sold to police units as far away Colombia and the Ukraine. Fewer freelance offers come up now that the Cold War is over, but opportunities still arise. A few months before the SOF convention he was asked if he wanted to return to Burma, where the junta continues to rule by terror. The day before I spoke with him, a fellow conventioneer offered him a job in an African nation he preferred not to identify (almost certainly Congo). "There's always action somewhere," he says. "This stuff never ends."

AS ROSSEY'S COMMENTS indicate, mercenaries are still a feature on the world's battlefields, being employed not only by states but also by insurgent groups. A UN Special Rappoteur report from 1994 notes a rise in mercenary activity, attributing this to armed conflicts arising as a result of the creation of new states and "a climate of acute ethnic, religious, and nationalist intolerance." However, today's freelance adventurers are more likely to be returning a job application to a private firm's personnel office than signing on with mysterious recruiters like Colonel Blue.

Further contributing to the corporatization of the mercenary field is the fact that with the Cold War over, the US and European governments have little strategic interest in great swaths of the Third World. Hence, Western powers are loathe to commit military troops to those regions, especially Africa. Such reluctance grew dramatically after eighteen American soldiers were killed in Somalia in 1993 when the Clinton administration dispatched troops to confront clan leader Mohammed Aidid. The following year, Rwandan Hutus slaughtered an estimated one million Tutsis using little more than small arms and machetes. Two hundred men with armored personnel carriers and twenty helicopter gunships could have stopped the genocide, but the world simply watched as the carnage unfolded. "Private companies fill a void in places where Western countries will not provide military force on the ground," says a retired US military man.

Multinational corporations also are turning to privatized mercenaries for protection, especially in countries where governments exert little control over their territory. Here again, Africa is a proving ground, with private companies increasingly called upon to guard mining sites, oil fields, and other economic installations. As Tom Reisinger of *SOF* puts it, "Industries want to maintain their turf. If the government is unstable, you don't want to invest and then lose your position. So companies hire private [security] firms to set up an enclave of safety. That way, regardless of which way the government goes, your interests are protected."

Israeli firms are among the more active players in the private military field. In 1997, a company called Levdan sent 200 former Israeli soldiers to train elite units in the Congo to protect President Pascal Lissouba. According to *Time* magazine, as part of the deal,

Lissouba's government agreed to buy $10 million worth of Israeli military equipment. Colonel Yair Klein, a former paratrooper, ran another company called Spearhead Ltd, which marketed "anti-terror" expertise to a variety of mass murderers. One of Klein's clients was the late Colombian drug lord Gonzalo Rodriguez, who paid the Israeli to instruct his killers in skills such as assassination and bomb-making. As a morale booster, Klein taught his pupils to chant "Communists, we drink your blood" during the instruction courses. In 1999, Klein was jailed in Freetown, Sierra Leone, for training the Revolutionary United Front. (As this book goes to press, Klein is set to be tried for treason. Israel, apparently with the help of the US, was reportedly exerting pressure on authorities in Sierra Leone to return him home.)

British companies are also well established in the booming privatized mercenary field. The *Sunday Times* reported that a security firm called Aims Ltd. had proposed to the Turkish government that it carry out a hit on Abdullah Ocalan, leader of the Kurdish guerilla group known as the PKK. The company submitted an eleven-page proposal offering to track down Ocalan, who would then be dispatched by a Turkish hit squad armed and trained by former SAS soldiers in Aims's employ. The plan was never carried out, but in 1999, Turkish Special Forces soldiers kidnapped Ocalan in Kenya. Aims and another British security firm provided military equipment and training in support of the operation.

Defence Systems Limited (DSL) of London offers corporate services that include hostage rescue, kidnap and ransom negotiation, intelligence operations, counter-insurgency and military training.

Retired British Army Major General Stephen Carr-Smith has said that DSL always works in "the dodgy type of countries, the remote, and the hostile—Angola, Mozambique, Colombia, Algeria, the former Soviet Union. Those sorts of countries where life is a bit tough at this stage." In Colombia, British Petroleum employs DSL to guard oil rigs from National Liberation Army guerillas in the oil-rich northeastern region of Casanare. To help carry out the job, DSL hired former army commander General Hernan Guzman Rodriguez, whose career highlights were featured in a 1992 report titled "State Terrorism in Colombia" issued by the Inter-American Commission on Human Rights. There is "abundant evidence and testimony" linking Guzman to a murderous right-wing paramilitary group called Death to Kidnappers, said the report. (Guzman, who was dismissed in a 1994 purge of the military leadership, denies the allegations.)

Another British firm, Sandline International, was created in the mid-1990s by retired officers and calls itself "an international military consultancy company specializing in the provision of advice and problem resolution to legitimate governments and international organizations." As Sandline's American representative, former US Army Special Forces officer Bernie McCabe, puts it, "We won't work for white powder gangs [cocaine barons] or rebel groups."

McCabe's job is to get Sandline hooked up with the US defense establishment. He says the company's operating concept is to "train the trainer," meaning Sandline instructs an elite group of locals, who are entrusted with spreading its wisdom to a broader cross-section of the recipient nation's armed forces. However, the firm leaves a few employees behind after completing its contracts so as to "guarantee that they [purchasers] are going to perform as we trained them to do." A good share of Sandline's employees are former staffers from the Pentagon, which McCabe calls "the greatest source of [military] manpower in the world . . . We take those guys on in a heartbeat."

Sandline received unwanted attention in 1997, when the prime minister of Papua New Guinea, Julius Chan, hired the firm—in exchange for a $36 million stake in a mine—to put down a decade-long independence movement. The contract included a provision stating that "all Sandline personnel will be furnished with the necessary multiple entry visas without passport stamps and authorization to enter and leave the country free from hindrance at any time." Some seventy Sandline personnel arrived in Papua New Guinea shortly after the ink dried on the contract but were forced to beat a hasty retreat when the deal was reported by the press, thereby provoking a wave of rioting.

In the aftermath of this PR debacle, Sandline's chief, Tim Spicer, defended his firm in an article in the *Sunday Times*:

I sometimes wonder if the people who have talked so disparagingly of "mercenaries" from the comfort of their armchairs . . . have any idea of what a dangerous world it is out there. Since the end of the Cold War smouldering ethnic conflicts have broken out all over the globe. In the old days, one or other of the superpowers would have snuffed them out. Now, the forces of the traditional "policemen" are depleted. Most have neither the resources nor the political will to involve themselves in far-away conflict, particularly if it is not nationally significant. Local armies can't always deal with conflict. So how can countries create a safe, stable, environment for peaceful existence and economic growth? Often they can't and are left on their own with catastrophic results. That's where private military companies come in.

Probably the best known of all the private mercenary companies is Executive Outcomes (EO), a Pretoria-based firm that was founded in 1989. Run by a former South African soldier and intelligence agent named Eeben Barlow, EO employed about 2,000 white and black veterans of South Africa's special forces—primarily the Thirty-two Buffalo Battalion, which was ultimately disbanded for its brutal intervention in South African black townships—and the Civil Cooperation Bureau, which was responsible for anti-insurgency operations during the apartheid years. "The Cold War left a huge vacuum, and I identified a niche in the market—we are selling the business of surviving," Barlow told one interviewer.

EO has been involved in several dozen African countries, generally carrying out small-scale security assignments. Unlike many mercenary firms, though, EO troops have also fought and led major combat operations. In 1993, the Angolan government hired EO to protect oil-producing territory against UNITA, paying the company with oil and diamond mining concessions. Most of EO's troops had fought with UNITA when it was backed by the CIA and South African apartheid leaders, and they used their knowledge to rout their former allies. An armored thrust in 1995 devastated UNITA's core force and ended with the capture of the Cafunfo diamond fields. Scattered and deprived off their financial support structure, UNITA was forced to join temporarily the government of President Jose dos Santos.

That same year, the government of President Ahmed Tejan Kabbah in Sierra Leone called on EO to assist in its war against the

Revolutionary United Front (which was also using mercenaries, in its case from the Ukraine and Belarus). When EO was hired, the RUF was within fifteen miles of the capital of Freetown and had seized control of mining operations that provided the country with most of its export earnings. The company's troops turned the tide in the government's favor, leading to free elections in 1996 for the first time in thirty years. Kabbah won and soon terminated EO's contract; before long, his government was overthrown (only to be reinstated by a Nigerian-led force in 1998). For its nearly two years of services, EO received about $35 million in cash and mineral rights from the government of Sierra Leone.

Executive Outcomes officially disbanded on January 1 1999, in response to a South African law that severely restricted mercenary firms. Nico Palm, EO's owner, put a clean face on the company's demise, writing in a press release, "African countries are busy working out solutions in Africa. Let's give them a chance." Another EO statement cited "the consolidation of law and order across the African continent" as a reason for the firm's presumed obsolescence. Some observers suspect EO has simply broken into unrecognizable corporate parts and will continue to operate from countries outside of South Africa. At least two security organizations originally tied to EO are still active: Saracen of Uganda (partly owned by Defense Minister Salim Saleh) and Lifeguard Security of Sierra Leone. A US government source told me that a group of EO vets had been hired by Israeli firms and were operating in Islamic countries in Northern and Eastern Africa. In 1999, downsized EO vets were reportedly hired to work in Sierra Leone as well.

American officials draw a sharp line between the firms described above and US companies like MPRI and Vinnell. The crucial difference, they say, is that the government prohibits American firms from directly participating in combat. "It's really apples and oranges," Phil Egger, head of the State Department's African Affairs bureau, says. "We don't want to give the impression that we'd hire a bunch of mercenaries." (Indeed, the distance MPRI keeps from the battlefield evokes disdain from more traditional mercenaries. "MPRI is so desperate to avoid being called mercs that they just scratch the surface," says Tom Marks, a contributing writer to *Soldier of Fortune*. "They're a glorified transportation corps, as opposed to a military outfit. They're like the FedEx of government service.")

Even if American companies aren't leading the charge on the battlefield, their advice and assistance are critical for combat operations. "Just as the distinction between combat arms and non-combat arms has become blurred during operations, the distinction between 'advising' and 'doing' for these contractors is similarly blurred," writes Major Thomas Milton of the Foreign Area Officer Association. "The reality is that most of these corporations' operations become an integral part of the foreign government's military capability. If these companies ceased work during hostilities, the host government's military would not be able to function near its perceived capability."

For the Pentagon, the privatization of military training programs is a win-win situation. In addition to providing plausible deniability about overseas entanglements, it allows Washington to shed military personnel while simultaneously retaining the capacity to influence and direct huge missions. "MPRI can send twenty former US colonels to Bosnia, while the US Army would have to strip more than an entire combat division to muster that many," says Colonel Bruce Grant of the Institute for National Strategic Studies. Looked at another way, private firms can train an entire foreign army. The Pentagon's IMET, on the other hand, generally provides instruction to no more than a few dozen soldiers. Its largest effort as of 1997 is in Honduras, where 266 soldiers and officers are being trained. Just as with IMET, American officers involved in the private training programs develop highly useful relationships with the foreign military leaders they work with.

The Pentagon is obliged to respond to inquiries, if not always in a forthright manner, when US troops are deployed abroad. Retired generals and private companies have far more leeway in evading questions from Congress or the press. Congress reviews and can restrict the dispatch of Pentagon military trainers abroad. It has no authority over private trainers, who need only obtain a license from the State Department, a process that occurs far from public view. Congress receives notification only if a contract is worth more than $50 million; most private training programs fall far below that mark. A former Congressional staffer who is familiar with the use of private military contractors described the system as a "non-sexy but far bigger Oliver North-style Enterprise . . . If the DoD was directly involved you'd have a whole network of Congressional offices providing oversight, even if it's not always sufficient. When you turn these tasks over to a contractor, the only oversight comes from an overworked civil servant in the federal bureaucracy." Grant concurs, saying that the US government has seized upon the use of private trainers "as an expeditious means to accomplish policy and bypass congressionally mandated law, regulation, and budget as well as the seemingly impenetrable bureaucracy that so often slows traditional security assistance actions."

The use of private firms is further attractive to government because the capture or murder of contractors carries almost no political fall-out. That's become especially important since Vietnam, after which American policymakers became increasingly averse to sending nationals to fight and die in foreign conflicts. Robert Brown of *SOF* says that for this reason, he's long felt the need for a US version of the French Foreign Legion. "The French government doesn't have to answer to whining mothers," he told me at the *SOF* convention. "So much of our policy is based on the question of, 'Oh my god, is anyone going to get hurt?' For the fucking faggots we've got in power, death is unacceptable. Every time we consider going into a foreign area there's this big worry about losing people. With the French Foreign Legion, if someone gets killed, it's tough shit."

Private firms also provide the Pentagon with perfect cover for its more sensitive overseas operations. Sometimes these are further obscured by the routine or even "humanitarian" nature of the duties for which the firms are contracted. In 1995 a company called Ronco was given a contract to perform demining duties in Ruwanda, which had recently become a close US military ally. At the time, Ruwanda was barred by UN embargo from receiving any military supplies. Kathi Austin, an Africa specialist and director of the Fund for Peace's Arms and Conflict program, was then in the region and learned that Ronco was actually importing small-scale military equipment, including explosives and armored vehicles. With the Pentagon's approval, she says, this was turned over to the Ruwandan military.

The private firms also serve to soak up military veterans cut loose by post-Cold War downsizing. One person I interviewed said that since ending his active duty status, he'd held posts abroad with three private companies: Vinnell, General Dynamics and MPRI. "Any time I looked around, I was able to find work," he says.

American firms involved in the military training field run the gamut from multinational behemoth to the equivalent of a Mom & Pop corner shop. As to the latter, James Woods, a former Deputy Assistant Secretary of Defense for African Affairs who now works as a Washington lobbyist at Cohen & Woods International, says there are numerous outfits that handle everything from training small units to helping foreign governments procure military equipment. The firms, generally headed by former Special Forces personnel and set up near domestic military bases, "basically consist of a retired military guy sitting in a spare bedroom with a fax machine and a Rolodex. They serve as a gateway to the large pool of retired military personnel. When they are in between jobs there's not much to do." But while this soldier-of-fortune element occupies a niche, it has had more and more difficulty landing anything beyond small-scale consulting contracts on counterterrorism or deals to provide protection for visiting VIPs. For projects of scale, the freelance warriors have lost out badly to well-connected corporations stocked with retired government and military officials.

WHEN IT COMES to military training, the biggest player is MPRI. It was founded in 1987 by retired Army General Vernon Lewis. Its corporate officers have included several dozen former high-rank-ing officers, such as General Carl Vuono, US Army Chief of Staff during the invasion of Panama and the Gulf War; General Ed Soyster, ex-head of the DIA; and General Frederick Kroesen, for-mer commander of the US Army in Europe. A brochure boasts that MPRI—which maintains a computer database with the names of 2,000 retired armed forces personnel—houses "The World's Greatest Corporate Military Expertise" and has "business cells and/or field representatives at military installations across the US and in overseas locations."

MPRI handles a variety of contracts for the Pentagon, helping out with curriculum for War Colleges and testing military equip-ment. It has also briefed the armed forces in countries like Sweden and Taiwan on American military strategy and tactics. Winning more substantive contracts sometimes runs into political and mili-tary obstacles. In 1994, MPRI sought to train the army of Zaire's dictator, Mobutu Sese Seko. The State Department rejected the company's initial license request due to political instability in Zaire; before MPRI could resubmit an application, guerillas led by Lawrence Kabila had toppled Mobutu. In 1996, the company entered into negotiations with Sri Lanka about a training program. According to *Jane's Intelligence Review*, Soyster traveled to the capi-tal of Colombo, where he was "extensively briefed by a senior local intelligence officer on the Tamil insurrection and the military mea-sures being used to combat it." The State Department issued a license for MPRI to train the Sri Lankan army, but the government there wavered and finally decided to turn the company down, presumably due to fear of negative political fall-out if MPRI's presence was exposed.

During the past five years, MPRI has played an important role in the Balkans. To facilitate its work, the company hired numerous retired US military officers with official experience in the region. Lieutenant General James Chambers served for thirty-six years in the Air Force, including a stint as director of contingency operational in Bosnia. Following his retirement, he became a vice president at MPRI. General John Sewall served as the Pentagon's special adviser to the Muslim-Croat federation, created in 1994 with US backing. The following year, Sewall and another officer made several trips to Bosnia and Croatia. European observers believed that their mission was to offer military advice, an activity then banned under a United Nations embargo. Following his retirement, Sewall also went to work for MPRI.

MPRI got its first big overseas contract in 1995, when Croatia hired the firm to advise and train its military forces. The company dispatched a team to Zagreb, headed by retired officers such as General Vuono, General Richard Griffitts and General Crosbie Saint (who commanded the US Army in Europe between 1988 and 1992). This was a period of intense fighting in the Balkans, with Croatia and Bosnia both having seceded from Yugoslavia. A State Department spokesman, John Dinger, said at the time that MPRI helped the Croatians "avoid excesses or atrocities in military operations." MPRI's spokesman, the retired DIA chief Ed Soyster, told me that the company merely "offered advice about the role of the army in a democratic society . . . The Croatians hope to join NATO, and if you want to join the club you have to look like the members."

Just months after MPRI went into Zagreb, Croatia's army—until then, bumbling and inept—launched a series of bloody offensives against Serbian forces. Most important was Operation Lightning Storm, the assault on the Krajina region during which Serbian villages were sacked and burned, hundreds of civilians were killed and some 170,000 people were driven from their ancestral homelands. "In terms of sheer numbers, it was the largest 'ethnic cleansing' of the war, though it was not as brutal as the worst Serb treatment of Bosnian Muslims during the war," the *New York Times* wrote of the Krajina assault. (In 1999, investigators at the international war crimes tribunal in The Hague recommended that three Croatian generals involved in the campaign be indicted for war crimes. The US not only refused to cooperate with investigators, but defended Croatian tactics before the tribunal. Two Canadian officers who were in Croatia during the attack said that the village of Knin was shelled indiscriminately and civilians were deliberately targeted. The Pentagon sent lawyers to argue that the shelling was a legitimate military tactic.)

Despite denials from the company, there is strong evidence that MPRI played at least an indirect role in Lightning Storm. A Croatian liaison officer told the local press that just weeks before the offensive General Vuono held a secret top-level meeting at Brioni Island, off the coast of Croatia, with General Varimar Cervenko, the architect of the Krajina campaign. In the five days preceding the attack, at least ten meetings were held between General Vuono and officers involved in Operation Lightning Storm. "No country moves from having a rag-tag militia to carrying out a professional military offensive without some help," says Roger Charles, a retired Marine lieutenant colonel and military researcher who has closely monitored MPRI's activities. "The Croatians did a good job of coordinating armor, artillery and infantry. That's not something you learn while being instructed about democratic values." (Mark Milstein, who reports regularly on the Balkans for *SOF*, was even more emphatic. As of early 1995, he says, the Croatian army "consisted of criminal rabble, a bunch of fucking losers. MPRI turned them into something resembling an army.")

In a sense, whether MPRI directed the Krajina campaign is secondary. "Once you provide training there's no way to control the way that the skills you've taught are used," says Loren Thompson, a military specialist at the conservative Alexis de Tocqueville Institution. Given Croatia's record in the twentieth century, he says—here he was referring to its collaboration with the Nazis—"I'm not sure you want that country to have a professional army."

Just months after the conclusion of the Krajina campaign, MPRI and Croatia signed a "Long-Range Management Program" intended to reorganize the Croatian Ministry of Defense. MPRI staffers also helped develop Croatia's military doctrine in conjunction with high-ranking officers. Zagreb viewed consummation of the agreement as evidence of official backing from Washington. "[The deal] serves as a response to the frequent conclusion that American-Croatian cooperation is undergoing a crisis," the state-run newspaper *Vjesnik* wrote at the time.

In 1996, after having won independence from Yugoslavia, the government of Bosnia also picked MPRI to train its new armed forces. Sarajevo signed on the dotted line after being pressed by James Pardew, the Clinton administration's Special Representative for Military Stabilization in the Balkans. The deal reportedly included a condition that Bosnia cut its military and intelligence ties to Iran, its close ally. Saudi Arabia, Kuwait, Brunei and Malaysia paid for the $400 million program, which was supplemented with large-scale shipments of US weapons to the Bosnian Army.

As in Croatia, MPRI's commitment to instilling respect for democracy is not entirely clear. One person who worked with the firm in Bosnia until 1998 said, "At the first sign that the human rights stuff in the classroom curriculum was making the students edgy, they deep-sixed it." Another of MPRI's Bosnia veterans says that the company "downplayed and removed references to the Geneva Convention and the 'laws of war' because it made the Bosnians uncomfortable." In early-1999, Washington suspended the "Equip and Train" program due to slow progress in creating a unified Moslem-Croat military. In August, the program was resumed and extended for an additional year, thereby netting MPRI another $9 million.

Elsewhere in Europe, MPRI is exploring deals with the new NATO countries: Poland, the Czech Republic and Hungary. British press reports from mid-1999 suggest that the company might be used to train the Kosovo Liberation Army as well. MPRI has also been seeking to expand its presence in Africa—as have its American and European competitors. In June 1997, the Defense Intelligence Agency sponsored a closed-door symposium, "The Privatization of National Security Functions in Sub-Saharan Africa," at the Sheraton

Hotel in Crystal City, Virginia. MPRI and other US private contractors were on hand, as was Eeben Barlow of Executive Outcomes,
Timothy Spicer of Sandline International and security consultants
for companies with investments in Africa such as Exxon and
Texaco. The DIA slapped a non-attribution policy on the event, but
one participant told me, "There was a consensus among government officials and the companies that this sort of activity is going to
greatly increase during the next few years."

The United States may have little interest in direct intervention
on the continent, but Africa is still of some economic importance.
It supplies one-fifth of America's oil needs, and is also a prime
source of diamonds and a variety of minerals. For much of the Cold
War, the French viewed Africa as their backyard. Jacques Foccart,
who for years ran a secret office within the president's office, wrote
a book in which he told of how the French virtually dictated policy
to a variety of African governments. By his account, Paris bumped
off an opposition leader in Cameroon and hand-picked the current
president of Gabon, the corrupt El Hadj Omar Bongo. French
ambassadors, he said, went so far as to have African heads-of-state
sign undated statements requesting French military intervention.

During recent years, though, France has seen its influence fall
in the region as close allies were overthrown in Rwanda and Zaire.
The US has sought to step into the breach. Between 1991 and 1995,
some 3,400 African officers were trained under the International
Military Education and Training program (the overwhelming
majority from authoritarian countries where the armed forces are
key political players.)

Private firms like Titusville and Florida-based AirScan have been part of the same process. Founded in 1989 and specializing "in airborne surveillance and security operations" (as well as oil spill and pipeline protection), that firm's operations are led by retired Brigadier General Joe Stringham, who ran US covert operations in El Salvador during the 1980s civil war. Company promotional literature says AirScan conducts operations around the world and that it works for the Pentagon, the Air Force, and unnamed multinational oil companies. "Many of our clients require discretion and their privacy is respected," the company says, adding that its "experienced crews, effective systems, and complete integration with ground forces" allow AirScan to "accurately direct ground personnel to the threat [and provide] observation and communication required for successful security operations."

Jane's International Review claims that AirScan "played a role" in the 1997 coup in Congo, in which Pascal Lissouba was removed from power by forces loyal to former dictator Denis Sassou Nguesso. The firm is also said to be operating out of northern Uganda in support of CIA-backed rebels across the border in neighboring Sudan. A French journalist who traveled to the region told me he met AirScan employees who were dropping equipment by air to Sudanese rebels.

Since at least 1997, AirScan has operated in Angola, a major supplier of oil to the US. During the Reagan years, the CIA backed Jonas Savimbi's UNITA guerillas in their war to overthrow president Eduardo dos Santos, then supported by the Soviet Union. After dos Santos embraced free-market reforms in the mid-1990s, the

Clinton Administration began to view Angola as a potentially important ally in Africa. It offered increasing support to dos Santos, especially after Savimbi, in 1998, walked away from a power-sharing arrangement with the ruling party and returned to guerilla warfare.

AirScan was called into Angola at the behest of multinational giant Chevron, which pressed the government to hire AirScan to provide surveillance of the oil-rich Cabinda province. Guerilla groups are active in the region, and AirScan uses Cessna 337s to monitor oil fields and prevent enemy infiltration. If security specialists detect rebel movement, they call in the Angolan military. "The rationale concerning the Cabinda venture among some authorities in Washington is that it does not matter if Angola again lapses into civil war," *Jane's* reports. "The priority is to keep the oil flowing."

MPRI, too, has been seeking business in Angola and in 1995 seemed to have locked up a major contract. That year, Clinton threatened to block United Nations aid to Angola unless dos Santos terminated his country's business agreement with Executive Outcomes. Dos Santos complied, and the State Department duly issued MPRI a license to train Luanda's army. The deal was worth millions of dollars and called for MPRI to implement a full-scale training program with the army and police, including, one Beltway Angolan specialist told me at the time, the notorious Rapid Intervention Police. Known as the Ninjas, the RIP—equipped with helicopter gunships, mortars, and armored personnel carriers—has attacked the unarmed opposition and committed serious human rights abuses. Renewed fighting between UNITA and the government has scuttled the dispatch of MPRI's trainers, at least until a peace agreement is signed.

MPRI had more luck in Liberia, where it trained the military to use US-supplied arms and equipment. It also has a significant role in implementing the African Crisis Responsive Initiative (ACRI), a program designed to strengthen US ties to African nations and create an indigenous "peacekeeping" force on the continent. Seven nations are participating—Benin, Ghana, Malawi, Mali, Senegal, Uganda and the Ivory Coast—several of which initially received training from Special Forces teams from Fort Bragg, North Carolina. In 1998, MPRI and LOGICON, a high-tech subsidiary of Northrop Grumman, were called in to provide "leadership training" for ACRI countries. The program has caused some consternation in Africa. As a March 1998 editorial in the *Johannesburg Mail and Guardian* put it, "An African security force [financed] by the US is likely to be pan-African in name only, for its core agenda will surely be set by those who provide the resources."

According to a 1997 State Department memo on the program, ACRI will only accept countries that "have military establishments that accept the supremacy of democratic civilian governments." A quick look at the armies MPRI is helping train through ACRI raises concerns about their credentials for peacekeeping. Uganda, which has emerged as one of the United States's closest allies on the African continent, was among the first to receive tutelage under ACRI. The country's president, Yoweri Museveni, has been in power since 1986, enforcing a "no party" system in which dissent is forcefully hampered. Secretary of State Madeline Albright has dubbed Museveni "a beacon of hope." Human Rights Watch, on the other hand, says his government displays little "commitment to the expansion of political freedoms." Meanwhile, several human rights groups have linked ACRI-trained battalions to murders, rapes, and beatings committed against Ugandan civilians in areas of the country contested by rebels.

This divide between rhetoric and reality grows wider yet in the case of Senegal. Just two months after Amnesty International released its 1998 special report on that country—which detailed the extensive use of arbitrary arrest, forced exile, extra-judicial killings, and torture by government security forces—President Clinton concluded a whirlwind tour of Africa by holding "extremely cordial" talks with Senegalese President Abdou Diouf. Convening at the Thies Army Base, just east of Dakar, the two leaders watched ACRI trainees perform military exercises. Diouf took the opportunity to boast of his government's "long-standing practice . . . to promote human rights and to strive for the perfect democratic process"—long-standing indeed, since Diouf has held office since 1981—while Clinton nodded his approval and lauded ACRI for shoring up political "stability" on the continent.

In Mali, another beneficiary of ACRI instruction, stability also holds top priority. There, President Alpha Oumar Konaré's security forces operate with considerable legal impunity, as demonstrated with the wholesale round-up of opposition leaders and student protesters during elections held in 1997. According to Amnesty International, the government has "not hesitated to use torture . . . to obtain information or confessions, but also to punish or intimidate members of civil society."

Beyond the issue of human rights, Dan Nelson says ACRI further separates African militaries from civilians. "It creates the impression that the armed forces have special importance and ties to the United States," he says. "It's like the School of the Americas, but now we're making house calls." Indeed, it appears that ACRI might serve as a model for other parts of the Third World. In mid-1999, President Clinton called for the creation of a US-led force for Latin America that would "protect democracy" by "intervening in threatened environments."

PRIVATE AMERICAN mercenary firms are also active in the Middle East, a region of huge economic and strategic interest to the United States. In Saudi Arabia, a clutch of companies are training every branch of the armed forces, so much so that they have in effect turned the Saudi security apparatus, infamous for its use of torture, into a private subsidiary of the Pentagon. The trail-blazer here is Vinnell, which in 1997 was acquired by Beltway mega-company TRW from The Carlyle Group, an investment firm headed by former Secretary of State James Baker, former White House budget chief Richard Darman, and former Secretary of Defense Frank Carlucci.

Vinnell worked for the Pentagon in Vietnam, prompting one US military official to describe it as "our own little mercenary army." Following the US withdrawal from Southeast Asia, Vinnell received a contract to train the Saudi Arabian National Guard, which protects the Kingdom from its internal enemies and guards strategic facilities such as oil installations. Deemed to be more reliable than the army, the National Guard has more than doubled in size during the past decade, growing to 75,000 men.

Vinnell has 1,000 employees in Saudi Arabia, many of them US Army Special Forces veterans. They are based at five National Guard Sites and, according to a person who once applied to work for the company, "instruct Saudi troops in using new weapons, supervise supply operations, and offer tactical training to mechanized units." During the Gulf War, Vinnell employees were deployed along with the Saudi units and got bonus pay for hazardous duty. "Those units couldn't operate without Vinnell personnel," says another person who worked with the firm at the time.

Another company active in Saudi Arabia is SAIC, a favored retirement spot for military officers and spooks. (See Chapter 5 for more on SAIC's place in the "revolving door" between the Pentagon and the private sector.) Officially SAIC assists the Saudi navy with no more than systems analysis. However, a person familiar with the firm's operations says it develops software that controls Saudi air defenses, and plays an important role running those operations. SAIC also brings Saudi military personnel to its headquarters in San Diego, where they are trained to run and maintain the navy's systems.

In conjunction with the US Navy and Marines, Booz-Allen & Hamilton—better known as one of the Beltway's biggest consulting firms—oversees the Saudi Marine Corps, which was created after the Gulf War. Booz-Allen also runs the Saudi Armed Forces Staff College. "It's a very sizable contract," says a person familiar with the agreement. "They're teaching senior-level military skills, including tactical training." O'Gara Protective Services, a private security business staffed by former CIA and Secret Service agents, was directly hired by Saudi Defense Minister Prince Sultan to protect members of the royal family (and their property). The company also instructs Saudi agents in the fine art of VIP protection. "The Saudi are beset by internal problems, so O'Gara's role is an important one," says the source. Meanwhile, defense giant General Dynamics runs a reconnaissance-training program with Royal Saudi Land Forces based in Tibuk. The official at the Office of Defense Trade Controls was clear about the relationship of all this corporate activity to US policy objectives: "Our troops are over there to protect vital US interests. Are we really going to put our people at risk because a host country's forces aren't sufficiently prepared to fight with us?"

IN LATIN AMERICA, the US's traditional backyard, private firms are also supplementing the Pentagon's security efforts. Florida-based Betac undertakes contract work for the CIA and works close-ly with the US Special Operations Command (SOCOM) based at MacDill Air Force Base. The command, which was created follow-ing the bungled rescue of fifty US hostages in Iran in 1980, oversees Navy Seals, Army Rangers and Delta Force. These elite units spe-cialize in covert operations in the Third World, train anti-drug police in Latin America, and assist US clients with "internal security." A former special operations officer now in the private sector says that SOCOM hired Betac to assist it in a range of activities, including overseas military training. Betac helped cement its relationship with the Command by retaining as consultants two of its past chiefs, retired four-star generals Carl Stiner and Wayne Downing.

DynCorp, a hydra-headed firm, is active across Latin America, especially in anti-drug operations. The company has more than

17,000 employees, over 550 operating facilities around the world, and annual revenues of about $1.3 billion. With major corporate offices in Virginia, DynCorp's interests range from environmental clean-up and information technology to the more murky areas of national security. Like Betac, DynCorp does work for the CIA. It also holds contracts with the Pentagon, the Drug Enforcement Agency, the Department of Justice, Environmental Protection Agency, Federal Communications Commission, Internal Revenue Service, and Treasury Department.

In 1997, DynCorp picked up a huge contract to build base infrastructure—everything from mess halls to the provision of electricity and water—when the Pentagon deploys troops abroad. The company has also assisted United Nations peacekeepers in Angola and in 1999 landed a contract with the State Department to provide the US contingent of cease-fire verifiers in Kosovo. Not all of DynCorp's contracts are so innocuous. In the early 1990s, the State Department hired the company for the ostensible purpose of maintaining helicopters then on loan to Peruvian anti-drug police. In 1992, three DynCorp employees died when one of those helicopters was shot down over a major coca-growing region. Among them was Robert Hitchman, and he was not in Peru to repair helicopters.

A one-time Marine Corps fighter pilot and covert-ops specialist, Hitchman worked in Vietnam and Laos for Air America during the 1960s. In 1964, he took part in a secret operation in which American pilots based in Taiwan flew helicopters off the coast of China to test Beijing's air surveillance systems. (The Chinese did not pick up the craft on their radars.) Fifteen years later, Hitchman turned up in Libya, where he helped run former CIA agent Ed

Wilson's military support and training operations for Muammar el-Qaddafi. In Joe Goulden's *The Death Merchant*, a biography of Wilson, one former colleague of Hitchman described him as a brilliant helicopter pilot and "a son of a bitch who could look death in the face and chuck it under the chin; absolute ice water."

An official US investigation never determined the cause of the crash in Peru, but suggested that crew fatigue was to blame. Meanwhile, Shining Path guerillas claimed responsibility. Hitchman's son, Robert III, who lives in Sacramento, confirms that his father was shot down by the guerillas, a fact, he says, that US government officials—including then-Secretary of State James Baker—asked him to keep quiet. "They didn't want the public to know the full extent of American involvement in drug wars in Latin America," he says. According to Hitchman III, his father and other DynCorp employees operated out of a base run by Peruvian police and the US Drug Enforcement Administration. Their real mission was to ferry in DEA agents to blow up cocaine labs, burn coca fields and coordinate aerial eradication programs. Hitchman was also training Peruvian pilots to fly helicopters in combat operations.

Hitchman III says his father worked with DynCorp and the DEA in Bolivia, Ecuador and Colombia as well. His colleagues included his commanding officer in Vietnam and another Air America veteran, James Sweeney (who was killed in the crash along with Hitchman). "They had no problem flying in that terrain, landing on little airstrips," he says. "It was just like Vietnam. They'd been doing it all of their lives."

DynCorp's International Technical Services division works closely with a State Department program called "Policing in Emerging

Democracies." Through it, the US has helped train police forces in Panama, Somalia, El Salvador, Bosnia and Haiti. In the latter case, the training took place after the Pentagon occupied Haiti and restored President Jean-Bertrand Aristide to power in 1995. DynCorp was one of several firms contracted by the State Department to train and deploy the Haitian National Police (HNP), which replaced the army as the country's leading security force. After American troops withdrew from Haiti, DynCorp's trainers stayed on as technical advisers to police units.

Although an improvement over the infamous Tonton Macoutes, the record of the HNP, in which 130 Haitian military officers assumed command positions, includes "extrajudicial executions, the unjustified or disproportionate use of lethal force, and beatings," according to Human Rights Watch. A confidential memorandum from the US Embassy in Haiti dated January 1997—at a time when the police training program was in high gear—and addressed to the Pentagon, the Joint Chiefs of Staff and the State Department stated: "Over 300 HNP agents have received specialized training in crowd control . . . Embassy expects crowd control to be major HNP task in 1997 as the stagnant economy engenders greater frustrations among the populace."

More recently, DynCorp has been working in Colombia, whose government is closely allied with the United States. Bogota's egregious human rights record has not prevented the Clinton administration from dramatically increasing military aid and sales to the Colombian government. The Pentagon has also dispatched several hundred Special Forces troops to Colombia. They run and defend surveillance facilities, train security forces, and provide intelligence on the activities of left-wing guerillas, who controlled about half of the country by 1999.

Officially, DynCorp employees in Colombia have no role in combat operations against guerilla groups, but are merely engaged in providing pilot training and technical support for the National Police's "illicit-plant eradication" efforts. But several reports suggest DynCorp personnel are actively involved in counterinsurgency in the south, where the guerillas are especially strong. In August of 1998, Tod Robberson of the *Dallas Morning News* wrote that DynCorp's activities went "well beyond the stated US mission of fighting drug traffickers."

DynCorp employees at the San Jose del Guaviare military base told Robberson they were under strict orders to stonewall reporters, but a few spoke with him off the record. They said that DynCorp's Colombian contingent was comprised of former Green Berets, Gulf War veterans, and a smattering of old CIA hands from the agency's wars in Central America. DynCorp's pilots, they said, had assisted the Colombian military deploy its counter-insurgency troops, and on several occasions had run into armed guerilla forces. (US-based officials are even less forthcoming. When asked about his company's operations in Colombia, Frank Henderson, DynCorp's director of international logistics support, responded, "You're getting into an area I wouldn't want to see in print.")

DynCorp's presence in Colombia was noted in the Latin American press. The Buenos Aires daily, *Clarin*, reported that a few dozen Vietnam vets were employed by DynCorp. "They walk around in

Bermuda shorts, they smoke wherever they want, and they drink whiskey," a Colombian anti-drug cop told the newspaper. According to the Bogota newspaper *El Espectador*, DynCorp's employees "refuse to subordinate themselves to Colombian officials."

Flying alongside DynCorp in Colombia are pilots working for East Inc. of Chantilly, Virginia. That firm was set up in 1983 to provide clandestine air transport services to the US government and was deeply involved in the Iran/contra affair. Founded and headed by retired Air Force Colonel Richard Gadd and set up with help from Richard Secord, East Inc. specialized in chartering flights that could not be traced back to the CIA or Pentagon. In late July 1998, just before a guerilla offensive, an East Inc. plane went down along the Guayabero River, near the San Jose del Guaviare base. Two pilots onboard were killed; the company called the accident the result of a technical failure (possibly true, but an assertion never tested by a public investigation).

In official government lexicon, the corporate activities discussed in this chapter—from training foreign armies to supporting covert operations abroad—fall under the category of "privatization." It's a bland word for what the trend signifies in foreign and military policy. Loren Thompson of the de Tocqueville Institution puts the case more vividly: "The only difference between what these firms do and what mercenaries do is that the companies have gained the imprimatur of government for their actions."

FIVE

STILL IN CONTROL
AFTER ALL THESE YEARS

Alexander Haig and the Revolving Door

"The intelligence world is a lot of fun, which is why so many guys retire and come back to it. You meet amazing and unique people all over the world, you're involved in incredible things, and you make money. At the end, you look back and say, 'I've had an interesting life'."

—Former Air Force officer, currently involved in the arms business, on the allure of the military field

ARMS MAKERS have plenty of ways to win influence in Washington, from campaign contributions to well-financed lobbying campaigns. But due to the tight links between the Pentagon and industry, companies find it especially useful to hire up military officials and defense staffers as they retire from public service. Ernie Fitzgerald is the Air Force official who was fired by President Nixon because he blew the whistle on cost overruns on Lockheed's C-130. Fitzgerald sued to get his job back and was reinstated four years later following a long court battle. Still at the Pentagon today, here's how he explains the inner workings of the revolving door:

Military officers for the most part are forced to retire when their family expenses are at a peak—they've got a couple of kids in college and they're still paying a mortgage. They won't starve on their retired pay. But at the same time, they can't keep up their lifestyle. What happens in our system is that the services see one of their management duties as placing their retired officers, just like a good university will place its graduates. And the place the services have the most influence at is with contractors. If you're a good clean-living officer and you don't get drunk at lunch or get caught messing around with the opposite sex in the office, and you don't raise too much of a fuss about horror stories you come across—when you retire, a nice man will come calling. Typically he'll be another retired officer. And he'll be driving a fancy car, a Mercedes or equivalent, and wearing a $2,000 suit and Gucci shoes and Rolex watch. He will offer to make a comfortable life for you by getting you a comfortable job at one of the contractors. Now, if you go around kicking people in the shins, raising hell about the outrages committed by the big contractors, no nice man comes calling. It's that simple.

The revolving door is a relatively recent phenomenon. In the years immediately following World War II, military officers did not commonly go to work for defense companies upon retiring from active duty (with the exception of the Air Force, which has always been the most corrupt service branch). A social stigma was attached to using influence and knowledge attained while serving one's country as tools for profiteering. By the 1970s, such inhibitions had broken down and revolving door stories provoked a national scandal. One particularly egregious case involved Malcolm Currie, who moved from the Hughes Aircraft Co. to become the Pentagon's director of defense research and engineering under Presidents Nixon and Ford. While at his government job, Currie approved the controversial "Americanization" of the French-West German Roland missile, a $104 million contract awarded to Hughes Aircraft. Soon afterwards, Currie returned to Hughes to take a corporate vice presidency. His duties included monitoring the Roland missile. In another high-profile case, General Dynamics in 1976 filed a claim with the Navy for cost overruns on the 688-class submarines, which the company had begun work on five years earlier. Though the claims were controversial, the Navy soon signed over a check to General Dynamics for $642 million. A few years later, the Navy secretary who awarded the settlement became a legal consultant to General Dynamics.

In response to efforts by Fitzgerald and other Pentagon reformers, Congress passed what came to be known as the "Proxmire Law," named after its chief sponsor, former Wisconsin Senator William Proxmire. The law required that Pentagon employees file a disclosure report upon taking a position with industry paying more than $25,000 a year. As Proxmire said at the time, "Nothing erodes the credibility of defense contracting more than the public perception that high military and civilian Pentagon officials are feathering their nest by doing favors for contractors. All too often, these Defense Department officials fulfill the public's low expectations by leaving government to work for the defense firms they were supposed to regulate. There is an appearance of wrongdoing here that overrides whatever contributions these individuals might make to the defense effort as private citizens."

The Proxmire Law allowed the public to keep track of who moved through the revolving door, but it certainly didn't stop it. Look at any major Pentagon weapons system and you'll find former military officials with a finger in the pie. Take Northrop Grumman's B-2 bomber, which at $2 billion per copy is the most expensive piece of military equipment ever devised. The plane was designed to penetrate the air defenses of the Soviet Union, a nation that no longer exists. "The B-2 is not about meeting threats to national security," says a Pentagon source. "It's just mindless bureaucratic momentum and pressure from the contractor." Northrop has helped to maintain support for the B-2 by hiring former officers as consultants or board members, including three retired Air Force generals. The company's B-2 team has also included Don Rice, a former secretary of the Air Force; Robert Helm, a retired Pentagon comptroller; and Togo West Jr., a former general counsel to the Pentagon under Jimmy Carter who after lobbying for Northrop in the early 1990s returned to public service under Bill Clinton to serve as Secretary of the Army.

A similar cast of characters can be found at other defense makers. Until 1997, Norman Augustine, a former secretary of the army, headed Lockheed. On that company's board sits retired General Robert Riscassi while top lobbyists at Lockheed's corporate offices in Bethesda, Maryland, include Alan Ptak, a former Navy deputy secretary of defense, and Jack Overstreet, ex-chief of weapons systems at the Air Force.

Nowadays, keeping track of the revolving door has become a more difficult task. At the request of the Pentagon, Congress in February 1996 quietly repealed the Proxmire Law. "It didn't really tell us anything, and took a lot of manpower to compile," says David Ream,

STILL IN CONTROL AFTER ALL THESE YEARS 193

director of the Defense Department's ethics office. (It's a sad commentary on the current state of defense reporting that more than four years later, the press had apparently not noticed the law's demise.)

The Pentagon took care to shred all records kept under the Proxmire Law except those for the years 1992 to 1995. A review of the remaining files, kept in seven large storage boxes at the National Archives in Suitland, Maryland, found that between those years 3,288 people poured through the revolving door, of whom 2,482 were officers with the rank of colonel or above. Upon reviewing the records it's easy to see why the Pentagon wanted the law repealed: conflicts of interest immediately leap out. Lieutenant General Gordon Fornell retired from the Air Force in 1993 and within fifteen months had picked up consulting contracts with ten defense contractors, including SAIC and Cypress International, an arms dealer based in Virginia. Lieutenant General John Jaquish retired from his Air Force job as principal deputy assistant secretary of acquisition on September 1, 1993. On November 1, he became a consultant to Grumman, Rockwell, and Vought. Three months later he signed on with Litton and Lockheed. All of the consulting jobs paid $25,000 a year or more. Admiral Huntington Hardisty served as commander in chief of the US Pacific Command until March 1 1991. Within two years Hardisty had six defense consulting jobs, of which four involved greasing the wheels for sales of weapons and equipment to Taiwan.

SAIC—a high-tech firm that translates and decodes intercepts for the NSA, provides the CIA with software to analyze intelligence data, and has a variety of contracts working on the "Star Wars" program and in the field of nuclear policy—offered career refuge to 198 former military officials and Pentagon employees. (The company's board members have included former Defense Secretaries William Perry and Melvin Laird, and former CIA directors John Deutsch and Robert Gates.) Next in line were Lockheed (168), Boeing (71), Northrop-Grumman (62), and Raytheon (56).

A lesser-known magnet for revolving door alumni is The Spectrum Group, a consulting firm located in Alexandria, Virginia where eighteen company officials are drawn from the armed forces and the Pentagon. A promotional brochure Spectrum sends to potential clients boasts that the firm's "team" includes more than a dozen former admirals and generals, whose "knowledge of [Pentagon] procedures and systems is unmatched." The brochure quotes Mark Goodfriend, CEO of a firm called Next Century Power—it markets rechargeable aircraft batteries to the Navy—as saying that The Spectrum Group "was instrumental in helping secure funding and getting us into the procurement loop."

Spectrum opened for business in 1994 and, according to one of a number of internal corporate memos that I obtained, the firm's revenues grew from just $287,648 that year to about $2.5 million in 1998. A confidential synopsis of activities performed for nineteen clients shows that all but one retained Spectrum to help gain access to or dollars from the Pentagon. In some cases, Spectrum Group claims to have inserted money directly into appropriations bills for its paying customers.

Spectrum avidly seeks to curry favor on Capitol Hill. "Our ability to communicate with Members of Congress through their staffs is paramount to Spectrum's success on the hill," Larry Ayres, the

company's executive vice president for government relations and a
former Army officer, wrote to other firm higher-ups. "It will be my
responsibility to go to staff members, introduce myself to them,
inform them of what we are doing with regards to our client (whose
place of business happens to be in their state or congressional dis-
trict), and to stimulate their interest in the matter." To further its
access on the Hill, Spectrum established a company PAC in March
1998. It soon held fund-raisers for Representatives Duncan Hunter,
Ike Skelton, Curt Weldon, Bill Young, all of the House National
Security Committee, and Senate Majority leader Trent Lott.

The Spectrum Group's chief strength, though, is its ties to the
Pentagon. One memo explains that the firm is assisting one client
"gain acceptance in DoD" while another confidently boasts of the
"outstanding personal contacts" of the firm's employees. Those
would surely include Jesse Brown, who resigned as head of the
Department of Veterans Affairs in mid-1997 and signed on with
Spectrum in September of that year. The agenda for the company's
next corporate meeting shows that Brown was already exploring
"opportunities" at the agency he had until so recently headed.

When the Pentagon targeted a number of military bases in
Arizona for closure, the state hired Spectrum to help keep them open.
The company deployed Air Force General James Davis, who was
appointed by House Speaker Newt Gingrich to serve on the 1995
Defense Base Closure and Realignment Commission, to handle that
account. (In its promotional brochure, Spectrum claims to have saved
eleven bases the Pentagon planned to close.) Spectrum slotted former Air Force Colonel Paul McManus to help Delta Air Lines win a

contract to repair aircraft engines for Air Force planes produced by McDonnell-Douglas, which helpfully was another Spectrum client at the time. "TSG was successful in bringing the Delta story to the US Air Force from the chief of staff . . . to the Commander of the Air Force Materiel Command," reads a memo.

Thanks to their connections, Spectrum officials are able to help clients win a competitive advantage—often an undeserved one—for their products. Former Air National Guard director John Conaway represents Lockheed, which racked up impressive sales to the Guard during Conaway's tenure there. He helps market Lockheed's AL-56M radar system to the National Guard and its ATARS reconnaissance system to the Navy. Both systems have been plagued by problems. According to a source that reviews weapons tests, during one trial run the AL-56M identified radar from a civilian airport as an enemy threat and repeatedly responded to what turned out to be false alarms. The ATARS system is supposed to send back reconnaissance photographs via a data link while it returns from its mission, thereby providing real-time intelligence and eliminating the need to develop film. But ATARS has performed so poorly that the Air Force, which originally intended to buy the system, has dropped out of the program.

An even worse boondoggle promoted by Spectrum is the Sense and Destroy Armor Project (SADARM), which is produced by California-based Aerojet. Helping Aerojet develop "the strategy to gain [Pentagon] support" for SADARM are Spectrum's Stephen Loftus, a former vice admiral, and Lieutenant General Gus Cianciolo, who retired in 1992 after serving as an adviser to the army's procurement czar. The SADARM consists of a 155 millimeter howitzer that opens up after firing to release a pair of sub-munitions. The sub-munitions descend by parachute and use a heat-seeking sensor to home in on and destroy enemy armored vehicles. "The sensor technology is incredible," raves Julie Rovegno, an Aerojet spokeswoman,

That's not a universally held view. The SADARM program is years behind schedule, way over budget and has suffered countless testing failures. Aerojet claims to have solved a problem that caused the two sub-munitions to routinely collide during their descent by parachute, but—according to a former Pentagon employee—SADARM's sensor is hopeless, and only "dumb ass luck" would enable the weapon to hit its target. "The sensor can't distinguish between an armored vehicle and a barbecue grill," the source says. "An opposing army could protect its equipment by lining Hibachis up and down the road."

In 1991, the House voted to kill SADARM, but the Senate saved it. In 1994, Congress reduced funding of the program after it flunked testing. The following year, the GAO concluded that SADARM "did not meet operational requirements." Yet like a vampire rising from the grave, SADARM lives on. The Army requested $56.5 million for the program in the FY 1999 budget and Aerojet, with Spectrum's able assistance, is trying to sell it to the Navy as well.

WHEN YOU WORK for some Pentagon bureaus, those "nice men" Ernie Fitzgerald talks about are almost sure to come calling when it's time to retire. One such department is the Defense Security Cooperation

Agency (DSCA), the Pentagon bureau that handles the government's Foreign Military Sales (FMS) program (see Chapter One for more on the Agency). Lieutenant General Howard Fish headed the DSCA during the Nixon and Ford administrations and, like most of the agency's directors, was an exuberant promoter of selling weapons to any and all buyers. Fish played a key role in watering down the Arms Export Control Act of 1976, which would have placed a ceiling on total foreign arms sales and given Congress the right to veto sales on human rights grounds. Fish was heavily involved in sales to Iran, then headed by the Shah, and to the Middle East.

Fish's work at the Pentagon provided him with the perfect resume when he decided to retire from government in 1978. He quickly found new employment with arms maker LTV, and within months of his resignation turned up in Malaysia, where he was hawking the company's A-7 fighters. Fish later worked at the head of international marketing for Loral, another big weapons maker, and then, in the late-1980s, took charge of the industry-backed American League for Exports and Security Assistance (ALESA). One of Fish's chief missions there was promoting the sale of weapons to the Middle East, especially to Saudi Arabia where Fish has intimate connections (he kept a picture of Saudi King Fahd on a bookcase at his office). Back in 1989, Fish met with chief of staff John Sununu and National Security Advisor Brent Scowcroft in a successful effort to convince the Bush administration to sell front-line tanks and supersonic fighters to Arab countries.

An impressive display of the ALESA's efforts came in the early 1990s, when at the behest of weapons makers it helped form the Middle East Action Group to press for deals then in the pipeline with the Saudis. In addition to Fish, other Action Group heavies included Dov Zakheim, a former deputy defense undersecretary for Reagan and an ordained rabbi with close ties to the American Jewish community; Sandra Charkjkhles, who served on the National Security Council as director for Middle East Affairs during the Bush years; and Robert Lilac, a former Air Force officer who commands a premium among weapons makers due to his close relationship with Prince Bandar, the long-time Saudi ambassador to the US.

Fish left the league in 1997 to become a consultant to Lockheed Martin. He wears a second hat as a member of a Pentagon policy review committee that advises the Pentagon on the international arms trade, and so is still intimately involved in the whole process of peddling US weapons abroad. Fish was in attendance at an industry-Pentagon luncheon in the spring of 1999 and complained that nowadays there is too much bureaucracy holding up sales. In his days at DSCA, the agency had something he called the "Gold Card," which allowed contractors to approve their own export licenses for specific weapons systems. "You fill out your own export license and report back to us," he explained. "If you do anything wrong, we'll kill you! That's what they should do now."

Fish's post-government career is fairly typical for DSCA directors. Of the last ten men to head the agency going back to 1971, nine went on to work for the arms industry (at least six for firms that sell weapons or military services abroad). The day after he retired from DSCA in 1993, Lieutenant General Teddy Allen took a job as a consultant to Hughes, offering the company advice on sales to Egypt—a major customer under FMS. A few months later Allen became an "international marketing" consultant with AEL Systems International, for whom he was to "provide advice and guidance" concerning FMS opportunities and also "provide recommendations and/or introductions to key customers." Lieutenant General Philip Gast stepped down from the agency in 1990 and is now a vice president for international operations at Burdeshaw Associates, a company whose self-described mission is to help clients "compete and win in global defense and government markets." Vice Admiral Ray Peet left the agency in 1974 and went on to work for several defense contractors, including Teledyne Ryan, where he currently serves as vice president for international affairs.

Lieutenant General Ernest Graves, who headed the DSCA between March 1978 and July 1981, is the only former head of the agency who didn't go on to work for the defense industry (other than a few freelance consulting jobs). Graves, who since retiring has worked as a military analyst at Georgetown's Center for Strategic and International Studies, says he turned down two offers from arms companies who wanted him to promote overseas sales. "I just wasn't comfortable with the notion of trading commercially on relationships I had formed when I was working for the government," he says.

A MYRIAD OF INDUSTRY trade groups and servicemen's associations—the Association of the United States Army (AUSA), the Air Force Association, the Navy League and Marine Corps League—make up one of the least noticed pieces of the Pentagon procurement puzzle. In addition to clamoring for bigger budgets and expanded mandates for their respective services, the groups provide a comfortable space where industry and government can informally gather to schmooze and politick. For former military men who want to stay involved in the field (while simultaneously desiring enough leisure time to keep up on their golf game), these outfits are a logical choice for post-government employ.

The servicemen's associations draw their legitimacy from active-duty and retired rank-and-filers, but it is industry that pays most of their bills. That's reflected in the groups' demands, some which verge on the absurd. During the 1998 Congressional battles for defense dollars, retired General Gordon Sullivan, AUSA's president, asked for a $30 billion supplement to the Pentagon's budget, an add-on twice as large as what had been requested by the Joint Chiefs of Staffs. Elsewhere, Sullivan has stated that defense spending should ideally be budgeted at five percent of the gross national product, which in 1999 would have come to $422 billion. "In the life of a republic there comes a time to challenge national policies," Sullivan wrote in an op-ed in *Army Times* in March of that year. "This is that time . . . We must recognize that three percent of the Gross Domestic product is not enough . . . [The world] has the potential of being chaotic and dangerous, with new challenges just around the corner. There will be tigers in the world—whether they are Saddam Hussein, Kim Jung II or Osama Bin Laden."

Like its sister organizations, the AUSA promises to keep its members plugged in at the Pentagon. In an advertisement in *Defense News*, the group solicits funds for its corporate "Sustaining Membership" program, which promises "face-to-face meetings" with Army decision-makers and government officials. It also trumpets special events that offer "a unique opportunity . . . to discuss policy, future plans and programs in a productive, collegial environment." Over at the Air Force Association, which represents over 200 aerospace and defense companies, an "Industrial Associates" program offers members similar "access to senior-level Air Force and DoD leaders."

Among the most important industry groups are the Aerospace Industries Association, which is headed by John Douglas, a one-time director of national security programs for Ronald Reagan, and the National Defense Industrial Association (NDIA), which bills itself as the "premier association" representing private companies and which is led by former Lieutenant General Lawrence Skibbie. With 900 companies and 25,000 individual members, the latter outfit works to ensure that "the Defense industrial base [is] considered in defense decisions." The Association's top ten issues for 1999 included increased budgets for new weapons systems, a tax credit for industry research and development spending, rapid progress on ballistic missile defense, and reforming defense export policy so as to "level the playing field" with America's international competitors. The latter is a special priority for the NDIA. A policy statement it circulated on the issue says that defense exports are "gaining increased prominence as the domestic market continues its precipitous decline. Export markets will not replace domestic sales, but can temper the decline. Exports can also sustain production lines for key military systems and components, thereby contributing to national security, supporting the defense industrial base, and preserving jobs for skilled defense workers."

In April 1999, Skibbie used his column in *National Defense*, the NDIA's glossy monthly, to lament the demise of the Soviet Union. "Many of us did not comprehend the dangers inherent in the disappearance of a single monolithic threat on which we could focus and concentrate our security efforts," he wrote. "Now we are faced with multiple, seemingly lower level, threats against which it is difficult to focus our efforts and enlist the energy and resources of the country." He complained that defense interests hadn't aggressively made their case to the public about a long list of national security threats, ranging from anthrax to North Korea. "You need to communicate to your lawmakers your concerns about these threats and how important it is for the United States to quickly prepare the home front, which has suddenly become the front lines in this new era of warfare," Skibbie urged members.

The NDIA's grassroots lobbying program puts those words into practice. It has thirty-four chapters across the country, from the Pacific Northwest to New England, and puts out a legislative alert to "inform the membership of pending legislation critical to the defense industry." The Government Policy Advisory Committee "serves as an effective vehicle for the exchange of views and information between government and industry on matters of common concern to the national security policy objectives of the United States as well as the commercial interests of its industry." Meeting for breakfast every other Tuesday when Congress is in session, the NDIA's Legislative Information Committee was chaired in 1999 by Jim Littig of Northrop Grumman and featured as guest speakers prominent members of congress and Pentagon staffers. The

Procurement Committee gives "NDIA membership access to the full spectrum of the governmental process," as well as the ability to "review and provide comments on major acquisition regulations and provide members with opportunities to sit on industry/government ad hoc boards."

In another of his monthly columns, Skibbie said the NDIA was "inundated with requests for support and input from the Pentagon." Answering the call of duty, the Association and its members testified before Congress on "defense modernization," convened a panel for the Army on the issue of contractors on the battlefield, joined the Air Force's Acquisition Leadership Council, facilitated a series of small business conferences across the country for the Navy, sat on Defense Export Competitiveness task force and helped win support for the Defense Export Loan Guarantee Program, which uses government money to underwrite loans to nations purchasing U.S weapons.

NDIA's cozy relationship with the Pentagon was seen at Defense Security Cooperation Day, held in June 1999 at the Hilton Hotel in Alexandria. A joint effort between the NDIA and the DSCA, Reform Day began with a 6:00 A.M. breakfast of coffee, stale pastries and fruit. Among the early arrivers was none other than Howard Fish. The fighting in Kosovo was at its height, and when another Reform Day participant commented on how many missiles had been dropped over the Balkans, Fish commented gaily, "Well, they'll have to make more of them!" Fish reminisced about his old days in charge of the agency, and all the top secret weapons deals DSCA was involved in. "I had a colonel who handled all the intelligence work for me," Fish shared, a roguish gleam in his eyes. "His name was Dick Secord. He later got in trouble with all the Iran/contra stuff. Afterwards I told him, 'Dick! You should've come to me, I would've kept you out of trouble.' But he didn't."

John T. Keels, a senior vice president for acquisition policy at Raytheon, made a beeline for my colleague Daniel Burton-Rose when he spotted his "Institute for Policy Studies" ID badge. Keels wanted to find a China expert at the think tank to talk to about the then-hot "Cox Report," which alleged that Beijing had swiped America's nuclear secrets. The report was triggering all kinds of rash anti-China legislation in Congress, said Keels, who explained: "I've been tasked with looking at external factors influencing policy to figure out how to balance security and economic interests such that we don't let our legislators overreact."

Also in attendance was Lieutenant General Michael Davidson, the current head of DSCA. Asked if issues such as human rights and regional stability were serious considerations in evaluating arms sales, he said his agency largely left those questions to the State Department. And what about the flip-side problem of customer countries becoming frustrated due to State or Congress holding up a transaction because of concern about those issues? That was indeed a sore point with some buyers, Davidson lamented, pointing specifically to Turkey: "They've expressed quite a bit of frustration with the US perception of the human rights problem being greater than the Turkish government perception and that things have not been delivered in a timely manner."

As the formal conference got underway, Diana Halvorsen of DSCA issued a warning to the attendees: "Bear in mind, there is

press here, so anything you say can and probably will be used pub-
licly." It was a heedless announcement since the more than 400
people in the crowd were drawn almost entirely from industry and
government, be it reps from a range of US agencies or customers
from a host of countries that buy American weaponry. Other than
one or two friendly industry reporters, there was no one at all from
the press or local think tanks (with the exception of Burton-Rose).

The backdrop to Reform Day was that DSCA and industry
believe that the Foreign Military Sales program is overly bureaucratic and slow in responding to buyers. Customers agreed. As Ken
Peru, director of the British military's Defense Procurement Office,
put it, "You are now dealing with buyers who have their own purchasing skills, who want to maintain their own internal production capability. You can no longer rely on the fact that you can
provide what industry cannot. So you have to become more cus-
tomer-oriented if you wish to succeed."

First up to address such concerns was Davidson, who said that
DSCA would try to be more efficient, but that to make the effort
work, "We're gonna need your assistance, we're gonna need your
ideas. It's got to be a team effort, to address the needs of government, to address the needs of industry, to address the needs of our
customers." After a few more speeches by Pentagon officials, the
conference broke into discussion groups. At the customer panel,
representatives from England, Singapore, Switzerland, South Africa
and Jordan discussed the pros and cons of the FMS program.
Amman's defense attaché in Washington, Hamed Sariah, gave it
good marks overall, but complained that "there were a few times

[during a war] when my country was in dire need of buying weapons or ammunition," and the US government dawdled in responding. John Wong, Singapore's counselor for defense procurement, was less equivocal: "The United States has helped my country build its military capabilities for the last thirty years, and we are very thankful for that. My country gets tremendous support from DSCA and all the Commands down the line."

Officials from United Defense Technologies, General Dynamics, Raytheon, Litton and Boeing headed up another panel called "Building a Working Partnership." The common theme here was that defense exporters need more help from Uncle Sam. Robert J. Ingersoll, a vice president at Boeing, said that the war in Kosovo had offered valuable lessons about the changing security environment, namely that the export process is "still steeped in a Cold War mentality" and unable to work through "regulatory impediments" in a timely fashion. "It is unlikely that we are ever going to see a conflict that will last very long," said Ingersoll. "Therefore, speed is imperative. FedEx can get something there in a day, but unfortunately, it takes us longer to meet the regulatory impediments."

Steve Delp, director of the Washington office of United Defense Technologies, put forth the idea that since "arms transfers are an integral part of US foreign policy," the government should at least consider picking up some of the tab for the transactions costs. "The customer is willing to pay its share, and industry is willing to pay its share, but we need to take a look at what government is giving for security assistance," he said, blithely ignoring the billions of dollars the government already doles out annually to subsidize overseas sales.

To seal the spirit of friendship and cooperation generated by Reform Day, DSCA officials handed out a draft of an "Arms Transfer/Technology Transfer White Paper" for participants to read at their leisure and then get back to the Pentagon with their input. "US defense industry and foreign customers perceive numerous problems with US processes for regulating arms transfers, technology transfer and disclosures of classified information," the draft began. "This paper attempts to address some of the more frequently raised problems and recommend a way ahead." The "way ahead" appeared to be a wish list of industry demands, such as speeding up the review time for export licenses and "identifying items and technologies that should no longer be controlled either because they represent low-risk transactions, or because of their widespread availability, are no longer controllable."

Within a few weeks, industry officials were already lobbying for changes proposed by the White Paper, with NDIA and Aerospace Industries Association leading the charge. The latter was urging that the whole licensing review process be privatized, and that some items be struck from the Munitions Control List. Meanwhile, the government had agreed to hire eight additional licensing officers in order to speed up reviews.

THE EARLY PART of 1999 found retired General Alexander Haig in constant motion. In February, Haig was off to Seoul, South Korea, where he was a VIP at Blessing 99, a Unification Church event at which 40,000 couples exchanged wedding vows at a local sports stadium during a ceremony conducted by the Reverend Sun

Myung Moon himself. The following month found Haig in Palm Beach, Florida—where he owns a mansion worth more than $4 million—for a party to commemorate the sixtieth birthday of former Canadian Prime Minister Brian Mulroney. The guest list for the affair ran the gamut from the Duke of Marlborough and Princess Ira von Furstenberg to former Senator Al D'Amato and TV personality Kathie Lee Gifford.

In April, Haig was in Washington, D.C. for yet another birthday party—NATO's fiftieth—and for a dinner sponsored by business groups at the Willard Inter-Continental Hotel in honor of Chinese Premier Zhu Wrong, who was then in the midst of an official visit to the US capital. Soon thereafter, Haig was named a "strategic board advisor" to SDC International Inc., a Palm Beach-based firm that had recently acquired Tatra, a Czech military manufacturer. The press release announcing his appointment said that Haig would "draw on his extensive contacts in government, business and diplomatic circles" in helping SDC export its equipment.

It was a busy period—though not unusually so—for the seventy-three-year-old Haig, whose years in government paved the way for his later career as a Beltway wheeler-dealer. Largely out of the public spotlight, Haig does not command the same clout or respect in the US as do better-known influence peddlers such as former national security advisors Brent Scowcroft or Henry Kissinger. But like those men he has many friends abroad, often in corrupt, dictatorial regimes that remain grateful for support Haig offered while serving in the Nixon and Reagan administrations. Thanks to such connections, Haig is able to rent out his services as a door opener for corporations seeking overseas investment opportunities, a lucrative recipe that has netted him tens of millions of dollars in fees. He also serves as an unelected foreign affairs mandarin, with interests that span the globe from Washington to Ankara to Beijing, and stature that permits him to promote the same policies he did as Reagan's first secretary of state: putting commerce before human rights, peddling weapons abroad, and maintaining Cold War military alliances with the world's most repressive regimes.

There are many people, including prominent conservatives in and out of government, who call Haig an especially cynical example of a public official who cashed in on his credentials. While many of those people demanded anonymity—especially Beltway power players, who are characteristically reluctant to go on the record—that was not the case with retired Army colonel and author David Hackworth. "Haig didn't become rich based on his military record or his brains," he says with characteristic frankness. "He's the ultimate Perfumed Prince who made his way to the top by being a horse-holder for a more powerful figure, from Henry Kissinger to Richard Nixon. He didn't invent the revolving door, but he became a master at making it spin."

A 1947 graduate of the US Military Academy and Korean War veteran, Haig took a job at the Pentagon during the Kennedy years. While there he served on a top secret unit called the "Subcommittee on Subversion," whose chief target was Fidel Castro in Cuba. At the same time, Haig was earning his graduate degree at Georgetown University. His 1962 dissertation, dryly titled "The National Security Act and the Professional Soldier's Role in National Security Policy," argued that military men should be given a greater role in establishing defense policy. Haig's thesis is notable for two things: first, its obtuse prose—there is talk of "interpretive vagaries," "thought modes" and a "permeating nexus"—reveals the origins of a public oratory style that the press later dubbed "Haig-speak"; secondly, the thesis shows that Haig's well-known intolerance for dissenting points of view has deep roots. At one point Haig argues that the military's role in policy formulation had been declining and that "facts render indictments to the contrary misinformed and even fraudulent."

In 1969, following a tour of duty in Vietnam, Haig was made an advisor to President Nixon's National Security Advisor Henry Kissinger. Like his boss, he was a hawk on the war and supported the secret bombing of Cambodia. Haig was also intimately involved in the US plotting against Chile's elected president Salvador Allende, who was overthrown in 1973 by General Augusto Pinochet. When Kissinger feared that National Security Council staffers were talking to the press, Haig coordinated with the FBI to have suspected leakers and journalists wiretapped. "It was Haig who . . . would formally transmit the names of NSC staff members and reporters to be wiretapped," Seymour Hersh wrote in *The Price of Power*, his biography of Kissinger. "It was Haig who repeatedly went to [the office of William C. Sullivan, assistant director of the FBI] to read wiretap transcripts and summaries . . . Haig truly seemed to enjoy the snooping."

By the time the Watergate crisis exploded, Haig had moved on to become Nixon's chief-of-staff and as others close to Nixon resigned or were indicted, he was the president's closest aide during his final months in office. It was then that the general first came into clear public view, and when Nixon was forced to resign in 1974, President Ford put the loyal Haig in charge of NATO's military operations. He stepped down in 1979, served a brief stint as president of defense manufacturer United Technologies, then signed on as secretary of state for the incoming administration of Ronald Reagan. In that post, Haig was a chief backer of big boosts in military spending, support for anti-Communist guerilla armies, such as the contras in Nicaragua, and increased confrontation with the Soviet Union.

In his memoirs, *Inner Circles: How America Changed the World*, Haig writes that throughout "my public career, I was a strong champion of human rights, and as secretary of state I believed myself to be in the forefront of American efforts to enhance and guarantee them throughout the world." That statement sharply clashes with Haig's public record. While serving as Reagan's secretary of state, he embraced the world's most repressive regimes, provided they allied themselves with the United States in the Cold War. He defended the apartheid government in South Africa, pushed for aid to the military junta in Turkey, coddled the Suharto dictatorship in Indonesia and was a staunch supporter of the Marcos kleptocracy in the Philippines. When right-wing government forces in El Salvador raped and murdered four American churchwomen, Haig informed a House committee investigating the atrocity that "the vehicles the nuns were driving in may have tried to run a roadblock." The women were found with bullets in the back of their heads, twenty miles away from the roadblock in question.

Haig's prickly personality and imperious demands often made his overseas trips difficult for US diplomatic personnel. One for-

STILL IN CONTROL AFTER ALL THESE YEARS   213

mer diplomat recalled to me that just prior to a major 1981 gather-
ing of regional leaders in New Zealand, the American embassy
there received precise instructions on how to arrange Haig's hotel
suite. Included was a diagram of how items were to be situated on
his dresser, including the exact spot where his bottle of bourbon
was to be placed. "This, from our view at the time, epitomized the
difference between the worst attributes of military officers—rigidi-
ty and absurd attention to detail—and the flexibility and inventive-
ness needed for real diplomacy," this person says. "No doubt we
were too harsh on the military . . . and too easy on our diplomatic colleagues, some of whom have been involved in great screw-ups. But
with Haig, I think there was some justice to our position."

Haig's hard-line views were in line with Reagan's, but his frequent
blunders and misstatements embarrassed the administration. He is
probably best remembered for his antics after John Hinkley shot the
president at the Washington Hilton Hotel March of 1981. Then-Vice
President George Bush was out of town and confusion reigned at the
White House. Ignoring the constitutional chain of command that puts
the speaker of the House as next in line to assume power, Haig tersely announced: "I am in control here." After a mere eighteen months in
office, Haig was pushed out by administration officials who feared that
his verbal gaffes, tightly-wound demeanor and cliff-edge politics—
Haig's aggressive posture towards deployment of nuclear weapons in
large measure produced the Nuclear Freeze movement—was seriously damaging the president's political standing.

In 1988, Haig made his first and only run for public office when
he stood for the Republican presidential nomination. It was not an

auspicious debut. The most influential person to endorse him was political comedian Mort Sahl, and Haig pulled out of the race following the Iowa caucuses, when he finished seventh in a field of six candidates. With 364 votes—0.3 percent—Haig had less than half the tally of the sixth place finisher, "No preference."

The general's political flame-out and lack of popular appeal did not diminish his marketability with Corporate America or the Beltway establishment. "His involvement in world affairs was a commodity to cash in on," says one retired military man who keeps a close eye on the revolving door. "When you're a former NATO commander and secretary of state, you don't have to go looking for [opportunities], they come looking for you."

AND COME LOOKING they have. Haig is affiliated with think tanks ranging from the conservative Hudson Institute, where he sits with former Defense Secretary Frank Carlucci and Star Warrior Frank Gaffney, to the pro-Israeli Washington Institute for Near East Policy, where his colleagues have included Secretary of State Madeleine Albright and Undersecretary of Defense Walter Slocombe. He was a founding member of the Trilateral Commission and currently holds spots on the Council on Foreign Relations, the Bretton Woods Commission, the Atlantic Council, the Free Congress Foundation and the Nixon Center for Peace and Freedom. Haig even made the *Palm Beach Post*'s 1999 list of "Who's Who" in local society, along with business moguls Donald Trump and John Kluge, and celebrities such as Yanni and Rod Stewart.

On the international front, Haig belongs to a variety of business-backed organizations that promote trade and fraternal relations with individual countries, thereby serving as a means for corporate executives to meet important foreign officials. One example is the US-China Policy Foundation—Haig is an "Honorary Advisor"—which sends congressional staffers on all-expense paid trips to China and otherwise seeks "the continued improvement of US-China relations." Haig is also affiliated with the American-Turkish Council, which works to bolster business and military ties with Ankara, and the Hannibal Club, which performs similar activities on behalf of Tunisia.

Haig's also still influential within the national security establishment and at the Pentagon, where many current top officers formerly worked under his command. General Wesley Clark, who in 1999 directed the war on Yugoslavia, wrote speeches for Haig in the late-1970s when the latter was in charge of NATO's military operations. After retiring from government service Haig served on a number of presidential commissions that reviewed military policy. In late 1997, he was invited to the Pentagon for a party welcoming incoming chairman of the Joint Chiefs of Staff, General Harry Shelton.

Haig's stature in military circles made him an effective advocate for the expansion of NATO, which in 1998 ratified as new members Poland, Hungary and the Czech Republic. Along with more than 100 other former government officials, Haig signed on to a series of newspaper advertisements urging the admittance of the former Soviet Bloc states. He also helped build support for expansion with a series of speeches around official Washington. Haig's role was important enough that he was invited by the White House to attend the Senate ceremony at which Poland's admission was formalized. Later, the American Center of Polish Culture threw a party for Haig and former National Security Advisor Zbigniew Brzezinski, another NATO expansion advocate, at Washington's Union Station.

Among Haig's more unorthodox ties is his relationship with Sun Myung Moon, leader of the Unification Church and a man who served a stint in prison for tax fraud. Haig has been a VIP at a number of Unification Church functions, including the Blessing 99 affair in Seoul described earlier. There he introduced Moon at a banquet that preceded the mass wedding and, in the words of a Church newsletter, "praised Father as the one who dealt a decisive blow to communism." (Chris Corcoran, a Unification Church spokesman, says he "assumes" Haig is paid for his appearances, though he would not provide information on fees.)

Haig also wrote the introduction to *The Truth is My Sword*, a two-volume Church offering that contains the collected thoughts and writings of Bo Hi Pak, Moon's second-in-command. Volume I of the set, *Collected Speeches*, runs 541 pages, while Volume 2, *Inspirational Messages and Personal Testimonies to Reverend Moon*, weighs in at 716 pages. In one essay, Pak speaks of his feelings of inadequacy in serving as Moon's translator: "It may take a millenium to explain even one sentence Father speaks . . . So I pray to God. God, let me translate in faith. I am desperately trying to somehow bring Father's spirit to you." In his introduction, Haig called Pak's tribute to Moon "a remarkable treatise on one man's devotion to his country, his faith, and indeed to the creation of a better world for all mankind."

Larry Zilliox, a Virginia private investigator who has followed the Unification Church for more than a decade, says Haig lends Moon credibility, a commodity that became especially important to the reverend after he served time in prison. "Other than George Bush, Haig is probably the most prominent American to work with the Unification movement," he says. "He doesn't seem to mind that Moon's a convicted felon who's been banned from entering a number of countries."

Another unusual alliance, at least in that Haig is no liberal on social matters, is his business partnership with transsexual author and telecommunications attorney Martine Rothblatt. (One can only wonder if Haig has read Rothblatt's book *The Apartheid of Sex: A Manifesto on the Freedom of Gender*, in which she writes that "There are persons with vaginas who think of their clitorises as small penises and, often with the help of strap-on dildos, obtain sexual satisfaction by penetrating rather than rubbing their lovemate.") The two are involved in a controversial plan to transmit the Internet and phone calls from giant zeppelins that will circle above major American cities.

Haig's primary source of income is his consulting shop, Worldwide Associates, located in a downtown Washington office building attached to the Madison Hotel. A curriculum vitae prepared by Worldwide says the firm assists corporations "in developing and implementing marketing and acquisition strategies in addition to providing strategic advice on the domestic and international political, economic, and security environment." Worldwide's client list is confidential—"People we work with wouldn't want us to talk about where we do business," explains Haig's long-time aide Sherwood Goldberg, who spoke to me when Haig himself declined an interview request—but a review of published accounts, public records and corporate records filed to the Securities and Exchange Commission (SEC) reveals some interesting details. Over the years Haig has worked—as an advisor or board member—for companies such as America Online, Interneuron Pharmaceuticals, MGM Grand, Metro-Goldwyn-Mayer, General Atomics, Chase Manhattan, Texas Instruments, and Quantum Computer Services. Not surprisingly, the general's client roster has also included a number of defense firms: Boeing, United Technologies, McDonnell Douglas, and International Signal and Control Corporation, a company which paid him to help market cluster bombs to Pakistan and weapons fuses to China.

Though Worldwide Associates' fee schedule is also confidential, it's clear that Haig is amply compensated for his services. In early 1999, the general netted $11.5 million by selling 147,488 shares—about 40 percent of his holdings—of stock options granted to him for serving on the board of America Online. In 1996, he signed a contract—obtained from SEC filings—with a Phoenix firm called Interactive Flight Technologies that called for him to be paid $50,000 per year plus "one percent of gross revenues received by the Company from customers obtained through the significant advice or assistance of General Haig."

All of Haig's seemingly disparate clients share a common interest in international markets, a realm in which the general's governmental experience and contacts are useful. When he signed on as an advisor to SDC International, the company enthused that his presence would assure it of "tremendous market growth, especially in the many regions where he has strong personal relationships." Those relationships span the globe. *Business Week* reports that when MGM was shooting a James Bond movie in Morocco, King Hassan II reneged on an agreement to provide tanks and fighters. After a phone call from Haig, the requisite military material was made available.

For United Technologies, Haig's ties to foreign leaders have proven golden. In 1983, the year after he was pushed out as secretary of state, he flew to Manila and helped persuade then-dictator Ferdinand Marcos to cancel a preliminary sales agreement with Bell Helicopter. Marcos instead signed a $63 million contract for Black Hawk military helicopters made by UT's subsidiary, Sikorsky Aircraft—a switch opposed by his own Air Force. A decade later Haig traveled to Turkey and helped nail down a $1.1 billion helicopter deal for his employer. "He was highly regarded and extremely well-received by senior officials in the military establishment," says Morton Abramowitz, US ambassador to Turkey under George Bush. "They don't necessarily buy things for that reason alone, but it certainly helps you get a foot in the door and make your case."

Haig's years in politics have put him on the Rolodex of Washington journalists as an all-purpose expert on foreign affairs. He's also a newspaper op-ed author and senior international affairs advisor for Rupert Murdoch's Fox TV network. As with super-consultant Henry Kissinger, it's often difficult to know where Haig's opinions end and his business interests begin. In 1995, at a time when he and a Texas natural gas entrepreneur were trying to put together an energy deal involving Turkey, he wrote an opinion piece in the *Washington Times* that attacked critics of Ankara's human rights record. "Those who support cuts in assistance or in support of Turkey are willfully blind to US strategic interests," said the article, which made no mention of Haig's financial ties to the country he was writing about.

For Goldberg, Haig's activities are entirely proper: "General Haig has been out of office for seventeen years. He's a private citizen. Former government officials also have the right to engage in business activities, particularly when those activities promote American interests. There's no one who cares more about this country than General Haig."

AS HE TROTS the globe putting together business deals, Haig works to influence American policy by promoting friendly ties with countries where he and his clients have business interests. In 1993, Turkmenistan's president, Saparmurad Niyazov, hired the general to advise him on winning US business and political support for a natural gas pipeline project that crossed over Iran. A long-time Communist Party hack, Niyazov was elected in 1992 with 99.5 percent of the vote and subsequently had his mandate extended in a referendum in which his popularity inched up to 99.9 percent. Human Rights Watch's world report for 1999 said his government "continued to deny its citizens nearly every civil and political right" while operating "a Soviet-style secret police" that allowed for "no political opposition, no freedom of assembly, no opportunity for public debate."

In seeking to sell the pipeline plan to the Clinton administration, Haig helped arrange an official visit by Niyazov to the US, where he sought to portray his client as a bold reformer. (The Turkmen ruler "should be a hero rather than a pariah," Haig told the *Associated Press*, adding that American officials who demand compliance with Western human rights standards were "shortsighted if not downright stupid.") Haig himself became one of Niyazov's most trusted advisors. In 1993, he flew to Ashgabat, Turkmenistan's capital, and appeared on the reviewing stand with Niyazov during independence celebrations. He also joined the Turkmen leader at the head table for a big state dinner that was part of the festivities. "For awhile there they were joined at the hip," Alan Moore, head of the US-Turkmenistan Business Council, says of the Haig-Niyazov romance. The pipeline deal was ultimately blocked by the Clinton administration, which has opposed any economic dealings with Iran. Haig, though, remains close to Niyazov. The two men met in 1998 when the Turkmen leader came to Washington for a second official visit, which included a stop at the White House.

Haig also lends business a helping hand in Indonesia (though his marquee value has no doubt diminished since his close associate Suharto was driven from office in 1998). In March 1997, he led a tour there of congressional staffers and corporate executives, including officials from Federal Express, Mobil, Caterpillar, and United Technologies. The trip was sponsored by the US-ASEAN Business Council, a conservative business group, and came on the heels of months of ethnic and religious riots during which hundreds of people had been killed. While in Indonesia, the tour group met with Suharto and a number of government ministers. Steven Clemons, then a staffer to Senator Jeff Bingaman, was on the trip and says Haig's presence on the delegation was one reason such high-level doors swung open. "He was a big deal over there," recalls

Clemons, who is now at the New America Foundation, a centrist think tank. Haig spoke on several occasions during the trip and, Clemons says, "It was all warm and fuzzy stuff . . . He never had a negative thing to say."

Haig is held in equal esteem in Singapore—an important Asian market for US firms –especially with former dictator Lee Kuan Yew, who held power for about three decades and now serves as a top government minister. In 1996, the Nixon Center for Peace and Freedom selected Lee to receive its first "Architect of the New Century" award, given to the world leader who most acts "in the Nixonian spirit of enlightened pragmatism in world affairs." The award caused a stink—Nixon's old speechwriter William Safire criticized the Center for "sucking up to a tinpot tyrant"—but Haig defended the choice, going so far as to tell the *New Republic* that Lee was "a paragon of Western capitalism and Western democracy." (Lee is even closer with Kissinger than he is with Haig. "Whenever Henry comes to Singapore, he is ushered around by protocol officers as though he was still secretary of state," a Singaporean journalist told me.)

But it is China where Haig has carved out a special niche as a door opener for American companies. The general has been a steadfast advocate of China since he led the advance team for President Nixon's historic 1972 visit, and he has continued to speak out for Beijing ever since. Perhaps the most spectacular example came when he turned up at Tianamen Square on October 1, 1989—four months after the notorious crackdown—to mark the fortieth anniversary of the founding of the People's Republic. The only

American to grace the proceedings that day, Haig knew that the US and all other Western ambassadors would be boycotting the event, but he shared the podium with then-Premier Deng Xiaoping, who congratulated him on his courage to appear.

It is conservatives who have been most angered by Haig's relentless support for Beijing. "It's tragic that a man who has contributed so much to his country would now become an apologist for China," says Edward Timperlake, a former assistant secretary of defense under Ronald Reagan. The Chinese, of course, are deeply grateful for Haig's support. Jin Zhu, a former military attaché at China's Washington embassy, has written an unpublished manuscript that describes how he worked with "Americans who might serve our interests." According to Jin, the embassy divided such people into three categories: Dear Friends, Important Friends and Regular Friends. He identified just three people as being in the first category: Scowcroft, Kissinger and Haig. "Each year, our office received a budget allowance for a specific number and kind of friends we could invite to Beijing," he writes. "For Dear Friends we pay air fare, hotels, and provide personal escorts as well as limousines."

The Chinese appear to be getting a good return on their money. When former Premier Deng Xiaoping's daughter, Deng Rong, came to the US in 1995 to promote a hagiography about her father—a book contracted by Rupert Murdoch—Haig threw a party for her at Worldwide's Washington offices. "His remarks that day were extraordinary," says a person who attended. "He was dripping with contempt for human rights activists who try to influence China policy." Haig even finds time to serve on the organizing committee of Florida

Splendid China, a seventy-acre theme park in Kissimmee that is owned by the State Council of the People's Republic. There tourists can stroll among detailed replicas of the Great Wall, the Imperial Palace and the Potola Palace of Tibet, where the Dalai Lama ruled until he was driven into exile following China's invasion of 1949. The park also offers acrobatic shows, though performances are sometimes understaffed. During Florida Splendid China's first three years of operations, more than forty acrobats requested political asylum in the United States.

According to Hill staffers, Haig has called members of Congress on China's behalf, be it to urge that Beijing be admitted to the World Trade Organization or to demand that China have its most favored nation trade status renewed. "He doesn't register as a foreign lobbyist, but he's effectively a voice for a foreign government," says Mark Lagon, a former foreign affairs advisor to the Republican House leadership. A current Hill staffer who closely follows China—and who asked to remain unidentified—says of Haig, "He's a guy we worry about because every time we try to put together a piece of legislation [critical of China], Haig gets on the phone to Republican members, and we suddenly find that we've got less votes than we thought we did."

Goldberg draws a distinction between lobbying and what Worldwide does. "General Haig does not represent any foreign government or lobby for foreign governments. Promoting American business interests in China or anywhere else is important to America's economy in an interdependent world. It's in that regard that we've assessed the China market [for clients]. He promotes a strong, stable mutually beneficial relationship with China."

If Haig is valuable to Beijing, the reverse is also true. Haig serves as an advisor to Chinese companies with interests in the US, including the China Ocean Shipping Company, the state-owned firm involved in the controversial bid to take over closed US Navy facilities at Long Beach, California. When he travels to China, Haig routinely meets with top officials, a level of access that has allowed him to help clients sell everything from air conditioning equipment to military materiel. To his critics, Haig's relationship with Beijing is based on an unseemly quid pro quo. As one former GOP government official remarked, "It's very simple. If he were critical of China on human rights or any other issue, his access would dry up and the companies that use him would no longer do so."

Those who question Haig's views on China swiftly discover that the general's well-known temper still runs hot. Haig called Representative Christopher Cox a few years ago to lobby him on China trade policy only to hear Cox suggest that Taiwan be admitted to the World Trade Organization ahead of Beijing. Haig, says a former Cox staffer, "went absolutely ballistic." Until 1997, Ross Munro was a fellow at the Philadelphia-based Foreign Policy Research Institute, where Haig is a board member. That year, Munro co-authored *The Coming Conflict with China*, which criticized Haig and other retired US government officials who do business in China. Haig was furious and, according to three sources, prevailed upon Institute director Harvey Sicherman to fire Munro. (Goldberg said the firing was "an internal matter" at FPRI while Sicherman said "It is our policy not to comment on relationships with former employees." Munro also refused to comment.)

Thus does General Haig go about the game of Realpolitik, a philosophy he learned from old masters such as Nixon and Kissinger, and that he has carried forward into the private sector. In diplomacy, the goal of Realpolitik is the pursuit of national advantage. In business, as Haig's adoption of the venerable doctrine demonstrates, it can just as easily be profit.

SIX

THE PHANTOM MENACE

Frank Gaffney and the Star Wars Crusade

> "*Whenever you have big money, and big bureaucratic interests, you're going to have people lying. What happens is they have to present arguments to justify things that are not necessarily justifiable in the terms that they claim they are.*"

—Theodore Postol, professor of Defense and Arms Control
Studies at MIT, in an interview with Gordon Mitchell

ADMIRAL HAROLD W. GEHMAN JR., Commander-In-Chief of the US Atlantic Command, was trying to wrap his mind around a critical conundrum. It was December 1998, and congressional support for a ballistic missile defense program was at a ten-year high. Meanwhile, as Gehman freely conceded at a symposium on the future of military efforts in space, Star Wars-inspired projects run by the Pentagon and defense industry leaders had been abysmal failures. "We've got to start hitting something," the admiral said plaintively, referring to a string of tests in which anti-missile weapons in the development pipeline failed to shoot down mock enemy targets.

Gehman finally got his wish the following year, when the Army's Theater High-Altitude Area Defense (THAAD), a key component of the current ballistic missile defense program, twice shot down mock missiles. Air Force Lieutenant General Ronald Kadish called the second hit "one of the watershed events in the technological history of our country." That claim was extraordinary, even by the normal standard of military hyperbole. THAAD's successes came in highly controlled tests that reduced the possibility for failure to near zero. As one critic said, the shootdowns were "akin to getting a hit in slow-pitch softball." THAAD's overall performance has been so poor that its prime contractor, Lockheed Martin, was ordered to pay the Pentagon $15 million in fines

The Pentagon's current anti-missile efforts grew out of President Ronald Reagan's Star Wars program. Reagan envisioned a system that would effectively amount to an "Astrodome" shield that would protect the United States from a missile attack by the Soviet Union. The Soviet Union no longer exists, but the program, which consumed $55 billion between 1983 and 1998, lives on. Advocates now say it is urgently needed to protect American soil from "rogue" states like Iran, Iraq and North Korea. Never mind that none of those countries is likely to develop a ballistic missile that can reach the United States for ten to twenty years, and that if they did launch such an attack they would face immediate obliteration. As John Pike of the Federation of American Scientists points out, "The United States could reduce their nations to a sea of radioactive glass. Dictators don't want to get vaporized. They have an instinct for survival."

The various spawns of Star Wars are uniformly years behind schedule and far over budget. In real terms, the US has spent three times more on missile defense as it did on the Manhattan Project that created the atomic bomb, all while the programs themselves have compiled a record that Pike aptly describes as being "unblemished by success." None the less, more money is on the way. In the fall of 1998, Congress gave the Pentagon an additional $1 billion to pursue Star Wars-style programs. The following spring, President Clinton—who back in 1993 had vowed to bring most research to a close—endorsed a bill mandating the future deployment of a national missile defense.

What accounts for the remarkable rebirth of Star Wars, which just a few years ago seemed to be dead in the water? Behind the revival is a tight-knit band of former national security insiders and nuclear policy wonks, whose political (if not intellectual) leader is Frank Gaffney, a Reagan-era Pentagon official who now directs the Center for Security Policy (CSP). Based on the edge of Georgetown in northwest Washington, the Center is a mix of think tank and lobby shop. It demands vast billions in funding for missile defense programs, makes wild claims about their effectiveness and attacks those who oppose its agenda—all while being heavily funded by defense contractors with a direct financial stake in Star Wars. As Robert Andrews, a Washington lobbyist for one of those contractors, Rockwell International, says of Gaffney, "Frank is the conservatives' rapid deployment force for national security."

THE ROOTS OF Gaffney's Center extend back to 1975, a time of despair for hard-line Cold Warriors. A conservative president,

Gerald Ford, was in office, but there was a nasty whiff of détente in the air. The US and Soviet Union had agreed to limitations on their nuclear arsenals and further arms control agreements seemed imminent. American involvement in the war in Vietnam had come to a humiliating close, and the US defense budget had sunk to $230 billion in today's money (which turned out to be a post-Vietnam low). The Pentagon and its allies rose to the challenge. Within five years, the field of battle was covered with dead or dying detentistas. The Soviet Union was successfully re-demonized, and American arms spending shot up to new levels.

Central to the conservative counter-attack was a momentous threat-inflation project called the Committee on the Present Danger. The group's architect was Yale professor Eugene Rostow, a conservative Democrat who had served Lyndon Johnson as an advisor on the Vietnam War and later helped form the Coalition for a Democratic Majority to back the 1973 presidential bid of defense hawk Senator Henry "Scoop" Jackson. On Thanksgiving of 1975—inspired, he said later, "by a couple of Bloody Marys"—Rostow wrote letters to a range of like-minded men, the most prominent of those being Paul Nitze, another nuclear hawk. As a young government scientist, Nitze was one of the first Americans on the ground at Hiroshima after the city had been leveled by an atomic bomb. Nitze—who later described his mission as putting "calipers on [the destruction] instead of describing it in emotive terms"—was struck by the fact that so many Hiroshima residents survived the blast. That apparently convinced him that atomic weapons could be fruitfully employed on future battlefields.

Rostow proposed a national campaign to get American national security back on track by building up both conventional and nuclear forces. He, Nitze and a few others began meeting at Washington's Metropolitan Club, where they drafted an activist blueprint. Among the early joiners were disgruntled conservatives such as Nixon's Secretary of Defense James Schlesinger, future CIA chief Bill Casey, Nixon administration veteran George Shultz, Admiral Elmo Zumwalt, and Richard Allen, who subsequently became Reagan's national security advisor. Amoretta Hoeber, a RAND veteran who had worked under the tutelage of Andy Marshall, was recruited when the group realized that the fairer sex had been excluded from its inner sanctum. Recovering Democrats such as Norman Podhoretz and Jeanne Kirkpatrick also came on board, as did a former California governor named Ronald Reagan.

Another important Committee member was Richard Perle, who had first grappled with the concept of nuclear annihilation when as a high-school student in Los Angeles he dated Joanie Wohlstetter, daughter of the RAND nuclear intellectual Albert Wohlstetter. Wohlstetter Sr. gave young Perle a copy of his seminal article critiquing the policy of nuclear deterrence, *The Delicate Balance of Terror*, which seems to have had a profound effect on his daughter's paramour. In 1969, Wohlstetter tapped Perle, then fresh out of graduate school, to work for the Committee to Maintain a Prudent Defense Policy, a new group he had helped establish. From there, Perle moved on to the office of Scoop Jackson of Washington state, otherwise known as "the Senator from Boeing." Jackson's office was known as "The Bunker," so named for its siege mentality. Jay

Winik evokes the environment in *On the Brink*, saying, "In their eyes, the inhabitants of the Bunker were a beleaguered few, fighting the lonely war against the left-wing forces of darkness, always on the precipice, about to be overwhelmed."

One of Perle's great victories while working for Jackson came in late 1975, when he sabotaged the SALT II treaty that called for limiting American and Russian nuclear stockpiles and restricted missile defense systems. While Secretary of State Henry Kissinger was in Vladivostok putting the final touches on the treaty, Perle hooked up *Washington Post* columnists Ronald Evans and Robert Novak with anti-SALT sources at the Pentagon. The columnists soon ran an article charging that Kissinger was seeking "a SALT II agreement at any cost," even if it meant selling out to the Soviets. Evans and Novak called upon Donald Rumsfeld, Ford's Secretary of Defense and Perle's friend (and later a member of the CPD), as the only man who could prevent concessions and save the nation from ruin. Along with Fred Iklé, the equally hawkish head of the Arms Control and Disarmament Agency (ACDA) and another soon-to-be Committee member, Rumsfeld pressed Ford to back away from SALT. Already reeling from the harsh attacks of Republican challenger Ronald Reagan, who accused Ford of coddling the Russians, the president declined to sign the treaty.

Nitze had been a member of a Korean War-era military lobby called the Committee on the Present Danger—the name came from Oliver Wendell Holmes's famous statement that no one had the right to shout "Fire" in a crowded room unless there was a clear and present danger—and the new organization selected the same moniker. Nitze drafted an early statement which explained that during the Korean War, the Berlin blockade, and the Cuban missile crisis, "the US had the strategic edge because of our superiority at the strategic nuclear level . . . To have the advantage at the utmost level of violence helps at every lesser level." Now, Nitze warned, "That edge has slipped away."

In the fall of 1976, Democrat Jimmy Carter defeated Ford to win the presidency. The victor's calls for cuts in military spending and his rhetoric about promoting human rights appalled the right-wingers mustered in the CPD. Two days after the election, the Committee held its inaugural press conference at the National Press Club in downtown Washington. A position paper it released that day, "Common Sense and the Common Danger," said that the "principle threat to our nation, to world peace, and to the cause of human freedom is the Soviet drive for dominance based upon an unparalleled military buildup. The Soviet Union has not altered its long-held goal of a world dominated from a single center—Moscow." As Anne Hessing Cahn of the American University notes in her book *Killing Détente*, the Committee was at this time considered to be so politically marginal and violently right-wing that the media all but ignored the press conference. There was no television coverage and not a single line about the affair appeared in the *New York Times* or the *Washington Post.*

Still, the hawks did manage to draw blood even before Carter was sworn in. At the time, the predominant view of American intelligence agencies was that the Soviet Union sought a rough parity with US forces. In 1976, George Bush, the new CIA Director, called in a group of hard-line "outside experts" (Team B) to "reevaluate" the finding of the Agency's professionals (Team A). The "Team B" members—including five from the CPD—were openly selected by Bush for their more pessimistic views of Soviet plans. They concluded that the Soviets were seeking military superiority over the United States and were preparing to fight and win a nuclear war.

All of this was nonsense. As Andrew Cockburn has shown in his book *The Threat*, by this time the Soviet Union's economy was already showing visible signs of strain, as was its military apparatus. The Red Army was in an unprecedented state of disarray and military ineffectiveness, manned by an ill-trained and drunken soldiery, and directed by a military-industrial complex even more insatiable than its American counterpart. Yet when the Team B report was leaked to the press, it won vigorous and sympathetic treatment. A front-page story in the *New York Times* on December 26, 1976 quoted a military source saying of the Team B report, "It was more than somber—it was very grim. It flatly states the judgement that the Soviet Union is seeking superiority over United States forces ... The questions begin on when they will achieve it." (As we will see later in this chapter, the Team B model became a favorite of the right-wing. In May 1990, as the Soviet empire was crumbling and hawks feared that peace might be breaking out, Frank Gaffney wrote an op-ed in the *Washington Times* saying, "Now is the time for a new Team B and a clear-eyed assessment of the abiding Soviet (and other) challenges that dictate a continued, robust US defense posture.")

The Team B success marked the onset of a dazzling PR offensive by the CPD and the Pentagon. Paul Nitze, Elmo Zumwalt and others took to the TV talk show circuit armed with a porta-pack of model Soviet and US intercontinental missiles. Their representations of Soviet missiles were significantly larger and more menacing than American ones. Such televisual props obscured the fact that neither size nor number was relevant to the effects of a nuclear exchange. Precise targeting of missile silos—the promise of a "preemptive strike" and "victory" in an atomic war—was impossible for reasons of atmospheric disturbance and gravitational pull.

In addition to strengthening offensive nuclear capabilities, the Committee also stumped for domestic missile defenses. Here, the hawks ran up against the 1972 Anti-Ballistic Missile Treaty. A keystone of the détente period, it virtually outlawed missile defense beyond the R&D stage and attempted to stop the arms race from extending into space.

By 1978, President Carter and all major media had largely accepted the CPD's premise of American "vulnerability" to a Soviet attack. Early that year, *Time* magazine convened a panel of conservative defense experts to answer the question: "Can the US defend itself? If so, not for long," the experts answered. "The Soviet Union's continuing nuclear and conventional military build-up is increasingly ominous and may jeopardize the delicate balance of power that has deterred nuclear war," the magazine said in summarizing their findings. "Disarmament negotiations like the SALT may not be capable, by themselves, of preserving the US-USSR balance." Edward Luttwak, a former adviser to Defense Secretary James Schlesinger, told *Time* that Moscow might soon "say to the West, 'Gentlemen, we are superior in ground forces, we can take most of Western Europe in forty-eight hours. You cannot checkmate that by strategic nuclear forces for you no longer have superiority. Now we want to collect'."

The new Red Scare was seen in the policy elite's changing view towards Afghanistan. In December 1973, when détente was near its zenith, the *Wall Street Journal* ran a rare front-page story on the country, titled "Do the Russians Covet Afghanistan? If So, It's Hard to Figure Why." Reporter Peter Kann, who later became the *Journal*'s chairman and publisher, wrote that "great power strategists tend to think of Afghanistan as a kind of fulcrum upon which the world balance of power tips. But from close up, Afghanistan tends to look less like a fulcrum or a domino or a stepping-stone than like a vast expanse of desert waste with a few fly-ridden bazaars, a fair number of feuding tribes and a lot of miserably poor people."

After the Soviets invaded to help prop up a friendly regime, this wasteland swiftly acquired the status of a precious geopolitical prize. A *Journal* editorial following the Soviet takeover said Afghanistan was "more serious than a mere stepping-stone" and, in response, called for US troops in the Middle East, increased military outlays, expanded covert operations and a reinstatement of draft registration. Drew Middleton, then a *New York Times* correspondent, filed a tremulous post-invasion analysis in January 1980. "The conventional wisdom in the Pentagon," he wrote, "is that in purely military terms, the Russians are in a far better position vis-à-vis the United States than Hitler was against Britain and France in 1939." Over at *Newsweek*, a correspondent reported that the "Soviet thrust" represented a "severe threat" to American interests. "Control of Afghanistan would put the Russians within 350 miles of the Arabian

Sea, the oil lifeline of the West and Japan," the magazine said. "Soviet warplanes based in Afghanistan could cut the lifeline at will." President Carter also concluded that the Russian conquest of Kabul was indeed serious. He swiftly called for a rapid upsurge in defense spending, and a rough new phase in the Cold War was underway.

It can be said without exaggeration that the Committee played an important role in killing détente and igniting the new Cold War. "They [the CPD's members] gave the appearance of thoughtful support to just throwing money at defense and directly contributed to the heightened fear of the Soviet Union," says retired Admiral Gene Carroll of the Center for Defense Information. "Their strategy was to scream at the top of their lungs that unless Congress approved more money for defense and a nuclear buildup, we're all going to die."

RONALD REAGAN's defeat of Carter in the 1980 election marked the final step in the transformation of CPD members from right-wing extremists to government insiders. Reagan's chief talent scout was CPD member Richard Allen, who helped see to it that more than sixty of his colleagues moved into high-level administration positions in the early 1980s. Rostow took the helm at the ACDA and called on Committeemen Rumsfeld and nuclear intellectuals William Graham and Colin Gray to be his official advisors. Nitze was appointed the administration's chief arms control negotiator. Richard Perle became an assistant secretary of defense for international security policy while Jeanne Kirkpatrick was named Ambassador to the United Nations. Amoretta Hoeber was picked to be the Army's deputy assistant secretary for research and development.

The Reaganites hit the ground running, calling for increased confrontation with the Soviet Union and a speed-up of weapons production lines. The administration's pronouncements on nuclear warfare were especially alarming. In 1981, Undersecretary of Defense Thomas K. Jones caused an outcry when he explained to *Los Angeles Times* reporter Robert Scheer that nuclear war was not nearly as devastating as people had been led to believe and that the US could recover from a full-out attack in two to four years. "If there are enough shovels to go around, everybody's going to make it," Jones asserted coolly. The shovels in question were for digging holes in the ground, that were to be topped by a slab of wood covered with dirt. There, Americans would safely hold out until high levels of radiation unleashed by a nuclear exchange had dissipated and life resumed as normal. ("It's the dirt that does it," Jones explained for the skeptical.) Later in the decade, Perle derided European opposition to the deployment of short-range nuclear missiles in Germany as "Protestant angst," saying, "It's a phase they will have to go through, and we will have to go through it holding their hand."

In the view of many on the CPD, nuclear weapons were designed for action, not to sit forever lifeless in missile silos and launch vehicles. Two Committee men, the ACDA's Colin Gray and Keith Payne, a Nuclear Use Theorist (NUT) at the Hudson Institute, made their names with a 1980 *Foreign Affairs* article entitled "Victory Is Possible." The piece argued that it was childish and hysterical to see Armageddon as the inevitable result of nuclear war. Instead, rational and effective military strategists must acknowledge that "nuclear war can have a wide range of possible outcomes." Indeed, nuclear war was not only survivable and winnable, but the US should consider initiating a first strike so as to ensure a favorable outcome. With proper "homeland defense" mechanisms in place, Gray and Payne said, the price of victory would be limited to twenty million American dead—a number compatible with their stated goal of "recovering sufficiently to insure a satisfactory postwar world order."

Getting "homeland defense" mechanisms in order soon became one of the administration's priorities. On March 23, 1983, Reagan went on national television and announced a plan to render "nuclear weapons impotent and obsolete." The means was to be a missile shield system that would crate an impenetrable Astrodome over the continental United States. This would end the threat nuclear weapons posed to mankind and, since America might be prepared to share the relevant technology with Russia, would allow for a move away from "mutually assured vulnerability to mutually assured survivability." Whether Reagan actually believed that Star Wars would usher in a period of peace and understanding is impossible to know. His advisors certainly understood that there would be no sharing of technology and that the Soviets would view US construction of a missile shield as a means of leaving their country vulnerable to an American first strike.

Following his Star Wars speech, Reagan appointed two panels to study the feasibility of implementing his Strategic Defense Initiative (SDI). "Many of the members of these panels were drawn from the ranks of private contractors who had been working on missile defense for years, [so] it was predictable that they produced largely rosy assessments," writes Gordon Mitchell, a professor at the

University of Pittsburgh, in a paper about Star Wars called *Placebo Defense*. Panelists gave little thought to the cost of implementing Star Wars, which were astronomical. A Defense Department study estimated full deployment of the Astrodome concept would come to $500 billion; others believed that to be half the necessary amount.

Not surprisingly, the program quickly developed quite a constituency among weapons contractors. The administration's original solicitation of ten plans for the overall system architecture reportedly received more bidders than any military contract in recent times. By 1985, the government had already committed enormous sums to Star Wars contracts. Lockheed was the leader of the pack with about $1 billion, while seven other defense firms had raked in $400 million or more. Consulting shops that owed their existence to SDI popped up like exotic mushrooms. One small outfit, Sparta, made fully three-quarters of its living from its missile shield unit. (The Government Accounting Office later discovered that Sparta spent more than $500,000 in taxpayer money to hold conferences for employees at resorts in Hawaii, Mexico, Jamaica and the Grand Cayman Islands.) System Planning Corporation, headed by Dov Zakheim, became another Star Wars profiteer by winning contracts to study—and inflate—the foreign missile threat to the United States. "Were we to proceed with deployment, it would be the biggest thing this industry has ever had happen to it, by far," Alan Benasuli, a financial consultant to defense firms, gushed to the *Washington Post* in late-1985. "It would be the greatest thing on earth." An employee at TRW was only slightly more contained, saying, "We're standing on the first turn of a defense development that will dominate the industry for the next twenty years."

Meanwhile, fierce disagreements erupted within the Star Wars policy world, with CPD members heading up competing factions. General Daniel Graham led the High Frontier, which pushed for the deployment of hundreds of space-based battle systems that would each carry a bevy of self-propelled "kill vehicles." Graham argued for deploying the backbone of the missile shield within a few short years, using "off-the-shelf technology" if need be. Graham's impatience led him to clash with a Star Wars group based at the Heritage Foundation that included two CPD members, scientist Edward Teller, the father of the H-bomb, and the brewer and right-wing funder Joseph Coors. They preferred to target ballistic missiles with a short-wave laser and favored a more protracted R&D process. Senator Malcolm Wallop led another faction of SDI advocates who envisioned shooting down incoming missiles with a long-wave chemical laser. (Perle initially opposed Star Wars, fearing it would cut into funding he preferred to see spent on a general defense buildup. He came on board after realizing the program could be used to sabotage the arms control process and was soon declaring Star Wars components to be "weapons of life.")

All the weapons options associated with the various approaches had one thing in common: none had even a remote chance of working, which led their proponents to gross exaggeration if not outright fraud. For example, Pentagon officials claimed that Brilliant Pebbles, a kinetic energy device designed to collide with and destroy its target, would cost between $40 billion and $60 billion. That was about half the price of their own in-house estimates and a fraction of the real amount if maintenance costs were figured in. Pentagon projections further showed that Brilliant Pebbles could remain in orbit for only a few days, not up to ten years as claimed by SDI advocates.

The Star Wars crew did rack up one impressive success. In 1984, a developmental interceptor homed in on and destroyed a Minuteman missile target. The Pentagon claimed immediately that the test showed that it was possible "to hit a bullet with a bullet" and proved that Star Wars could work. Nine years later, the *New York Times* revealed that the exercise had been faked. Scientists had placed a homing beacon on the Minutemen and heated it up before launch, which greatly increased its visibility to the interceptor. In case this failed to get the desired result, the scientists had also secretly put high explosives on the Minuteman, which would detonate spontaneously in the event of a near miss. "We would lose hundreds of millions of dollars in Congress if we didn't perform successfully," one of the conspirators explained to the *Times*.

Houston Rice, a retired Lockheed engineer, said during a phone interview that contractors were aware from the outset that the Astrodome concept was fundamentally unattainable. During the bidding process on one Star Wars component, he said, "the company made promises that we, the engineers, knew to be ridiculous. They simply out-lied the competition, and when they got the contract they tuned it over to engineers who knew it couldn't be done."

TESTING SETBACKS produced political opposition, but a core of true believers remained committed to the fight for Star Wars. In this regard, no one was more fanatical than Frank Gaffney. Like so many prominent atomic hawks, Gaffney came to nuclear maturity inside

Scoop Jackson's "Bunker." From there he moved to the office of Senator John Tower, a high-ranking member of the Armed Services Committee, where he stayed until 1983, when Perle tapped him to be deputy assistant secretary of defense for nuclear forces and arms control policy. In *Hard Line*, the autobiographical novel Perle published after leaving government, Martin Waterman (Perle) considers Scott Bracken (Gaffney) to be "a younger version of Waterman himself, which is probably why he'd hired him in the first place . . . If he (Waterman) was the department's watchdog, Bracken was *his* watchdog—loyal, smart, effective."

In his position as deputy assistant secretary of defense, Gaffney helped organize the Pentagon's campaign against Star Wars critics, most notably at the State Department. Gaffney was known unaffectionately by his peers as "Perle's bulldog," for the frequency and viciousness of his attacks. He was also known for his slavish devotion to the boss. In 1986, the State Department initially succeeded in blocking Gaffney's participation at arms control talks in Reykjavik. By the time Perle won a spot for his deputy all suitable hotels were booked, so Gaffney slept on the floor in Perle's room. (As recounted in Winik's *On the Brink*, Gaffney's tasks in Iceland included looking after Perle's kosher salamis, a mission that ended in disaster. Perle placed the succulent sausages on a window ledge to chill, but the Arctic wind swept them to the ground. Before Gaffney could intervene, vigilant security guards dispatched the salamis by bayonet.)

Even within the rarefied crackpot atmosphere of the late-Reagan years, Gaffney stood out as something of a crank. Perle's resignation in 1987 left him without a patron, and new Secretary of Defense

Frank Carlucci soon pushed him out. A brainstorming session of former high-level national security staffers the following year prompted Gaffney to found the Center for Security Policy. "What we need is the Domino's Pizza of the policy business," Perle, one of the participants, is reported to have said. "If you don't get your policy analysis in thirty minutes, you get your money back."

Over the years, the Center became a refuge for former members of the Committee on the Present Danger (as well as what William Hartung of the World Policy Institute calls "a virtual Star Wars Hall of Fame"). As of late-1999, at least eleven Committee members sat on Gaffney's Board of Advisors, including Edward Teller, Amoretta Hoeber, Fred Ikle, Jeanne Kirkpatrick, and Henry Cooper, a former director of Reagan's Strategic Defense Initiative Organization (SDIO). Perle, of course, is also represented, as are a number of other inveterate Cold Warriors: Midge Decter, a former head of the Committee for the Free World; Elliott Abrams, Reagan's point man on Latin American policy; William Bennett, the former secretary of education and current head of Empower America; and Dov Zakheim, head of SPC International. Also gracing the board are six executives from Lockheed Martin, as well as representatives from Star Wars contractors such as Titan Corporation, Allied Signal and Rockwell International.

Gaffney found no paucity of financial support in getting the Center off the ground, and his budget has grown from $244,000 during its first year to about $1 million today. Around one-quarter of that money comes from defense contractors, while much of the rest is donated by right-wing funders such as Richard Mellon Scaife, Joseph and

Holly Coors, the John M. Olin Foundation, the Readers' Digest Association, and the Sophia and William J. Casey Foundation.

Gaffney's agenda stretches beyond Star Wars, and bears more than a passing resemblance, at least in broad terms, to that of the old CPD. He calls for a big increase in defense spending and promotes specific weapons systems such as the B-2 bomber that are dear to his funders. "The nation will, if anything, need far more of these aircraft than the twenty-one currently planned," Gaffney wrote in an op-ed in the *Washington Times* in August 1997, just as the bomber's fate was going before a Congressional appropriations committee. Gaffney also points to the depleted Red Army as a continuing menace, part of his lasting fixation with Russia. ("There are times when I think Frank must have suffered food poisoning from a bowl of bad borscht given his reflexive hostility to things Russian," Ted Galen Carpenter of the Cato Institute told *National Journal* in a 1995 interview.) For Gaffney, any type of arms control is strictly verboten. He's sought to rally opposition to the Strategic Arms Reduction Talks II and feverishly opposed the Chemical Weapons Convention, which was negotiated by the Reagan and Bush administrations and finally approved by Congress in 1998 (after virtually every other country in the world had already signed it). A few years ago, he tried but failed to force the United States to withdraw from the ABM treaty.

Another specialty of Gaffney's is shooting down government appointees he sees as being too liberal. He launched a violent campaign against Morton Halperin—a card-carrying member of the American Civil Liberties Union—after the Clinton administration nominated him to a Pentagon post in 1993. Gaffney was widely credited with sinking Halperin's chances, though in doing so he angered Republican Senators John McCain and Strom Thurmond by providing them with heavily distorted biographical information about the nominee. ("I can't believe all this information I have received from a reliable authority is incorrect," Thurmond is reported to have said when he discovered Gaffney's deception.) Gaffney had less luck when it came to Derek Shearer, an economics professor who Clinton nominated to be ambassador to Finland. "A pedigreed radical socialist whose enthusiastic embrace of central planning and government diktat is a matter of record," said Gaffney. The senate deemed Shearer to be less alarming and sent him off to Helsinki.

Gaffney's primary interest, indeed obsession, is promoting Star Wars-related schemes. "The threat is now!" blared the headline on a September 1998 op-ed that he penned for the *Washington Times*, his primary outlet. The story warned that North Korea would soon have the capability to launch a missile attack on "not only Japan and all of America's other Asian allies, but the US states of Alaska and Hawaii as well." Another column in the same month quotes retired Air Force Lieutenant General James Abrahamson—the founding director of SDIO under Reagan and a man who now works for a number of companies with a financial stake in Star Wars—as saying, "The problem with moving into a real ballistic missile defense system has not been technology. It's really been the [financial and political] restraints that have been put on the program." In a January 1998 op-ed, Gaffney said that since the US did not have a ballistic missile defense in place, it was "a safe bet that at some point in the foreseeable future, weapons of mass destruction will be used against the United States, its allies and/or its interests. This may happen as early as [this year]; if not, chances increase for an attack in the following few years . . . Thousands, perhaps hundreds of thousands, of people will die . . . The witch hunt to determine culpability for the surprise attack at Pearl Harbor will likely pale by comparison with the wrath that will justifiably be felt toward those responsible for deliberately leaving an unknowing American people vulnerable to incalculably greater destruction."

Gaffney's writings frequently serve as an echo chamber for his own supporters. In March 1999, he hailed the publication of "a superb legal analysis" co-authored by former Reaganite Deputy Assistant Secretary of Defense Douglas Feith. The paper, he wrote, had conclusively demonstrated that the ABM Treaty had "lapsed" since the Soviet Union, the only other signatory nation, no longer exists. Therefore, "the United States no longer has any obligation to continue to constrain, dumb-down or otherwise deny itself technologies that could prevent ballistic missiles from destroying American communities." Gaffney didn't mention that Feith is a financial contributor to his CSP, sits on its board of advisors, and serves as its legal counsel. Another Gaffney dispatch lauded Senator Jon Kyl of Arizona—also a CSP advisor—as "one of the Senate's most influential members on national security matters," and congratulated him for adding hundreds of millions of dollars to the 1998 budget for missile-killing technology.

Gaffney gets his message out with regular fax blasts of Center press statements and publications, including its weekly "National Security Alert." In a typically colorful dispatch from May of 1995, the Center said that the then-popular movie *Crimson Tide*, starring Denzel Washington and Gene Hackman, had exposed millions of Americans "to a singularly powerful argument for missile defense." After explaining that the movie's story line revolved around a rogue Russian commander who was preparing a first strike on America, the alert concluded ominously: "Although it is never mentioned in the movie, there is only one reason why such a nightmare scenario might arise: the United States has no defense against ballistic missile attack." Gaffney further seeks to influence public opinion with the Center's Military Committee, which consists of sixteen former three- and four-star officers. Their job is to "stimulate and inform the security policy debate by exposing decision-makers, the media and the public to the experience and judgment of some of the nation's most distinguished retired senior military commanders."

The Center also produces informational videotapes such as "America, the Vulnerable," which "offers a brief tutorial about how it is that the United States came to be completely vulnerable to missile attack as a matter of state policy, and what can be done to correct this increasingly perilous condition." Released in 1998, the video opens with a melodramatic sequence from Colorado Springs, where amidst the frenzy of a ballistic missile streaking toward the US— fired from "somewhere in the Middle East"—a panic-stricken General admonishes, "No, Mr. President, we can't shoot it down. We have no defense against a missile attack. There is nothing I can do to stop it." The mood set, Gaffney presents an all-star line-up to weigh in on the urgent need for a missile defense initiative. First, we hear from Newt Gingrich and former California Governor Pete

Wilson, the latter indignant at a "government completely unwilling to defend its own people." Next, Jeane Kirkpatrick and Keith Payne provide a quick history lesson on Russian untrustworthiness and the futility of arms control agreements. Richard Perle follows with a dire psychological analysis of our contemporary adversaries. For those foolhardy enough to find comfort in the end of the Cold War, James Woolsey informs viewers that the world is in fact a far more dangerous place than before. "Having slain the dragon," Woolsey explains, "we find ourselves in a jungle full of poisonous snakes— Iran, Iraq, Hezbollah—and these poisonous snakes are much harder to keep track of than the dragon was." The video is punctuated throughout by scenes of mushroom clouds and cowering school children, frenzied mobs of Ayatollah fans, an ever-animated Saddam, and a podium-banging Quaddafi. However, the video concludes on a happier note. Before a final clip from Reagan on the moral imperative of the Star Wars, former SDIO director Henry Cooper restores calm with his estimation that missile defense security is but "$2 to $3 billion dollars and three to four years away."

EVEN AS GAFFNEY fought the good fight on behalf of ballistic missile defense programs, continued testing failures and cost overruns were badly undermining political support for his Star Wars dream. The collapse of the Soviet Union contributed to his difficulties. In 1991, Congress cut the budget for SDI for the first time ever, slashing funding by twenty-three percent. Two years later, Clinton's Defense Secretary Les Aspin officially decreed "the end of the Star Wars era." In making this pronouncement, Aspin didn't refer to the practical difficulties of building a ballistic missile shield, but simply said that in his estimation the threat of a nuclear attack on the United States had "receded to the vanishing point." That left a door open to Gaffney and other true believers: if they could concoct a threat, Star Wars could be resurrected.

During this Dark Age, Gaffney kept missile defense alive with the help of key Republicans in Congress. Representative Bob Livingston (who resigned after being outed as a serial philanderer by *Hustler* publisher Larry Flynt in 1998) made a national missile shield a tenet of the GOP's 1994 Contract with America. The following year, CSP and the Heritage Foundation produced a report that called for a fresh $7.3 billion in Star Wars funding—money that would be used to put an end to "the Clinton administration's policy of intentionally leaving American cities and territory open to missile attack." Meanwhile, Gaffney was cranking out rigged polls that purported to show that US public was petrified about the American vulnerability to a missile strike. All this convinced Bob Dole to try to make Star Wars a big issue in his 1996 presidential campaign, during which he said that "national missile defense must be America's top defense priority."

The problem here was that Americans in fact were not overly concerned about the threat of a ballistic missile attack, as seen in independent polls conducted at the time. One such survey, from May 1996, found that just three percent of Americans believed it likely that the US would be subjected to a nuclear missile attack during the next five years. Clinton, well aware of such polling numbers, attacked GOP plans to accelerate missile defense programs. "This plan is misguided," he said of a Republican attempt to double research monies. "It would waste money. It would weaken our defenses by taking money away from things we know we need right now. It would violate the arms control agreements that we have made and these agreements make us more secure. That is the wrong way to defend America." Republicans soon ditched the whole issue. Even Dole only obliquely referred to the topic at the Republican convention in August.

A bigger obstacle for Gaffney and the Star Warriors came in the form of unexpected opposition from the intelligence community. In 1995, the CIA delivered a report to the president that found that "no country, other than the major declared nuclear powers, will develop or otherwise acquire a ballistic missile in the next fifteen years that could threaten the contiguous forty-eight states and Canada." Clinton cited the CIA report in December 1995 when he vetoed a defense authorization bill that mandated the deployment of a missile defense system.

Gaffney responded by calling the CIA study a "Pollyannish and highly politicized judgment." He and his Congressional allies demanded a "second opinion," and further investigation was duly organized, this time under the aegis of CIA Director Robert Gates. However, Gaffney's hopes were dashed when Gates and his colleagues issued their findings in December 1996. They reaffirmed the CIA's earlier report, saying that the US was unlikely to face a new ballistic missile threat until at least 2010.

Gaffney and other Star Warriors now created a clamor for a third opinion and scored a major coup when Congressional Republicans created the nine-member Commission to Assess the Ballistic Missile Threat to the United States. The commission, in essence a new Team B, brought together a group of intelligence outsiders to assess the earlier judgements. Its chair was Donald Rumsfeld, the former secretary of defense, founding member of the Committee on the Present Danger, and advisor and donor to Gaffney's Center for Security Policy. Two other Committeemen and CSP advisors, William Graham and William Schneider, joined Rumsfeld on the panel. So, too, did ardent Cold Warriors Paul Wolfowitz, an under-secretary of defense under George Bush, and James Woolsey, the former CIA Director. Those summoned to testify—for example, Andrew Marshall of the Pentagon's Office of Net Assessment and Caspar Weinberger, a Reagan Defense Secretary—shaped the report as much as the hard-line stance of the majority of its members. The Commission also employed a number of politically reliable consultants, including Star Wars contractor Zakheim.

Needless to say, Gaffney finally got what he wanted. The "Rumsfeld Commission," as it came to be known, delivered its report to Congress in July 1998. It found that the threat of an Iranian, Iraqi or North Korean ballistic missile attack on the US was "broader, more mature, and evolving more rapidly than has been reported in estimates and reports by the intelligence community." As Rumsfeld explained to the press, "We are in an environment, potentially, of little or no warning."

Lost in the uproar that greeted the report were some important facts. As subsequently pointed out by Commission member Robert Garwin in the *Bulletin of Atomic Scientists*, the Rumsfeld panel "did not say that an ICBM threat to the United States from Iraq, Iran, or North Korea would actually emerge in the next few years or less . . . We simply judged that these nations have the capacity to develop ballistic missiles if they assign a sufficiently high priority to their missile programs, fund them fully, and make good use of foreign assistance." With Iran in a state of prolonged economic crisis, North Korea facing starvation, and Iraq utterly impoverished by United Nations sanctions, the threat here seems insignificant. Furthermore, the Rumsfeld panel didn't examine simpler, cheaper means by which enemy states or terrorists might seek to attack the United States—such as smuggling in a nuclear, chemical or biological weapon by land or boat. Instead, observe Liseth Gronlund and David Wright, both physicists at the Union of Concerned Scientists, the report makes missile attack appear "uniquely threatening [and suggest] that addressing it should have a higher priority than countering other threats to US security."

There's also no reason to believe that missile defense scientists can ever succeed in building a shield with a 100 percent success rate. "Give them enough time and money, and missile defense programs are going to work better than they do now," says Pike of the Federation of American Scientists. "But is it ever going to work well enough that you'd bet the country on it? The answer is no. Something is always going to get through, and you're going to want to nuke whoever shot at you. That's no different than the situation now."

Gaffney's congressional helpers ignored such finer points, and seized on Rumsfeld's findings as cause for an urgent revival of missile defense systems. The very day it was released, then-House Speaker Newt Gingrich stated: "This is the most important warning about our national security since the end of the Cold War." House National Security Committee Chairman Floyd Spence appeared before the press the same day to proclaim that the Rumsfeld report should lead to an "aggressive effort" towards missile defense.

To celebrate Rumsfeld's achievements, Gaffney awarded him the Center's "Keeper of the Flame" award for 1998. Alexander Haig, Senator Kyl, and former Senator Wallop were among the attendees at the black tie award dinner at Washington's Four Seasons Hotel. When he summarized the lessons to be drawn from the Commission, Rumsfeld drew a parallel to Pearl Harbor, saying, "We provided an undefended target, and if we know anything from history, it is that weakness is provocative . . . Weakness invites others in adventures they otherwise would avoid." He also quoted Al Capone as saying, "You get a lot more with a kind word and a gun than you do with a kind word alone," then added, "You can substitute the word 'ballistic missile' and put in the name of some regional Al Capone, and it is every bit as appropriate today."

The release of the Rumsfeld report set the stage for the near complete collapse of the Clinton administration's previous position on missile defense. The president subsequently signed the National Missile Defense Act of 1999, which mandates deployment of a national missile defense system "as soon as technologically feasible." (The president was to decide in the summer of 2000 whether to commit to a five-year deployment plan.) In its Clinton-era version, a land-based missile shield would protect all fifty states from the menace posed by "rogue" states. The anti-missile web would also be able to catch an accidental launch from Russian or Chinese arsenals, though it is explicitly stated that it is not able to protect against a full-fledged nuclear attack from those countries.

To further the Act, Clinton announced a new pledge of $6.6 billion for ballistic missile defense over the next six years, bringing the total for the period to $10.5 billion. Boeing is overseeing systems integration for the whole program, which will fatten its bottom line by billions over the next ten years. The company is also the prime contractor for a lucrative project to build an Airborne Laser to take out SCUD missiles, and is to assemble rocket boosters for a ground-based interceptor as well. Lockheed Martin, which is building the THAAD system, will also benefit substantially. In the year 2000, the company will get $611 million in taxpayer money for the project, which is budgeted at $15.4 billion overall. Dozens of other contractors, big and small, are riding the gravy train as well.

Gaffney is also nearing his long-cherished goal of destroying the ABM Treaty. Clinton's Secretary of Defense William Cohen has stated that he believes there is an imminent ballistic missile threat to the US and that the Treaty therefore will have to be, at minimum, amended. There are those who argue that whilst Clinton's ground-based interceptors technically fall within the ABM's boundaries, a sea-based program the Navy is pushing for does not. Meanwhile, defense hawks and contractors are drawing up more offensive missile defense schemes in the hope that Congress keeps replenishing the Star Wars budget.

And so the old foot soldiers of the Committee on the Present Danger, along with their spiritual heirs, ceaselessly toil on. Some are now elderly and largely out of action—Eugene Rostow seems limited to firing off an occasional letter to the editor—but many are still in the thick of national security battles. Amoretta Hoeber went to work for weapons contractor TRW following her years in the Reagan administration, and today runs a defense consulting shop out of her home outside of Washington. Keith Payne heads up the Fairfax, Virginia based National Institute for Public Policy (NIPP), a non-profit consulting firm he founded with Colin Gray. He continues to be a vocal opponent of nuclear abolition and remains committed to ballistic missile defense, positions he pushes in frequent appearances before Congress. The NIPP advises the Pentagon's Ballistic Missile Defense Organization and several agencies within the office of the Secretary of Defense, and sponsors seminars on national security for Hill staffers. It also runs a High School Education program, which provides social studies teachers with a curriculum supplement on "key issues of democracy and its global challenges."

Gray is still affiliated with the NIPP but lives in England, where he holds the Chair of International Politics at the University of Hull, Yorkshire. He, too, remains active in the nuclear field and has joined the hunt for a new threat to replace Russia. In a 1996 article for *Orbis*, he wrote menacingly of China in this regard, describing it as "a superstate" with "weight and position." "Unlike the unlamented, erstwhile USSR, China is not a landlocked power, and she cannot be landlocked by a prudent US containment policy . . . Because of size, character of territory, population, social habits, and location, it would be difficult to exaggerate the potential positive or negative contribution of China to international order."

Perle is one of the most active of the old Cold Warriors. After retiring from government, he set up a consulting business and soon was helping Raytheon sell Patriot missiles to Turkey. He currently holds a post at the American Enterprise Institute, where he chairs a Team B-type defense review that evaluates military needs for the coming century. In 1997, Perle testified before the National Defense Panel on ideas for "reinventing" the Pentagon. Perle recommended reducing troop levels by one-third and using the savings to buy stealth and other high-tech weapons. Perle is still a foreign policy guru for Republicans and played a crucial role in building support for the Iraq Liberation Act, which Congress passed in November 1998. The Pentagon and the Clinton administration opposed the bill, which authorized the president to distribute $97 million in military equipment and training to opposition groups seeking to overthrow Saddam Hussein. In testimony before Congress, General Anthony Zinni, US military commander for the Gulf region, called the Act a "dangerous" piece of legislation and said he didn't see a single Iraqi opposition group "that has the viability to overthrow Saddam Hussein at this point."

(A number of other Cold Warriors were also involved in the drive for the Iraqi Liberation Act, including Paul Wolfowitz, who along with Perle lobbied on the Hill. Meanwhile, the Iraqi opposition received military advice from retired General Wayne Downing, a special forces expert, and former CIA officer Duane "Dewey" Clarridge. The latter is best known for his work in support of the contras. It was his idea to mine Nicaragua's harbors, Clarridge recalls in his 1997 memoir, *A Spy for All Seasons.* The inspiration came to him as he was relaxing at home and wondering how to fulfill an order from then-CIA director William Casey to step up pressure on the Sandinista government. "I remember sitting with a glass of gin on the rocks, smoking a cigar, and pondering my dilemma, when it hit me . . . Sea mines were the solution . . . To this day I wonder why I didn't think of it sooner." When I asked Clarridge and Downing how they came to be part of the effort to overthrow Hussein, both men were murky. "That's sort of private," Clarridge said from San Diego, where he now lives. "For me it's a bit of a hobby." Downing, who works out of the Colorado Springs offices of defense contractor SAIC, would say only that "some people called me and asked me to get involved.")

Finally, there is Gaffney, who runs an outfit that Hoeber describes as "the intellectual heir of the Committee on the Present Danger." Undeterred by yet another missile defense testing failure that was revealed in early-2000, he relentlessly carried on the crusade for "homeland defense." In January, the Center put out a "Decision Brief" titled: "Try, Try Again: In Light of Threat, the Appropriate Response to Missile Defense Test Failure is a Redoubled Effort." The brief said that even skeptics had come to realize the growing threat posed by rogue states, including North Korea, which posed a "real danger" of launching a future ballistic missile attack on the US

The Center's brief was published one week after the American people got their first look at North Korea's only operational test center, the Nodong facility. Images of the center were taken courtesy of Space Imaging Inc., the first private spy satellite, and showed that Pyongyang's efforts in the field of ballistic missiles is not nearly as menacing as Gaffney suggests. As John Pike told one reporter, the Nodong facility consists of nothing more than "a shed, a dirt road, a launch pad, and a rice paddy."

Index